WHAT DOES THE ALLIANCE REALLY BELIEVE?

SORTING OUT ESSENTIALS, DISTINCTIVES, AND
OPEN QUESTIONS IN UNIFIED LOVING LIBERTY

PAUL L KING, TH.D., D.MIN.

COMMENDATIONS

"This is worth doing, I taught Christian Doctrine this year, and this framework was very helpful in discussing theological positions."—*Alliance missionary and adjunct professor*

"Three thumbs up!"—*Consecrated Woman in Ministry*

"The Christian and Missionary Alliance and its hermeneutics is a vital subject."—*retired Alliance pastor*

"I believe this would help a lot. Especially new people coming into the Alliance. It would benefit by being translated into some other languages like Spanish."—*pastor, New York City*

"Helpful addition to Alliance material for ordination/consecration." —*Alliance associate pastor*

"I think it would be great. I could see it being used to help with accreditation preparation."—*Former Licensing, Ordination, & Consecration Council member*

"The worthiness of the endeavor is beyond question. We need this book. Years ago, I read the list of Systematic Theologies produced by different denominations in James Leo Garret's *Systematic Theology*, Volume 1. When he reached The Alliance, I was saddened to read that our offer was one book: Dr. George Pardington's *Outline Studies in Christian Doctrine*. A book that was from 1916!!! Maybe, from your book, Dr. King, someone (or even yourself!) will feel motivated to produce a Systematic Theology from the peculiar standpoint of the Christian and Missionary Alliance."—*Alliance worker, Puerto Rico*

Alliance Heritage Press/Paul King Ministries, Inc., Owasso, Oklahoma

What Does The Alliance Really Believe? Sorting Out Essentials, Distinctives, and Open Questions in Unified Loving Liberty

by Paul L. King

Printed in the United States of America

International Standard Book Number: 9798826973905

CONTENTS

ABOUT THE AUTHOR

Dr. Paul King, Th.D., D.Min., is a retired ordained Official Worker of The Christian and Missionary Alliance, born and raised in the C&MA. He has served more than 50 years in ministry as a pastor, theologian, historian, and biographer. Currently, he serves as adjunct professor at Crown College, and serves the Alliance South Central District as an Interim Pastor and Oklahoma Regional C&MA Church Multiplication Facilitator.

Dr. King was a former Member of Southwestern District C&MA LOCC, has taught Alliance History and Theology for the Canadian Central District of the C&MA, conducted ordinand and consecrant seminars on Alliance heritage, and authored 14 books and 60+ articles, including numerous articles and books on Alliance history, biography, and theology. He served as Scholar-at-Large at Alliance Theological Seminary and as 2006 Scholar of the Year at Oral Roberts University. He founded the Higher Life Alliance Heritage Renewal Network, dedicated to preserving and promoting the Higher Life and Alliance Heritage, and has been one of the leaders of Rekindling the Flame Gatherings, dedicated to Holy Spirit renewal in the C&MA.

Dr. King conducts seminars on Alliance Heritage, Healing, Spiritual Warfare, Holy Spirit Renewal, Elder-Deacon Training, Ministry and Leadership Development, Creating a Healing Community, and more! For more information, see his website www.paulkingministries.com.

Dr. Paul King and his wife Kathy were married in 1975, live in Owasso, Oklahoma, and have two married adult children and five grandchildren. His hobbies are writing, genealogy, and watching birds and wildlife on their pond.

DEDICATED TO

Bob Petty,
Midwest C&MA District Superintendent,
and his wife **MaryK.**

who challenged me to mentor
the younger generations
in our Alliance Heritage.

ACKNOWLEDGMENTS

As I sensed the Spirit stirring within me the monumental task of writing a book on Alliance theology and hermeneutics, I was trying to discern if this was my desire or God's. I soughcounsel from several friends and mentors who speak into my life. These are just a few of the many who have encouraged me to take this on:

- **Rev. Bob Petty (now Midwest DS) and his wife MaryK** were mentors to me during a transitional period of time in my life. They challenged me, and commissioned me, as it were, to write and to mentor others in our Alliance heritage.
- **Dr. David Chotka,** Canadian Alliance pastor, prayer leader, and author, challenged me, "Write, write, write—that's right!"
- **Dr. David Smith,** pastor of Queens Alliance Church, Queens, New York, and author, affirmed this is needed and I am the one to do it.
- **Rev. David Jones,** retired Alliance missionary, urged me, "You are the go-to person on this."
- **Rev. Ron Walker**, pastor, Westview Alliance Church, Fort Wayne, Indiana, kindled a fire in me to do this, and even break it up into sections, producing multiple simpler summary booklets, which I hope to do.
- **Dr. Jerry Breedlove,** Alliance church planter, author, leadership coach in Kansas City, like Bob and MaryK Petty, envisioned my ministry as one of coaching people in Alliance heritage, the Higher Life, and the life of the Spirit.

- **Dr. Franklin Pyles,** former president of the Alliance in Canada, whom I consider a mentor—after reading the summary manuscript and making suggestions, he stirred me, "Yes, go with this!"
- **Rev. Dick LaFountain,** retired pastor, mentor, and friend, prayed an anointing over me to write and to keep alive the Alliance Heritage.
- **Rev. Kenneth Cluck,** pastor, adjunct professor, freind, and former LOCC colleague, gave me good positive critical input for the manuscript, saying it would be of great value to LOCCs and the licensing process.

Many others have influenced and impacted the writing of this book as well: especially **Dr. John Stumbo and Rev. Terry Smith,** current President and Vice President of the U.S. C&MA—through their courageous leadership for dialogue and change yet holding fast to the founding message and ministry of the Alliance and to the authority of Scripture—they have encouraged me to continue writing and urging people to the fullness of the Alliance deeper life message. **Dr. Kelvin Walker,** U.S. corporate Vice President and Metro District Superintendent; **Dr. David Hearn,** former president of the Canadian C&MA; **Dr. Bill Meyer,** friend, LOCC member, and pastor of Alive Again Alliance Church; **Dr. Patrick Blewitt,** Dean, Tozer Theological Seminary; **Dr. Alexander Zell,** Director, forGraduate Online Programs at Crown College, **Dr. Bernie Van de Walle,** Canadian Alliance professor and District Superintendent; **Drs. Mark and Reatha Searing; Rev. Jon Rich;** and so many more!

PREFACE

This book is the result of several requests that I put into print and make available as an e-book my PDF mini-book *Essentials, Distinctives, Open Questions: The Three-Tier Alliance Hermeneutic.* I had originally put it together hurriedly to have it available for the discussions at the 2021 C&MA US General Council. Many have been saying this will be an important resource for decisions to be made at the next General Council and following. Others are saying that it is needed for use in our Districts, especially for the Licensing, Ordination, and Consecration processes. Still others want to share it with their lay leaders. I have received requests to make it available for use internationally, as well as in series of booklets, which I hope to do.

As I began to prepare and re-format the mini-book for publication, I realized how skimpy it was. Therefore, I have revworked and added content in some place for further explanation and documentation in important areas, yet uneven and still skimpy in other areas to avoid becoming too bulky a book. So this is a revised, expanded edition of the PDF mini-book. However, the full Alliance systematic theological book will still have to wait until the dust settles over the Statement of Faith issues. Yet I hope that this book will be helpful in clarifying the matrix used by A. B. Simpson and early Alliance leaders in sorting out what is essential, what are distinctives, and what are open questions, and to bring consistency across the board in application of that matrix for The Alliance today in the 21st century.

Although this book is aimed mainly toward those who have had some theological training, whether Bible college or seminary, increasingly, more of our present and future leaders are coming from lay backgrounds and second career callings without formal training, so I try to explain theological terms such as hermeneutics (principles of biblical interpretation), or exegesis (the actual process of explaining or interpreting the meaning of the text), or ecclesiology (doctrine of the church), or eschatology (doctrine of the end times). I have tried to maintain academic integrity for complex theological and exegetical issues, simplifying as much as possible and briefly putting the more technical discussions in endnotes or appendices. Full exegetical engagement of various issues and interpretations will need to wait for the fuller systematic theological book. Some have suggested that I produce for lay leaders a simpler version or divide it into shorter booklets. I welcome ideas for how best to do that.

Sorting out essentials and non-essentials is a vital task. Choosing a title was difficult. Many worthy titles and sub-titles have been proposed that express practically what I hope to accomplish through this book. This book will discuss issues we agree on and issues we agree to disagree on agreeably, and how The Alliance navigates theological discussions and arrives at theological conclusions.

Ultimately, it is our goal to maintain unified faith with loving liberty. That is The Alliance!

PART I

ALLIANCE THEOLOGICAL FOUNDATIONS

INTRODUCTION: WHY THIS BOOK?

As I read and study the writings of A. B. Simpson and other early leaders of the Christian and Missionary Alliance (C&MA), what vitality and depth I encounter, far beyond the basics of the great foundation of the Fourfold Gospel than most Alliance people have read. As I have dialogued with other Alliance leaders on Facebook, over Zoom, telephone, and in conferences and seminars, I have seen how little many Alliance leaders really know about our heritage and theology.

Dr. Arnold Cook, former president of the C&MA in Canada, wrote for our times, warning about "generational slippage" or "historical drift": "Historical drift is the inherent tendency of human organizations to depart over time from their original beliefs, purposes, and practices, which in the Christian context results in the loss of spiritual vitality."[1] Of course, what one person calls drift and another person calls drift may vary. This study is intended to ferret out what Simpson and the early leaders intended to be our essential standards from which to avoid drift, and what are open questions or secondary issues that have greater flexibility. I will cite doctoral dissertations and numerous other sources who have documented some of this this drift within the C&MA.[2]

WHAT DOES THE ALLIANCE REALLY BELIEVE?

Or a little more formally, "What is the theology of The Christian and Missionary Alliance?" These are questions that have been simmering and perhaps coming to a boiling point in the 21st century. Because of the nature of The Alliance "big tent," Alliance theology and hermeneutics (principles of interpretation) have not been articulated clearly across the board through the years. Consequently, various theologies and hermeneutics have been propagated as "Alliance," some of which are actually in conflict with Alliance theology and hermeneutics or have been elevated to the level of 1st or 2nd tier doctrines, when our founders intended them to be 3rd tier non-essential open questions.

Since we are a "big tent," pastors and leaders coming into the Alliance from other varied backgrounds have brought with them their favorite Bible teachers and preachers on every end of the theological spectrum—such as John MacArthur, R. C. Sproul, Paul Washer, Tim Keller, John Stott, C. Peter Wagner, Kenneth Hagin, and Bill Johnson, to name just a few. They often have great biblical teaching in some areas, but unfortunately do not necessarily share Alliance beliefs and values. Further, some of their teachings or emphases actually clash with Alliance theology, values, and practice. I have also heard others in the Alliance express regarding a vast array of issues that they want to move away from, dis-identify with, or significantly modify and/or discard some historic Alliance doctrines and practices:

- "Well, this is what the Alliance believed in the past, but we know better now."
- "We can't go back to the past." We need to look forward, not backward."
- "Since we are a denomination now, we can't go back to the flexibility and exceptions we made when we were a movement."
- "We have learned from the mistaken theology of Simpson and the early Alliance."
- "I am not interested in old dead guys."

- "Early Alliance exegesis was loose; ours is more precise today."

These are statements I have actually heard some Alliance leaders make. What comes to my mind is the Scripture: "All that generation also were gathered to their fathers; and there arose another generation after them who did not know the Lord, nor yet the work which He had done for Israel" (Judges 2:10).

Of course, the first clause does not apply to these Alliance leaders, because this new generation *does* know the Lord, and for that we are grateful. However, the second clause may apply in a way. They *do* know the Lord, but later generations often *do not know* the mighty works of God He had done in and through the early Alliance and the truths He had revealed to Simpson and the early Alliance. Some don't have a clue about vital Alliance roots in Covenant Theology, the Higher Life, the supernatural, and as well what have been considered non-essential open questions throughout Alliance history.

Thus, I would rephrase this as, "All the original generation of the Alliance passed on, and a new generation arose who know the Lord, but don't know the Lord like A. B. Simpson did and the mighty works the Lord did in and through the early Alliance." They don't have a personal understanding and appreciation for the foundations of our wonderful message and ministry.

I shared this about a few years ago with a couple I consider mentors in my life, Bob and MaryK Petty (Bob has since become the Superintendent of the Alliance Midwest District). They urged me, challenged me, even commissioned me, as it were, to present the treasure of writings and Higher Life message of A. B. Simpson to this generation and mentor this new generation in the vital rich heritage of Simpson and The Alliance. This book is a result of that challenge.

This is not to say that we should not be critical of Simpson and early Alliance leaders if they had some unsound teaching. Certainly, there are aspects of the teachings and practices of Simpson and early Alliance leaders that we need to adjust or abandon.[3] I admit that I tend to be a Simpson-ite and a Tozer-ite, but I assure you that don't agree with everything Simpson or Tozer taught. I like what another District Superintendent once said, "I would die for Jesus, but not for the Alliance." (Although sometimes I might come close to dying for the Alliance as well!).

Nonetheless, we miss a lot of the vital depth, strength, and vibrancy of our heritage if we become too critical or indifferent about our past. Dr. Arnold Cook provides wise counsel those who would "celebrate drift":

> If this becomes the first response to drift, we would be doing an end run around the Holy Spirit's commitment to renewal. Unlike secular structures, the church is first an organism, secondly an organization. God designs organisms for renewal. Organizations can only be restructured.
>
> Second, much of drift is intertwined with generational issues. God is committed to working through generations, the art of Christian leadership, not around them. The art of Christian leadership is the challenge of blending in generations into dynamic synergism to a watching and fragmented world.[4]

These issues are not easy to discern. When is something an end run around the Holy Spirit, and when is the Holy Spirit doing something new? To what things of the past should we be anchored, and what things should be let go of for new generations? Are we like Tevye, in the classic Jewish musical *Fiddler on the Roof*, bound to the past, for "without our traditions our lives would be as shaky as a fiddler on the roof?" What are the legitimate anchors to which we need to hold, regardless of generations? This study explores those anchors for the Alliance.

Partly as a response to Dr. Cook's book, I was commissioned in 2000 by Dr. K. Neill Foster (Board of Managers member and publisher of Christian Publications) and Dr. Donald Wiggins (then Vice President of Church Ministries) to research and write a document on *Hermeneutical Implications in the Christian and Missionary Alliance Statement of Faith*, which would be co-authored by the three of us and possibly be used in ordination studies. It was never published, due in part to the closure of the Alliance publishing house, but several Alliance leaders have affirmed to me that the need for a similar book is even more pressing now.

The earliest systematized Alliance theology was theologian George P. Pardington's work entitled *Outline Studies in Christian Doctrine*, but as aptly named, it was only an outline of theological lectures with some notes), and it did not flesh out or fully explain Alliance doctrines. No other thorough systematic work covering Alliance theology has been published. Dr. Scott Borderud concluded through his dissertation research that systematic theology is "the theological discipline most neglected in the history of the Alliance."[5] Others have given summaries of Alliance theology, like Dr. Keith Bailey's brief *Bringing Back the King* and more recently *The Whole Gospel for the Whole World* by Dr. Franklin Pyles an d Dr. Lee Beach. Others have written about some aspect of the Fourfold Gospel.[6] Though not a developing a systematic theology, Daryn Henry, in his recent dissertation published as *A. B. Simpson and the Making of Modern Evangelicalism*, presents a fresh insightful examination of Simpson and the early Alliance, combining biographical, historiographical, theological, and sociological reflection.[7]

Dr. Bernie Van de Walle from Canada is, I believe, the premier theologian of A. B. Simpson today. His excellent book, *The Heart of the Gospel*, is the closest in recent years to a systematized presentation of the history and theology of the Fourfold Gospel and the theology of Simpson and has been used in ordination studies.[8] It does touch in varying degrees to aspects of systematic theology. Nevertheless, it was not intended to cover all of Alliance theology systematically or historically. Nor is this book intended to do that. If there is interest, hopefully Bernie or myself or someone else will tackle that in the future.

Until that tome is written, the intent of this book is to provide a valuable Alliance theological and hermeneutical resource (with documentation for further research) for Alliance seminary students; Licensing, Ordination, and Consecration Councils members; and candidates for licensing, ordination, and consecration, as well as for pastors, elders, boards, and lay leaders. When I served on Licensing, Ordination, and Consecration Councils, we did not want to know only what the interviewee believed, but *why* he or she believed and *how* they articulated it, to have scriptural support, but also why that Scripture supports it and how to communicate it with others.

THE ALLIANCE THEOLOGICAL HERMENEUTIC

Every denomination or theological group has its own theology and hermeneutic, its own perspective of doctrine and interpretation: a Reformed theological hermeneutic, a Wesleyan theological hermeneutic, a Baptist theological hermeneutic, a Pentecostal theological hermeneutic, a Lutheran theological hermeneutic, etc.[9] The Alliance hermeneutic is none of these and all of these! The Alliance theological hermeneutic is comprised of three tiers that embrace or give liberty to all of these theologies, expressed in one dimension or another or to one degree or another, without fully embracing or dogmatizing any of them. The Alliance theological hermeneutic is not Reformed or Lutheran or Methodist, or Arminian, or Episcopal, or Quaker, or Baptist, or Pentecostal although, as we will see below, it may be in some ways inclusive of all of them in the 3rd tier.

Because of the nature of the Alliance "big tent," Alliance theology and hermeneutics have not been articulated clearly or consistently across the board. Hence, various theologies and hermeneutics have been propagated as "Alliance," some of which are actually in conflict with Alliance theology and hermeneutics or have been elevated to the level of 1st or 2nd tier doctrines, when our founders intended them to be 3rd tier non-essential doctrines and practices to be held as open questions. What has sometimes happened is that one side begins to emphasize and to push, so then the other side feels a need to push back.[10] Our strength, having an inclusive harmonized unity of doctrinal viewpoints, has also been a weakness when the lack of a strong, clear centerpiece of the three-tier doctrinal foundations has allowed for one theological viewpoint to rise up and take dominance.

Some in the Alliance try to impose a Reformed hermeneutic or an Arminian hermeneutic or a dispensational hermeneutic, etc., upon the

Alliance. The Alliance "big tent" allows for each of these hermeneutics to "co-exist" in the Alliance without imposing that particular conviction upon all.

I use the word "co-exist" with fear and trepidation, for when I have used it before in a Facebook discussion, it was implied that I was accommodating to the one-world religious universalist "co-exist." We are in a day in which the vocabulary shifts and terms like "gay" and "rainbow" take on very different meanings than they once did. So, by "co-exist," I do not mean compromising our essentials, but rather living in harmony while disagreeing on secondary or tertiary issues.

SIMPSON'S "LIVING THEOLOGY"

A.B. Simpson was not a systematic theologian in the academic sense. He did not try to systematize theology. Rather, all theology needed to relate to life. He was a practical biblical theologian. He was not interested in abstract concepts, but in concrete application to Christian living in the world. Although he believed in the ideal, he recognized the real, the living.

Living Truth or Dead Theologies?

Introducing the first issue of his periodical *Living Truths* in 1902, Simpson asserted that there are "living truths and dead theologies."[11] Theology had to be alive and had to relate to life. Preeminently, theology related to Jesus Christ as the way, the truth, and the life (John 14:6).[12] Simpson's theological hermeneutic included these principles (summarized in this book and hopefully elucidated more completely in the proposed full systematic theological book):

Living Theology Is Christocentric. All of theology, then, revolves around Jesus Christ. Simpson's hermeneutic is Christological. Every doctrine is Christo-centric:

> Salvation is not to embrace a creed, but to meet the Saviour. Sanctification is not to find an experience, but to receive the Christ and the

Holy Spirit to abide within and relive His life in us. . . . To reveal Him, to make Him real to human hearts, to bear witness to Him who is 'the Way, the Truth and the Life' is the first object of *Living Truths*.[13]

Simpson illustrated this through his preaching, teaching, and writing, especially through his expositional *Christ in the Bible* series. For Simpson, all truth is found in Christ, for He is the Truth Incarnate.

Living Theology Is Confirmed in Experience with Christ. For Simpson, all truth is not merely found in Christ, but in a personal encounter with Christ. Simpson asserted,

Back of every error lies a lost truth. . . . Let us not merely condemn the error but seek to find the point of contact with every human soul, and gently lead it back to the lost truth and the Living Christ, who is God's answer to all questionings, and God's resting place for all tired and homeless hearts.[14]

All heresy and theological error come from looking for the living truth in the wrong place: In some sense, some of Simpson's theology was derived in part from his experiences—especially his experiences of healing and sanctification, though he would insist that his experience was rooted in Scripture and stemmed from his personal encounter with the Living Truth.

Living Theology Must Be Biblical. While Simpson was not fully a systematic theologian in the academic sense, he might be considered a biblical theologian in the sense that he was an expositional preacher and teacher. His *Christ in the Bible* series was comprised of a series of expositions on Scripture—especially emphasizing Christ in every book of the Bible. His pneumatological work was a biblical-theological approach to the Holy Spirit, again finding the Holy Spirit in almost every book of the Bible. *The Gospel of Healing* also contained a biblical-theological framework for divine healing.

Living Theology Is Flexible in the Non-Essentials. When we look at A.B. Simpson's theology, sometimes we need to distinguish between early Simpson and later Simpson, just as we might distinguish early

Bonhoeffer and later Bonhoeffer or early C.S. Lewis and later C.S. Lewis. When we examine Simpson's earlier and later views, we discover that Simpson modified his views on such theological issues as the end times, faith and healing, the role of tongues in evangelism, women in ministry, etc. He was dogmatic on the essentials of the faith, but flexible and teachable on other matters.

In an article on "Side Issues and Essentials," Simpson used the biblical image of wineskins to illustrate the difference between them. The wineskin itself is the container for the new wine of the Holy Spirit. This represents the essentials of the faith. The structure is necessary but making non-essentials or side issues essentials makes the wineskin brittle and inflexible:

> These skins when new were elastic and susceptible of stretching with the fermentation of the wine and expansion of its volume. The bottle grew as the wine swelled and there was no rupture. But new wine put into old skins would have no allowance for stretching and hie result would be the rending of the bottles and the loss of both bottles and wine. And so, the Lord teaches that it is impracticable to try to combine things that are not essentially adjustable to each other. The result will be failure and disaster. . . . The same struggle still goes on when people try to hold on to old forms, habits and methods of worship, and work which are not in themselves essential.[15]

Living Theology Sustains the Essentials. On other issues, especially doctrinal essentials, Simpson maintained consistency in views throughout his life and ministry. Simpson was more of a practical theologian than a systematic theologian, so we might not be comfortable with all of his views on a variety of issues. As with the Alliance hermeneutic as a whole, we need to discern levels of doctrinal importance in Simpson. Because Simpson himself informally created the three-tier Alliance hermeneutics of essentials, distinctives, and non-essentials, Simpson's hermeneutic for his own belief system was virtually the same as the Alliance hermeneutic he created.

Living Theology Is Demonstrated in Typology. This approach is to be distinguished from the allegorical method. Typological interpretation "affirms the historical meaning of the text but also notes that entities (people, objects, events) mentioned in the texts prefigure subsequent and corresponding entities (for example, King David is viewed as a *type* of Christ)."[16] This methodology can be valid as long as it is not taken to extremes. The tabernacle, for example, does provide many valid typological examples, based on the typology presented in Hebrews 9 and 10. However, this does not give legitimacy to attempting to find typological symbolism in every detail of the tabernacle, for that would lapse into allegorization.[17]

Simpson and other early Alliance leaders did make more use of typology than some interpreters are comfortable with today.[18] This was typical of other evangelical leaders of his time (Charles Spurgeon, Andrew Murray, etc.). Yet he was not as extreme as some have become. His typology was almost always distinctly Christological. He did not get into esoteric mystical symbolism, but always pointed to Jesus. Simpson's use of typology was Christ-centered and cross-centered. He believed that typology confirmed truths of the Word and truths of the Word confirmed typology. Especially what stands out is Simpson's typology of the tabernacle, which he applies in three different arenas: the tabernacle as a type of Christ, the church, and the Christian life.[19]

Living Theology Can Be Drawn from or Confirmed by Diverse Sources. Simpson gleaned from the teachings and interpretations of the church fathers such as Polycarp, Irenaeus, Tertullian, Origen, Cyprian, Eusebius, Jerome, and Augustine. He mined gems from Puritans such as Samuel Rutherford and Richard Baxter; mystics such as Brother Lawrence, Fenelon, and Madame Guyon; Reformers such as John Calvin, Martin Luther, John Wyclif, John Knox; Pietists such as Francke and Blumhardt; and other Christian leaders such as Whitefield, Wesley, Wilberforce, Coleridge, Finney, Spurgeon, Hudson Taylor, George Mueller, and the list goes on. He criticized the theology of "Romanism," but cited Catholic leaders such as Bernard of Clairvaux and Thomas a Kempis.

He studied academic commentaries and Greek and Hebrew scholars such as Albert Bengel, Conybeare and Howson, Henry Alford,

Franz Delitzch, Marvin Vincent, and George Pember. He discussed what he called "controversies of exegetical theology."[20] Simpson embraced some aspects of dispensational teaching, but also warned against "rigid dispensation teachers" and dangers of dispensation teaching.[21] Simpson was familiar with classic philosophers like Socrates and Plato and pseudepigraphal literature such as the Book of Enoch. He consulted all these sources critically, separating wheat from chaff and sifting through Scripture.

Ultimately, Living Theology Calls People to a Deeper and Higher Life in Christ. For Simpson, "the Alliance has a broader basis" than even a worldwide missional movement. "It also aims to accomplish an equally important work for the promotion *of a higher Christian life* and *full salvation for both soul and body.*[22]

1

THE BIBLICAL AND HISTORICAL BASIS FOR THE ALLLIANCE HERMENEUTIC

EARLY ALLIANCE "BIG TENT" FRATERNALISM

From its inception in 1887, The Christian and Missionary Alliance was formed to be an "ecumenical" interdenominational organization (including Methodists, Baptists, Presbyterians, Episcopalians, Lutherans, Mennonites, Brethren, and Quakers, among others, and later, Pentecostals), focusing on missions and the Higher Christian Life with the motto of Jesus Christ as Savior, Sanctifier, Healer, and Coming King.

The term "ecumenical" was often used in a positive sense in early Alliance literature of cooperative ventures of various evangelical, Bible-believing groups, uniting around a common cause for the gospel, not the negative connotations often associated today with watering down the Gospel through theological and moral compromise.[1] "Fraternal," "inclusive,"[2] "broad platform," "big tent," among others, are terms that have been used throughout Alliance history to describe endeavoring within evangelical orthodoxy to live the motto: "Unity in things essential; liberty in things non-essential; love in all things."[3]

Early on and throughout early Alliance growth and development, Simpson emphasized a big tent attitude toward various doctrinal differences, yet with boundaries.[4] The adaptability of Simpson is observed in his 1900 policy: "God's methods in matters of outward form are flexible enough to allow for exceptions and adjustments."[5] It would seem that Simpson intentionally surrounded himself with leaders from diverse theological backgrounds: George Peck and George Watson (Methodist); Peter Updegraaff (Quaker); Henry Wilson and Kenneth MacKenzie (Episcopal/Anglican); Frederick Farr and A. J. Gordon (Baptist); Carrie Judd Montgomery (Episco-pal/Salvation Army/Pentecostal), among others, just to name a few.

COVENANT THEOLOGY—THE THEOLOGICAL-HISTORICAL FOUNDATION FOR THE ALLIANCE HERMENEUTIC

Although the Alliance is not distinctly Reformed in theology (as we will see that Calvinism and Arminianism are 3rd-tier open question doctrines), certain aspects of Alliance theology and hermeneutics are rooted in Covenant Theology. Developed by Reformation leaders such as Zwingli and Bullinger, Covenant Theology set the foundation for much of the 19th century Higher Life teaching. It was adopted by one strain of the Calvinist Reformed tradition and especially found its consummation in the Dutch Puritan theology of Cocceius and the Scotch Covenanter movement. Anabaptists and Wesleyans also adopted elements of Covenant Theology.[6] Its appeal to diverse theological groups also laid a foundation for Simpson's ecumenical "broad platform."

The Covenant Theology hermeneutic is centered around God's covenants as a central theme of Scripture. It interprets from Scripture that the Church is spiritual Israel in covenant relationship with God. The promises of God to the nation of Israel are fulfilled on a higher, spiritual plane through the Church, through what Covenant Theology writers called the "covenant of grace" and "covenant of redemption" through Jesus Christ. Just as Israel had covenant rights and privileges through their covenant with Yahweh, so through these covenants from Christ the Church has similar parallel rights and privileges.

These doctrinal foundations of the Reformation period were

further developed by the Puritans and Pietists, were adopted into 19th-century Reformed holiness beliefs, and provided a foundation for 19th and 20th-century Higher Life movements, as taught especially by William Boardman (Presbyterian), Andrew Murray (Dutch Reformed), A. B. Simpson (Scotch Presbyterian), A.T. Pierson (Presbyterian), and others in the Higher Life/Keswick Reformed holiness movement, as well as by Charles Spurgeon (Baptist), who is sometimes called the last of the Puritans. Simpson promoted Covenant Theology through the Alliance, which became a major stream of the Higher Life movement.

A Caveat to Covenant Theology

Some varieties of Covenant Theology developed what is called "replacement theology," namely that the Church supersedes and replaces God's covenants made with Moses and Israel, therefore, God's covenants with Israel are null and void. This was not the position of Simpson and the early Alliance. Alliance leaders believed God's covenants with Israel remain in effect, although there was a variety of interpretation regarding just exactly what that means. Missionally, throughout its history, The Alliance has always ministered to both Jews and Palestinians, recognizing both the special place of Israel in God's economy, and, at the same time, equality and oneness between Jews and Gentiles. This is important for the intertwining of mission and eschatology (end-times).

THE ALLIANCE ECUMENICAL HERMENEUTIC: ESSENTIALS, NON-ESSENTIALS, AND LOVING LIBERTY IN UNITY

Simpson and the early Alliance sought to represent unifying factors within evangelical orthodoxy, living the motto: "Unity in things essential; liberty in things non-essential; charity in all things."[7] Simpson and the early Alliance modeled a "unity-in-loving-liberty" big tent biblical hermeneutic that allows for varying viewpoints on the role and meaning things considered to be non-essential or secondary or "open questions."

Unity in Things Essential—Non-Negotiables and Distinctives (2 Thess 2:15).

These are the non-negotiables of the faith passed down through the apostles and the New Testament writers. Regardless of denominational or theological persuasion, we are united around the central doctrines and issues of the Christian faith, about which we will not compromise. In addition to the non-negotiable essentials of the faith are the distinctives that make the Alliance "The Alliance." These are not essentials to faith in Christ, but they are essentials to the vision and ministry of The Alliance, the core values and doctrines that are unique and specific to The Alliance.

Liberty in Things Non-Essential.

Romans 14:5-10, 22 give us principles and examples of freedom of personal convictions and beliefs without judgment. Paul recognizes that a variety of beliefs and practices are not essential doctrines of the faith. Paul stipulates, "The faith which you have, have as your own conviction before God" (Rom 14:22). On this basis, A. B. Simpson and The Alliance granted people "liberty to present the truth . . . in such as their convictions warrant." Many other doctrines and issues are secondary, and in those The Alliance has granted liberty of conscience and belief. These secondary issues can be interpreted in different ways by evangelical, Bible-believing Christians, and thus regarded as "open questions."

Charity in All Things (Col 3:14-15).

The Alliance gave liberty to teachers in presenting various opinions, so long as they "shall not be pressured in an aggressive or controversial spirit toward those who differ," and "with the understanding that any spirit of antagonism and strife toward those who may hold different opinions is discountenanced." Alliance leaders agreed to disagree peacefully on those things in an attitude of love, charity, and acceptance.

HISTORICAL BACKGROUND OF THE ALLIANCE STATEMENT OF FAITH

Originally, the early Alliance as an interdenominational parachurch organization did not have an official Statement of Faith. However, when questioned whether the Christian Alliance was an evangelical organization, Simpson and the Board of the Christian Alliance responded with an official statement: that they did not "feel to publicly recognize or allow any to speak upon its platforms any who are known to hold views contrary to evangelical truth."

Earliest Alliance Statement of Faith—1892.

Such truth was thus defined in Article III of Constitution and By-laws of International Missionary Alliance:

> The Board and all missionaries and members of the Society shall be required to subscribe to the following declaration of principles: "I believe in God the Father, God the Son, and God the Holy Ghost, in the verbal inspiration of the Holy Scriptures as originally given, in the vicarious atonement of the Lord Jesus Christ, in the eternal salvation of all who believe in Him, and the everlasting punishment of all who reject Him."[8]

1906 Statement of Alliance Testimony.

The 1906 "Conference for Prayer and Counsel Regarding Uniformity in the Testimony and Teaching of the Alliance" expanded upon this statement and the principles of the Fourfold Gospel.[9] The focus of this meeting was on Alliance distinctives and what constitutes open questions.

The Five Fundamentals of 1910.

The Alliance subscribed to the Great Fundamentals presented formally and shared interdenominationally in 1910 and following by evangelical Christians of all stripes. These included 1) the verbal inspiration and inerrancy of Scripture, 2) the Virgin Birth, 3) the deity of Christ, 4) the substitutionary atonement of Christ, and 5) the resurrection and the literal, visible Second Coming of Christ.[10]

C&MA Affirmation of the Fundamentals by Alliance Theologian George Pardington (1912).

These included the inspiration and inerrancy of Scripture, the Virgin Birth, the deity of Christ, the substitutionary atonement of Christ, and the resurrection and the literal, visible Second Coming of Christ.[11]

Note: But don't confuse "The Fundamentals" and Fundamentalism. It is important to note that the writing of *The Fundamentals* should not be confused with the Fundamentalist movement which would later emerge out of this. Many who affirm the Fundamentals of Faith would not be considered Fundamentalist, including the C&MA.

Expansion of the Fundamentals--1919.

The 1919 World Christian Fundamentals Association (WCFA) expanded the Five Fundamentals into nine points: (1) verbal inerrancy of the Scriptures, (2) personal, premillennial, imminent return of Christ, (3) one God in three persons, (4) deity of Jesus, (5) sinfulness of man, (6) substitutionary atonement, (7) bodily resurrection of Jesus, (8) justification by faith, (9) bodily resurrection of the just and unjust.[12]

Note: C&MA Leadership's Prominent Role in Drafting the Fundamentals—1919ff. The WCFA also received strong input and representation from the C&MA by Paul Rader (pastor of Moody Church and president of the C&MA following Simpson's death) and Dr. Charles Blanchard (President of Wheaton College and an honorary Vice President of the C&MA), who was a leading member of the executive committee and spokesman for this Association.

Further C&MA Affirmation of the Fundamentals—1920s.

- 1922—Board of Managers statement: "the distinctive testimony of the Alliance" for Alliance schools, reaffirmed the 1906 declaration as well as "the historical fundamentals of the faith as embodied in 'The Apostles Creed' and 'The Niagara Creed' [The Great Fundamentals]."[13] **(see Appendix 1 for the Niagara Creed).**

- 1927—document entitled "The Message of the Christian and Missionary Alliance" included the "Great Fundamentals," as well as Alliance distinctives.[14] This document became the basis of the 1928 C&MA Statement of Faith for Alliance schools.

1928 Statement of Faith for Alliance Schools.

According to Alliance historian Robert Niklaus, "The 1928 doctrinal statement, . . . was used in all Alliance Bible Schools and had to be signed annually by each of the teaching staffs. Framers of the statement simply took the nine articles of the Christian Fundamentals Association and attached to them the distinctive Alliance testimony embodied in the Fourfold Gospel."[15]

Note: Separation from Fundamentalism. Even though the 1928 Doctrinal Statement was grounded in the statement of the WCFA, since the Alliance doctrinal statement included an article about belief in healing and the Alliance believed in all of the gifts of the Spirit, it parted company from the WCFA in 1928 when the WCFA passed a resolution against Pentecostal teaching, including speaking in tongues and healing.[16]

Growth Brings Need for Theological Clarity and Boundaries.

Dr. Scott Borderud writes,

> Its status as an interdenominational society really prevented a formulation of creed until necessity demanded it. This interdenominationalism was so strong and so pervasive in the Alliance that many would question the need for a doctrinal statement applicable to the entire denomination, right up to the point of its adoption in 1965. But the growth of the Alliance, along with the various theological conflicts in 20th century American Christianity called for clear articulation of doctrinal positions.[17]

Official Statement of Faith—1965.

The C&MA Statement of Faith of 1965 was adapted almost completely, with only minor changes, deletions, and additions, from the "Doctrinal Statement of 1928," and adopted by General Council and the C&MA Bible schools.[18] It is also the Statement of Faith of the Alliance World Fellowship. A full-length book on Alliance theology, hermeneutics, and Statements of Faith awaits decisions to be made at the US General Councils.

Canadian Statement of Faith.

After the Canadian C&MA became self-governing, the 1965 Statement of Faith was updated and revised in 1985, 1998, and 2000. **See Appendix 2 for both the C&MA and Canadian Statements of Faith as of 2020.**

2

ALLIANCE HERMENEUTICAL PRINCIPLES

THE BIBLICAL FOUNDATION FOR THE ALLIANCE HERMENEUTIC

Hermeneutics are vital to the beliefs of the Alliance. Especially significant in the 2nd century of our movement is the importance of maintaining our theological foundations and avoiding historical drift. Former Canadian C&MA president Dr. Arnold Cook admonished: "A weakened commitment to Scripture, more than any other factor, has facilitated historical drift. It renders us vulnerable to the subtle accommodation to culture."[1] That weakness provides a slippery slope away from the authority of Scripture toward relativism and enculturalization. We want to affirm that The Christian and Missionary Alliance maintains the authority and inspiration of the Bible as God's infallible and inerrant Word, and that our principal beliefs are based on sound exegesis and interpretation of Scripture.

The Alliance Statement of Faith, as with any document, was written with certain assumptions in mind. Alliance doctrine and hermeneutics are based primarily on grammatical-historical assumptions. Simpson was an expository preacher, trained in the art of the grammatical/historical exegesis of the original languages of Scripture, as standardly taught in ministerial training of his time. While Simpson often made use of typological significance, his studies were based on grammatical-historical principles and Christocentric and Covenant theological presuppositions.

THE ALLIANCE HERMENEUTIC OF GRAMMATICAL-HISTORICAL EXEGESIS

The Alliance Hermeneutic has been based upon the basic accepted principles of grammatical-historical exegesis, which included *the principles of Plain Intent, Scripture Comparison. Literal Priority; Grammar, Syntax, and Context; Culture, History, and Genre; using critical methodology reverently and discerningly; and being Spirit-taught, not just Word-taught.*

These will be explained and illustrated in a future full-length systematic theological book. We can see from this brief overview that Simpson and early Alliance leaders and other evangelical leaders of their time were acutely interested in hermeneutical soundness.

2nd Tier Hermeneutics of Alliance Distinctives

The hermeneutics of Alliance Distinctives followed grammatical-historical exegesis above, just as with the Fundamentals of the Faith, and added these biblically-based principles:

Stay Christocentric. "Jesus only is our message" as Savior, Sanctifier, Healer, and Coming King.

Affirm __All__ Scripture as Useful for Doctrine (Didaskalia) and Practice (2 Tim 3:16). The Alliance thus affirmed that we can get doctrine from both didactic Scripture (Epistles) and historical Scripture (Acts). This is against the teaching of those who teach the opposite, such as John Stott. Alliance scholar Dr. Bob Willoughby affirms the Alliance position. See Appendix 8, Exegetical Evidence #4.[2]

Maintain the Essential Distinctives Flexibly without Compromise. The Alliance Distinctives are what make The Alliance "Alliance." They are regarded as essentials to the foundation and ministry of The Alliance, but not essentials of the faith at the same level as the Fundamentals. They are non-negotiables within the Alliance, yet flexible wineskins in expression and application.

Follow the Principle of "We Believe This, But We Allow That." The genius (as well as the tension) of The Alliance is strong belief, but with loving allowance without disharmony for certain differing views. See Chapter 18 for examples.

Be Flexible, But Not Loose. The early Alliance found it challenging at times, even during the first 25 years of Alliance history, to maintain those essential distinctives flexibly without compromise. Simpson wrote in 1909 of concerns:

> The Alliance cannot afford to compromise. . . . Loose views about sanctification, the baptism of the Holy Spirit, the definite experience of union and fellowship with Christ and Divine Healing through the name of Jesus are out of place on such a platform.[3]

Beware of Drift. Firm that the sanctifying baptism/filling of the Spirit was *not* a 3rd tier optional belief for the C&MA, but rather an essential 2nd tier distinctive, Simpson was concerned about drift and asserted that in the Alliance, "*We should deeply deplore any drift from this high and established standard.*"[4]

3rd Tier Alliance Ecumenical Hermeneutics

As Inclusive as Scripture Allows, as Exclusive as Scripture Mandates. Simpson and the early Alliance understood, on one hand, that they needed wineskins to contain the fresh movement of God— wineskins that were defined, yet that were flexible, not rigid. The Alliance was thus as inclusive as Scripture allows (flexible wineskins for the moving of the Spirit) and as exclusive as Scripture mandates (definite wineskins or containers with biblically- decreed limits).

The Alliance believed in interdenominational cooperation and evangelical diversity and unity. Simpson modeled an endeavor to be a bridge-builder across denominations and theological viewpoints. Board of Managers member John MacMillan later called it "harmonized diversity," saying, "Where there is this Christo-centric attitude, differences of doctrine and variations in forms of worship are recognized as non-essentials of faith."[5] While maintaining all of the 1st and 2nd tier hermeneutical principles mentioned above, Alliance leaders maintained additional principles for 3rd tier liberty regarding open question non-essentials.

Tozer's Principles for Determining What Is Essential and What Is Non-Essential. A.W. Tozer became one of the C&MA's most articulate and influential communicators of this Alliance hermeneutic. His writings include the following principles among others (explained in more detail in my book *Anointed Women,* Chapter 3).

- Distinguish between majors and minors.
- Recognize that truth has two wings.
- Don't hold tightly to one text.
- Balance Scripture with Scripture.
- Maintain the Spirit of the Word, not the letter.
- Follow the principle that internal essence is most important.

Other Alliance 3rd Tier Hermeneutical Principles

- **Harmonize seemingly contradictory texts.** Rather than pit one against the other, hold both in balance.
- **Acknowledge that normal does not necessitate a norm.** That which is common does not automatically make it binding. Consider a broader, more charitable hermeneutic.
- **Realize "the final exegesis is not always found in the lexicon and grammar."—A. J. Gordon.**[6] Even with the use of sound grammatical-historical hermeneutics, evangelical Christians disagree oN how to interpret certain texts.
- **Leave room for divine ambiguity in Scripture** in such issues as the end time events, variations in church government, biblical support for Calvinism and Arminianism, roles for women in ministry and other issues. About the essentials, there is no ambiguity.
- **Follow The Alliance hermeneutical ethic:** Maintain unity, liberty, and love.

3

THE THREE-TIER ALLIANCE
HERMENEUTIC

As mentioned in Chapter 1, all denominations or theological groups have a hermeneutic, a perspective of interpretation of Scripture: a Reformed, a Wesleyan, a Pentecostal, a Baptist hermeneutic, etc. The Alliance hermeneutic is none of these and all of these! The Alliance hermeneutic embraces or gives liberty to all of these, expressed in one dimension or another or to one degree or another without fully embracing or dogmatizing any of them. [1] Recognizing that godly people who use sound biblical hermeneutics disagree on how to interpret the same Scriptures, The Alliance allowed for these variances to be downplayed for the sake of harmony and the greater purpose—evangelizing the lost.

Because of the nature of the Alliance "big tent," Alliance theology and hermeneutics have not always been articulated clearly across the board. Thus, as stated in Chapter 2, various theologies and hermeneutics have been propagated as "Alliance," some of which are actually in conflict with Alliance theology and hermeneutics, or else have been elevated to the level of 1st or 2nd tier doctrines when our founders intended them to be 3rd tier *liberty* doctrines.

Some people have thought these three-tier classifications and categorizations were my invention, but they are not. A.B. Simpson himself used the terminology of "essentials" (of Christian faith), "distinctives" (or "essentials for the Alliance"), and "open questions" (or side issues, non-essentials, etc.), to designate levels of interpretation and importance. From its inception in 1887, The Alliance has indeed had an informal 3-tier hermeneutic throughout out our history, although not always expressed in a clear or consistent manner. These three tiers have been ascertained and compiled from numerous Alliance documents and various sources, including Simpson's writings, Alliance periodicals, and official Alliance documents, such as board minutes, Council documents, etc. These three tiers have been utilized throughout Alliance history as follows:

1ST TIER: ESSENTIALS/NON-NEGOTIABLES "Unity in things essential" (2 Thess 2:15; 1 Cor 15:1-4)
2ND TIER: ALLIANCE DISTINCTIVES Supernatural Christocentric Fourfold Gospel ("the rallying point"—A.B. Simpson)
3RD TIER: NON-ESSENTIALS, OPEN QUESTIONS, SIDE ISSUES "Liberty in things non-essential; Love in all things" (Rom 14; Col 3:14-15)

Modeling a "unity-in-loving-liberty" hermeneutic, The Alliance has allowed for varying viewpoints on the role and meaning of things considered non-essential, secondary, or open questions. As stated earlier, the early Alliance was thus as inclusive as Scripture allows and as exclusive as Scripture mandates, building bridges of interdenominational cooperation in what John MacMillan called "harmonized diversity,"[2] including three levels of doctrinal importance and flexibility of interpretation.

FIRST TIER: ESSENTIALS/NON-NEGOTIABLES

These are what Simpson called the "great essential principles that we cannot compromise," or what Alliance theologian George Pardington called the "fundamental doctrines,"[3] which were the same as the "Great Fundamentals." These included the following cardinal doctrines of evangelical Christian faith: Trinity; deity and humanity of

Christ; person and work of the Holy Spirit; lostness of man and need of new birth; substitutionary atoning death of Christ; reality of heaven and hell; salvation/justification by grace through faith; inspiration, authority, infallibility, and inerrancy of Scripture; incarnation and virgin birth of Christ; physical resurrection of Christ; visible physical 2nd coming of Christ.

Simpson and early Alliance did draw a line in dealing with questionable doctrinal issues that would water down or compromise the above doctrines. Maintaining soundness in these would be essential. Simpson and early Alliance leaders called out heresies such as the "carnality of Christ" (Christ had a sinful nature) and "second probation" (people have another chance to be saved after they die).[4] These were not open questions; but rather, such teachings threatened the foundation doctrines of the Christian faith.

SECOND TIER: ALLIANCE DISTINCTIVES
(with some 3rd tier liberty)

The Alliance Distinctives are what make The Alliance "Alliance." These are the doctrines considered essential to the ethos and vision of The Alliance as founded by A. B. Simpson. These are the Fourfold Gospel and vital related truths. As Simpson maintained, "The points essential to our united testimony are Salvation, Sanctification, Divine Healing and the Lord's Coming."[5] They are based on the foundations of Scripture, the Higher Life message, and Covenant Theology.

Christocentric

Jesus only is our message." The hermeneutical grid for The Alliance is "Christ in the Bible," interpreting all of Scripture—every book—Christologically.

Christological Continuism

The priority of "Jesus only is our message" exemplifies a high

Christology, putting special emphasis on the unchangeable character, purpose, and work of Christ, expressed through Hebrews 13:8. As Simpson articulated it, "If the Christ of Christianity is the same yesterday, today and forever, the Christianity of Christ ought also to be the same yesterday, today, and forever."[6] The clear implication, Simpson asserts, is that all supernatural gifts of the Spirit continue today, what is called "continuism." Thus, The Alliance takes a stand for continuism and against cessationism or dispensationalism, the belief that certain gifts of the Spirit ceased after the end of the apostolic age/dispensation or the completion of Scripture. This belief is implicit in the sanctifying filling of the Spirit and Christ as Healer as 2nd Tier Distinctives.

Christ Our Savior

"Jesus Christ, a living reality and all-sufficient Saviour. . . . It is a message of supernatural power, available through our risen Lord for every believing soul."[7] "Salvation is not to embrace a creed, but to meet the Saviour."[8] Christ is the Savior of the whole person—spirit, soul, and body—what Simpson called "the gospel of full salvation." Jesus saves from sin and hell, but also lifts the believer into a higher life.

A Distinctive Within a Distinctive: Believer's Baptism by Immersion. This a 2nd tier extension with 3rd tier liberty. For Simpson, believer's baptism was not a creed, but an encounter with Jesus Christ our Savior. It is a part of the fuller, higher life in Christ—but not a doctrine to be imposed; rather, a life to be experienced.

Christ Our Sanctifier

The sanctifying baptism/filling with the Holy Spirit, firmly held as a 2nd tier doctrine with 3rd tier liberty allowing for different terminology and variations of understanding.[9]

Christ Our Healer

Healing is a provision of the atonement but allows for 3rd tier liberty for variations or nuances of interpretation and practice.

Christ Our Coming King

The premillennial 2nd Coming was a 2nd tier doctrine with 3rd tier liberty. The founding Constitutional Statement of The Alliance, August 1887, reads:

> Inasmuch as many persons who desire to become members of this Alliance and are in full accord with its principles in other points, cannot yet fully accept the doctrine of Christ's Pre-millennial Coming, *it is agreed that such persons may be received into full membership provided they receive the first three points of testimony*, and are willing to give this subject their candid and prayerful consideration.[10]

THIRD TIER: LIBERTY IN THINGS NON-ESSENTIAL

With a hermeneutic of "unity in loving liberty," the early Alliance was as inclusive as Scripture allows (based on Romans 14) and as exclusive as Scripture mandates, building bridges of interdenominational cooperation in "harmonized diversity." Simpson and The Alliance affirmed a *broad platform and bridge-building* with *flexibility*; *liberty*; and *balance*, avoiding extremes and side issues such as "fads, frauds, phases, and hobby horses."[11] Such things were considered "open questions" or "side issues" in the following areas, among others:

- Calvinism and Arminianism
- Church government (including roles of women in ministry
- Beliefs and practices regarding baptism, Communion, and foot washing
- Forms, habits, and methods of worship; modern hymns and

tunes; beliefs and practices of Communion; fasting; when to worship (sabbath, Sabbatarianism, etc.)
- Varying views on Creation (but not evolutionary theory)
- Views on "phases and phrases" of sanctification
- Views on end times: details, order of events, antichrist, role of Israel; etc.
- Catholicism vs Protestantism
- And more![12]

The following chapters describe what is entailed in each of these three tiers.

PART II

TIER 1: ALLIANCE ESSENTIALS

4

TRINITARIAN ESSENTIALS
THEOLOGY PROPER

EXPOSITION OF THE STATEMENT OF FAITH ON THE TRINITY

The proposed full systematic theological book will examine each phrase of the US and Canadian Statement of Faith Article 1 on the Trinity, citing scriptural support from the grammatical-historical hermeneutical approach and quotes from Alliance leaders, such as Simpson and Pardington, and exposition from the Great Fundamentals. This chapter will provide a concise summary.

There is one God, who is infinitely perfect, existing eternally in three persons: Father, Son, and Holy Spirit.

This statement above is affirmed in the US and Canadian Statements of Faith Article 1—The Trinity. The C&MA statement on the Trinity, with the exception of the phrase *who is infinitely perfect*, in both the 1928 and 1965 statements, is word-for word identical to Article 2 of the World Christian Fundamentals doctrinal statement. It is based upon traditional grammatical/historical exegesis of several passages of Scripture, combining several hermeneutical principles, including the plain meaning of the text, context, and comparing Scripture with Scripture. According to early Alliance theologian George Pardington, the Bible affirms both the unity of God in Exodus 20:3-7 and Deuteronomy 6:4, 5 and the "distinction of persons in the Godhead" in Matthew 28:19; John 14:16, 17, 20-23 and 2 Corinthians 13:14.[1]

APPLICATION TO THEOLOGICAL AREAS OF CONTROVERSY TODAY

Particular areas of relevant controversy today include God as Creator and the nature of creation, openness theology, and Simpson's meaning of "Jesus only is our message" vs non-Trinitarian "Jesus Only" oneness Pentecostalism.

The Doctrine of Creation and God as Creator as Fundamental

Simpson and the Alliance did not accept any view that did not involve direct creation: "The Holy Scriptures distinctly teach that a creation of this universe by the direct power of God is an article of faith and *not open to question or discussion*. . .. *the doctrine of creation is fundamental* to every other doctrine in the Scriptures.[2] The position of Simpson and The Alliance thus affirmed:

- Creation is direct by the power of God, not by Darwinian evolution.
- Creation is *ex nihilo*.
- Creation is historical, accepting "without question the historicity of the early chapters of Genesis."[3]
- These points are essential non-negotiables, not open to question.

Alliance Theology and Open Theism

Openness theology basically teaches that there are some things that are logically unknowable, even to God, and that God is ever-learning.

This grew out of the process theology concepts of the 1960s, and the "evangelical" version (if it can be considered evangelical) has been taught by scholars such as Clark Pinnock, Gregory Boyd, John Sanders, etc. This is one of those issues our founders never imagined would be an issue, so, of course, it was never directly addressed. Some would claim, then, that this is an open question in the big tent of The Alliance. However, our earlier leaders give us a glimpse of how they would answer today as they affirmed the sovereignty of God.

The hermeneutics of current openness theology ignores or downplays the straightforward meaning of these Scriptures, and changes and limits the meaning of the unchangeableness of God: Thus, the Alliance Statement of Faith stands in opposition to any form of openness theology that makes God less than God. A. W. Tozer presents the clear grammatical/historical meaning of Scripture concerning God's infinite perfection upheld by the C&MA. For more Alliance perspectives on openness theology, see Toccoa Falls professor of religion, Dr. Jon Tal Murphee, *Divine Paradoxes: A Finite View of an Infinite God*,[4] and Appendix 3 for a listing of an extensive listing of sources of Tozer's answers to Openness theism questions.

Alliance "Jesus Only" vs Modalistic Oneness Pentecostal "Jesus Only."

On "Jesus Only" and the Trinity this section in the proposed systematic theological book would discuss criticism of Simpson's "Jesus only" motto, providing biblical, hermeneutical, and Alliance support of the Trinity, as distinguished from the Oneness Pentecostal "Jesus Only" theology. Briefly here, A. B. Simpson's "Jesus Only," message is in no way to be confused with the "Jesus Only" Oneness Pentecostal movement, which was modalistic, not Trinitarian. Pardington, an Old Testament and Semitic scholar, especially weighs in on this by means of the hermeneutical *principles of Scripture comparison and grammar and syntax.*

5

CHRISTOLOGICAL ESSENTIALS
THE PERSON AND WORK OF JESUS CHRIST

DEITY AND HUMANITY OF CHRIST, INCARNATION, VIRIGIN BIRTH, SUBSTITUTIONAL ATONING DEATH, PHYSICAL RESURRECTION

The Alliance at its core is Christo-centric ("Jesus only is our message"). The Christological non-negotiables of the Christian faith are summarized in Article 2 of the Alliance Statement of Faith on "The Person and Work of Christ."

Jesus Christ is true God and true man. He was conceived by the Holy Spirit and born of the Virgin Mary. He died upon the cross, the Just for the unjust, as a substitutionary sacrifice, and all who believe in Him are justified on the ground of His shed blood. He arose from the dead according to the Scriptures. He is now at the right hand of the Majesty on high as our great High Priest. He will come again to establish His kingdom of righteousness and peace.

This article, stated the same in both the U.S. and Canadian Faith Statements, is a merging together of Articles III, V, and VI of the World Christian Fundamentals Doctrinal Statement, with some reorganizing and rewording. In one paragraph it stresses and summarizes the deity and humanity of the person of Christ, the Incarnation and virgin birth, and the work, death, atonement, resurrection, and ascension of Christ.

This chapter in the proposed full systematic theological book will cite scriptural support from the grammatical-historical hermeneutical approach and quotes from Alliance leaders, such as Simpson and Pardington. It also includes sources from which the statement is drawn, especially exposition from the Great Fundamentals of 1910-1919. The chapter also deals with application to current Christological issues such as various orthodox and non-orthodox kenotic theories and various atonement theories.

The C&MA Manual cites Philippians 2:6-11 as the scriptural basis for this doctrine. The plain intent of the text clearly identifies Jesus as both God and man. In the form of God Jesus is true God; made in the likeness of man, Jesus is true man. Of the phrase "in the very nature God," using the hermeneutical principles of grammar and syntax, Simpson notes, "The language has the force and bears the construction that He was equal with God, that He was a possessor of the very nature of God, was Himself a divine Person."[1] Further, he explained, "Christ gave up a place of dignity and position in heaven, where He was known as God and God alone. And now, He is forever known as man, still divine, yet not exclusively divine, but united to the person, flesh, and form of a created being."[2]

James Orr, one of the originators of the Fundamentals, explained why the Virgin Birth is vital: "Those who accept a full doctrine of the Incarnation—that is, of a true entrance of the eternal Son of God into our nature for the purposes of man's salvation—with hardly an exception accept with it the doctrine of the virgin birth of Christ, while those who repudiate or deny this article of faith either hold a lowered view of Christ's person, or more commonly, reject his supernatural claims altogether."[3]

Pardington gives much attention in his *Outline Studies of Christian Doctrine* to the exegetical and theological basis of the death of Christ, and especially the substitutionary nature of the Atonement.[4] In particular, he notes that in Matthew 20:28 and Galatians 2:20, "There are two Greek prepositions which express the substitutional or vicarious idea, viz: *huper*—in behalf of, and *anti*—instead of. Some regard them as equivalents."[5] The compilers of the Great Fundamentals emphasized the importance of the substitutionary understanding for the Atonement, as opposed to those would water down the meaning of the death of Christ to the moral influence theory.[6]

EXCURSUS: CHRIST'S HUMANITY, KENOTIC THEORIES, AND THE ALLIANCE

There is much misunderstanding, misinformation, and controversy about the doctrine of "kenosis" based on the Scripture "Christ emptied (*kenoo*) Himself" (Phil 2:7), including in Christian and Missionary Alliance circles. This is a very complex theological issue, and some popular "discernment" groups are quick to cast judgment on what they perceive to be "heresies" of the doctrine of kenosis purported by "false teachers."

Although I myself have concerns about some of the things taught by alleged "false teachers," I have found that there is often a rush to judgment in misunderstanding and mislabeling such teachings as "heresies" and such people as "false teachers," especially as it has caused confusion in Alliance circles. As we will see below, these accusations of heresy when applied to the kenotic statements of A. B. Simpson and A.W. Tozer (as well as many other evangelical leaders) would brand them as heretics and false teachers.

Simpson wrote against a kenosis theory that makes Jesus less than God. He also refuted the belief in the "carnality of Christ," the teaching that Jesus had a sinful nature, but did not sin.[7] This theory allegedly arose out of Scottish Presbyterian pastor Edward Irving and others in the 1830s. These were not and are not debatable issues or open questions for the Alliance.

At the same time, Alliance leaders did maintain an orthodox view of kenosis, what is known in theology as a "sub-kenotic" theory. He maintained that Jesus did His miraculous works, not as God, but as man. Other evangelical leaders associated with the Alliance also affirmed this, including A.W. Tozer and Simpson's Baptist friend colleague A. J. Gordon. **See Appendix 4 for a summary of orthodox sub-kenotic functional theologies, and the orthodox kenotic teaching of Simpson and Tozer.**

EXCURSUS: ALTERNATURE ATONEMENT THEORIES .

While affirming substitutionary atonement, Simpson also accepted the ransom theory of atonement. Both views can be held without conflict. So long as another view of the atonement also accepts the substitutionary view, the views can be held concurrently. However, some current theology holds to what is called a non-violent view of the atonement, which appears in conflict with the substitutionary view. Such a view would not be considered an open question if it conflicts with or waters down a substitutionary view of the atonement.

6

HOLY SPIRIT ESSENTIALS

THE PERSON AND WORK OF THE HOLY SPIRIT

The Holy Spirit is a divine person, sent to indwell, guide, teach, empower the believer, and to convince the world of sin, of righteousness, and of judgment.

Article 3 of the Alliance Statement of Faith on "The Person and Work of the Holy Spirit" is essentially the same in both the Canadian and the U.S. Faith Statements. This chapter cites scriptural support from the grammatical-historical hermeneutical approach and quotes from Alliance leaders, such as Simpson and Pardington. It also includes sources from which the statement is drawn, especially exposition from the Great Fundamentals of 1910-1919.

"THE HOLY SPIRIT IS A DIVINE PERSON . . ."

The World Christian Fundamentals Doctrinal Statement had no statement regarding the person and work of the Holy Spirit, except as stated in Article One as one of the persons of the Trinity. The leaders of the World Christian Fundamentals Association did regard the person and work of the Holy Spirit as vital, as R. A. Torrey wrote an article on the Holy Spirit for *The Fundamentals*.[1] Pardington's *Outline Studies* on the Holy Spirit appear to be based on Torrey's Fundamentals article.

The C&MA in 1928 thus determined a need to give further definition to the person and work of the Holy Spirit.[2] The Alliance Manual cites John 14:15-18; 16:7-11, 13; and Acts 1:8; as scriptural support for this doctrine.

Alliance and Great Fundamentals writers cite scriptural evidence that divine attributes and characteristics and acts of personality are ascribed to the Holy Spirit.[3] Both the writers of the Fundamentals and the C&MA recognize that the Holy Spirit is not an "it," not an impersonal force, but is a person. This article of faith stands against unorthodox teachings and religious groups at the time that denied the Trinity and the divine personhood of the Holy Spirit, regarding the Spirit a force, such as Unitarians, Jehovah's Witnesses, and Oneness ("Jesus Only") Pentecostals, or Seventh Day Adventists who regard the Holy Spirit as "the Law."

"... SENT TO INDWELL, GUIDE, TEACH, EMPOWER THE BELIEVER, AND TO CONVINCE THE WORLD OF SIN, OF RIGHTEOUSNESS, AND OF JUDGMENT."

This portion of the doctrine of the Holy Spirit contains simple summary of verses of Scripture describing the role of the Holy Spirit: John 14:17; Romans 8:9-11 (indwelling), John 16:13 (guiding); John 14:26 (teaching); Acts 1:8 (empowering); John 16:8 (convincing of sin, righteousness, and judgment). This article of faith lays the foundation for the Alliance distinctive of sanctification and the baptism in the Holy Spirit.

7

SCRIPTURE ESSENTIALS (BIBLIOLOGY)

INSPIRATION, AUTHORITY, INFALLIBILITY, AND INERRANCY OF SCRIPTURE

This chapter discusses Article 4 of the Canadian and US Alliance Statements of Faith on "The Doctrine of Scripture." This article is based on Scripture and Article I of the WCFA Doctrinal Statement and very similar in wording.[1] Because this Faith Statement is so critical to all we believe, I am devoting more time to this foundation than the other essentials in this summary.

> <u>US and Canadian:</u> *The Old and New Testaments, inerrant as originally given, were verbally inspired by God and are a complete revelation of His will for the salvation of people. They constitute the divine and only rule of Christian faith and practice.*

Keith Bailey affirmed The Alliance "has from its beginning held a very high view of the Holy Scripture. The Bible is the Word of God and is therefore authoritative."[2] Simpson asserted, "The Bible is either everything or nothing. Like a chain which depends upon its weakest link, if God's Word is not absolutely and completely true, it is too weak a cable to fix our anchorage and guarantee our eternal peace."[3]

Early on after the founding of the Alliance, A. B. Simpson originated the first informal Statement of Faith, in his words identifying

Scripture as *"verbal inspiration as originally given."*[4] This belief has continued throughout the history of the Alliance, continued intact in the official Statement of Faith 77 years later in 1965.

The Alliance recognizes that the texts as we now have them may contain discrepancies due to errors in transmission but affirms that the original manuscripts were without error. There is no scriptural basis for claiming that transmission will be inerrant. Unlike some who would claim that the Scriptures are inerrant in basic truths, but not in historical matters, the Alliance affirms that the original manuscripts were historically true. When a discrepancy is found that is not apparently due to error in transmission, there is another valid scriptural explanation.

The question first arises about what is meant by inerrancy—what view of inerrancy is held by The Alliance? H. Wayne House identifies four "evangelical" views on inerrancy: 1) Complete Inerrancy, 2) Limited Inerrancy, 3) Inerrancy of Purpose; 4) Irrelevancy of Inerrancy.[5] David Dockery, one-time President of the Southern Baptist Theological Seminary, is more nuanced, identifying nine possible positions held by various theologians with regard to the doctrine of biblical inerrancy. See the endnote for an explanation of each of the positions.[6] The positions are summarized in this chart:

Wayne House Categories	Proponents (according to House)	David Dockery Categories	Proponents (according to Dockery)
		1. Mechanical Dictation	John R. Rice
1. Complete Inerrancy	Harold Lindsell Roger Nicolle Millard Erickson	2. Absolute Inerrancy	Harold Lindsell
		3. Critical Inerrancy	Roger Nicolle Millard Erickson
2. Limited Inerrancy	Daniel Fuller Stephen Davis William LaSor	4. Limited Inerrancy	Howard Marshall
		5. Qualified Inerrancy	Donald G. Bloesch
		6. Nuanced Inerrancy	Clark Pinnock
3. Inerrancy of Purpose	Jack Rogers, James Orr	7. Functional (Purposeful) Inerrancy	G. C. Berkouwer, Jack Rogers, Donald McKim
4. Irrelevancy of Inerrancy	David A. Hubbard (Fuller Seminary)	8. Irrelevancy of Inerrancy	David A. Hubbard
		9. Biblical Authority	William Countryman

WHERE DOES THE ALLIANCE FIT ON THIS CHART?

From statements throughout Alliance history by Alliance leaders, it can be determined that the C&MA takes House's #1 (Complete Inerrancy), a position that blends Dockery's #2 and #3, or is positioned somewhere between #2 and #3. It is clear from C&MA statements that the C&MA does *not* embrace House's Categories 2-4 or Dockery's Categories 1 and 4-9. Thus, it can be reasonably concluded that its credentialed ministers who sign and affirm the Statement of Faith should, in their views of inerrancy, fall within the parameters of House #1 or Dockery #2 and #3.

The C&MA position in some ways fits Dockery's Absolute Inerrancy category but differs in the issue of taking seriously the human element, as affirmed by early Alliance theologian George Pardington: "While it maintains the superintendence of the Holy Spirit, rendering the writers of Scripture infallible in their communications of truth and thus making their writings inerrant, yet it leaves room for the freest and fullest play of personality, style, etc."[7]

Further, The Alliance (following The Fundamentals of 1910-1915) accepted cautious limited use of critical scholarship.[8] At the same time, the scholars of The Fundamentals recognized that critical study and grammatical/historical exegesis is not enough. R.A. Torrey, a Yale, and German university graduate who was well-versed in biblical study in Hebrew and Greek, noted that a person may be well-educated but not Spirit-taught and the need for balancing human education with divine education. Torrey and Pierson understood that some scholars who study the original languages and do critical study do not have the illumination of the Holy Spirit. They discerned that the Fundamentals, upon which much of the C&MA Statement of Faith is based, are recognized, and accepted only through Spirit-enlightened study.

"Limited" inerrancy, which declares that all that the Bible teaches is without error, but historical elements may not be totally true, contradicts the hermeneutical principles of plain intent and literal priority. It is clear that The Alliance does *not* accept the view of limited inerrancy as defined by both House and Dockery or the other views that waterdown inerrancy. An article in the *Alliance Witness* in 1971 by Nyack College professor David H. Moore, commissioned by the National Office. then located in Nyack, New York, clearly spells out the Alliance position against this view:

> There are those who hold to inerrancy in theological matters but not in the nontheological. This raises the problem of how one goes about extracting the spiritual message from the historical details in which it is framed. If inspiration has only to do with doctrine it would mean that inspiration suddenly ceases when the Biblical writer turns to matters of history. The Bible speaks the truth on every subject it touches. Yet one must be careful to distinguish between what the Bible says and what men say that it says![9]

THE ALLIANCE POSITION ON THE AUTOGRAPHS

Throughout Alliance history, The Alliance has maintained Scripture's own claims to inerrancy. In full theological book I will mention examples from four C&MA scholars: 1925—Dr. T.J. McCrossan (Hebrew and Greek professor, C&MA minister, President of Simpson Bible Institute)[10]; 1971—Nyack professor Dr. David Moore[11]; 1971—Dr. Arthur P. Johnston, President of St. Paul Bible College[12]; 1985—Dr. Keith Bailey, District Superintendent, Vice President of North American Ministries:[13]

THE ALLIANCE POSITION ON INERRANCY, HISTORICITY, AND AUTHORSHIP

The Alliance position throughout its history from its inception to today, has affirmed the relationship of inerrancy and verbal inspiration with historicity of biblical accounts.[14] The Alliance agreed with *The Fundamentals*, which upheld evangelical belief in historicity of the biblical accounts. These included inerrancy of the original autographs;[15] verbal inspiration, substantial Mosaic authorship of the Pentateuch, creation, the flood, the exodus, the defeating of Jericho, authorship of the book of Isaiah by one Isaiah, not two or three; authorship of the book of Daniel in the 6th century Babylonian period, not the 2nd century; [16] and genuine authorship of letters attributed to Paul, among other issues. The Alliance has remained in agreement with *The Fundamentals* on these issues, as crucial to inerrancy. Research of Alliance sources demonstrates documentation of Alliance support for all of these, in particular, substantial Mosaic authorship and early date of the Pentateuch,[17] one author of Isaiah, 6th century authorship of Daniel, and genuine authorship of the letters attributed to Paul.[18]

THE ALLIANCE AND ARTICLE 10 OF THE CHICAGO STATEMENT ON BIBLICAL INERRANCY

Since Article 10 of the Chicago Statement on Biblical Inerrancy deals specifically with inerrancy of the original autographs, we will compare the Alliance position with Article 10.

Paragraph 1—Accuracy of Available Texts

<u>Chicago Statement</u>: "We affirm that inspiration, strictly speaking, applies only to the autographic text of Scripture, which in the providence of God can be ascertained from available manuscripts with great accuracy."

<u>Alliance Affirmations:</u>

"Technically, however, inspiration applies only to the original manuscripts or autographa."—Dr. David Moore, *Alliance Witness*, 1971[19]

"Since we have only copies of copies and our English Bible is necessarily a translation of those, we allow for possible human error in the transmittal: "inerrant *as originally given*. But a comparison of manuscripts copied over a wide span of time gives us confidence that our Bible today is *essentially what it was in its original form*. The copyists and translators have been amazingly faithful." (italics mine)."—H. Robert Cowles, *Alliance Witness*, 1982[20]

Paragraph 2—Copies and Translations as the Word of God

Chicago Statement: "We further affirm that copies and translations of Scripture are the Word of God to the extent that they faithfully represent the original."

Alliance Affirmation: "How can you say that the Old Testament is inerrant right down to the very jots and tittles when we don't have the original writings and the copies contain obvious errors? In the first place, we do not claim inerrancy in the copies and translations of Scripture. The doctrine of inerrancy holds that the original autographs were inerrant right down to the jots and tittles. Further, the minor mistakes made by copyists do not prevent the reconstruction of a pure text. This is the task of the scholar as he works with the manuscripts. As he compares the manuscripts, he labors to reconstruct a pure text, one that is accurate right down to the jots and tittles."—Andre Bustanoby, *Alliance Witness*, 1967.[21]

Paragraph 3—No Faith Tenets Are Affected by Lack of Autographs.

Chicago Statement: "We deny that any essential element of the Christian faith is affected by the absence of the autographs."

Alliance Affirmation: "The effect of inspiration continues in copies and translations in proportion as those copies and translations correspond to the autographa. . . . Every Bible reader today owes an incalculable debt to those who in former days tediously and laboriously copied manuscripts. In more recent generations we are indebted to the scholars who have devoted themselves to the exacting science of textual criticism. From the combined efforts of scribal copyist and textual critic has come a text amazingly accurate, with a minimal number of variants, none of which affect major doctrines."—David Moore, *Alliance Witness*, 1971[22]

Paragraph 4—Lack of Autographs Does Not Make Inerrancy Invalid or Irrelevant

Chicago Statement: "We further deny that this absence renders the assertion of biblical inerrancy invalid or irrelevant."

Alliance Affirmation: "A frequently heard complaint is that to argue for inerrant autographa is irrelevant since we cannot produce inerrant autographa. That no one can produce inerrant autographa is, of course. true. However. it was the testimony of Paul that the *graphe*, or Scripture, was 'God-breathed.' It is unlikely that Paul would use *theopneustos* if by *graphe* he meant copies."—David Moore, *Alliance Witness*, 1971[23]

These comparisons demonstrate that **The Alliance affirms what the Chicago Statement on Biblical Inerrancy affirms.**

THE ALLIANCE POSITION ON VERBAL INSPIRATION

After exegeting 2 Timothy 3:16 and 2 Peter 1:21 and quoting other authors discussing proper and improper interpretation of the syntax of the passages, Pardington commented,

> If we are to have accuracy and authority, there can be no such thing as inspired thoughts apart from inspired words; for language is the expression of thought—its embodiment and vehicle. The Bible is the Word of God. The very words of Scripture are inspired.[24]

He makes it clear that the Bible not only contains the Word of God but *is* the Word of God. Pardington authenticates the verbal inspiration of Scripture through hermeneutical principles.

Throughout Alliance history, The Alliance has always affirmed verbal inspiration of Scripture, even before the drafting of The Five

Fundamentals. So what, then, is meant by "verbal inspiration?" The question often revolves around two Latin phrases: *ipsissima vox* and *ipsissima verba*. *Ipsissima vox* is Latin for "the very voice." *Ipsissima verba* is Latin for "the very words." Does inspiration mean that the Holy Spirit moved the writers of Scripture to write *every word* of Scripture —*ipsissima verba*? Or does inspiration mean that the Holy Spirit moved the writers of Scripture to write *the general idea* of Scripture—*ipsissima vox*? Does inspiration cover the details or the general "gist" of meaning? Does inspiration refer to the "very words" or the "very voice"?

Since the Alliance Statement is based on the Fundamentals of 1910 and their exposition, we look to those explanations given to understand the foundation of authorial intent. The essay on the Fundamentals explains very clearly: "The doctrine of verbal inspiration is simply this: The original writings, *ipsissima verba*, came through the penmen direct from God."[25] I have not found anywhere that Alliance writers use the term; however, Alliance writers throughout Alliance history do very clearly refer to the meaning of *ipsissima verba*.[26]

". . . AND ARE A COMPLETE REVELATION OF *H*IS WILL FOR THE SALVATION OF MEN. *T*HEY CONSTITUTE THE DIVINE AND ONLY RULE OF *C*HRISTIAN FAITH AND PRACTICE."

This statement is based on a literal rendering of Paul's declaration (2 Tim 3:15). Paul's syntax demonstrated that "because they are 'God-breathed' (v 16), coming from the very mouth of God, they have been enabled to teach powerfully what is true concerned salvation."[27]

They are divine because they are God-breathed and inspired by the Holy Spirit (2 Tim 3:16) and are not from human interpretation (2 Pet 1:20). Simpson affirms, on the basis of the *plain intent* of these passages, that "they had an authority and value that which put them in an absolutely distinctive class from all human literature."[28] Pardington calls the Scriptures the "final court of appeal" and the "Supreme Court," the ultimate authority for mankind.[29] The validation of the authority of Scripture is itself thus derived from grammatical-historical hermeneutics.

8

HUMANKIND AND SALVATION ESSENTIALS
(ANTHROPOLOGY AND SOTERIOLOGY)

LOSTNESS OF MAN AND NEED OF NEW BIRTH; SALVATION AND JUSTIFICATION BY FAITH

This chapter examines Articles 5 and 6 of the Alliance Statement of Faith on "The Doctrine of Man," (Canadian: titled "Sin") and Article 6, "The Doctrine of Salvation" (titled in the Canadian Faith Statement as "Freedom from Sin").

US: The Doctrine of Man: *Man was originally created in the image and likeness of God: he fell through disobedience, incurring thereby both physical and spiritual death. All men are born with a sinful nature, are separated from the life of God, and can be saved only through the atoning work of the Lord Jesus Christ. The prospect of the impenitent and unbelieving person is existence forever in conscious torment, and that of the believer in Christ, is to have everlasting joy and bliss."*

Canadian: Sin: *"Humankind, originally created in the image and likeness of God, fell through disobedience, incurring thereby both physical and spiritual death. All people are born with a sinful nature, are separated from the life of God, and can be saved only through the atoning work of the Lord Jesus*

Christ. The destiny of the impenitent and unbelieving is existence forever in conscious torment, but that of the believer is everlasting joy and bliss."

This article is adapted from the World Christian Fundamentals Doctrinal Statement, combining Article IV and the second part of Article IX.[1] The Canadian Faith Statement has only minor wording changes. Regarding Article 5, this includes man's original creation, the fall of man through sin, sinful nature, need of salvation through Christ's atonement, the state of the lost and believers.

"HE FELL THROUGH DISOBEDIENCE, INCURRING THEREBY BOTH PHYSICAL AND SPIRITUAL DEATH."

The story of the fall of man in Genesis 3 is viewed by The Alliance as a literal true event, not merely a symbolic myth. God told Adam in Genesis 2:17, "In the day that you eat [of the fruit of the forbidden tree] you shall surely die." Although physical death did not occur immediately, spiritual death—alienation from God—began the process of physical decay and loss, eventually leading to physical death.

"ALL MEN ARE BORN WITH A SINFUL NATURE, ARE SEPARATED FROM THE LIFE OF GOD, . . ."

The Alliance lists Romans 3:23 as scriptural support for this doctrine: "For all have sinned and come short of the glory of God." Further, the aorist tense here can mean both the final judgment (as in 2:12), and "the decisive and universal character of man's fall."[2] Pardington notes the testimony of several Scriptures that humankind has a sinful nature: all are under a curse (Gal 3:10), all are children of the devil (John 8:44; 1 John 3:8-10), the natural man is a stranger to the thing of God (1 Cor 2:14), the natural heart is deceitful (Jer 17:9), the mental and more nature is corrupt (Gen 6:5, 12; 8:21; Ps 94:11; Rom 1:19-31).[3]

". . . AND CAN BE SAVED ONLY THROUGH THE ATONING WORK OF THE LORD JESUS CHRIST. . ."

The C&MA Manual cites 1 Corinthians 15:21-22. Taken by plain intent, it is the death and resurrection of Christ that makes people alive spiritually. Jesus had to be the second Adam.

"THE PROSPECT (PORTION) OF THE IMPENITENT AND UNBELIEVING PERSON IS EXISTENCE FOREVER IN CONSCIOUS TORMENT." This portion of Article 5 comes from the plain intent of Revelation 21:8: "But the cowardly, the unbelieving, the vile, the murderers, the sexually immoral, those who practice magic arts, the idolaters and all liars—their place will be in the fiery lake of burning sulfur. This is the second death." Referring to the lake of fire, Pardington writes that the lake of fire "is described as a place of conscious and unending torment."[4]

ARTICLE 6—THE DOCTRINE OF SALVATION

US: The Doctrine of Salvation: *Salvation has been provided through Jesus Christ for all men; and those who repent and believe in Him are born again of the Holy Spirit, receive the gift of eternal life, and become the children of God.*

Canadian: Freedom from Sin: *Salvation has been provided only through Jesus Christ. Those who repent and believe in Him are united with Christ through the Holy Spirit and are thereby regenerated (born again), justified, sanctified and granted the gift of eternal life as adopted children of God.*

This article is based on the World Christian Fundamentals Doctrinal Statement, Article VIII: "We believe that all who receive by faith the Lord Jesus Christ are born again of the Holy Spirit and thereby become children of God."[5] The Canadian Faith Statement expresses the same intent with updated wording and clarifications. This article is adapted from the WCFA Doctrinal Statement, combining Article IV and the second part of Article IX.[6] The proposed full systematic theological book will cite scriptural support from the grammatical-historical hermeneutical approach and quotes from Alliance leaders such as Simpson and Pardington and would also include sources from which the statement is drawn, especially exposition from the Great

Fundamentals of 1910-1919. This article is retained almost verbatim from the 1928 Alliance Statement of Faith for Alliance schools.

The C&MA takes the exclusive claims of Christ at face value when He asserted of Himself, "I am the way, the truth, and the life, no one comes to the Father but through Me." On the basis of Jesus' claim, Peter proclaimed, "Salvation is found in no one else, for there is no other name under heaven given to men by which we must be saved" (Acts 4:12). Peter's statement has Old Testament basis from Isaiah 12:2; 49:6-8; 52:10). It also recalls statements such as "I, even I, am the Lord, and apart from me there is no savior" (Isa 43:11, see also Deut 4:35, 39; Isa 44:6, 8; 45:5, 6, 14, 18, 21, 22; 46:9; 47:8). Expanding on the claims of Jesus and the teachings of Peter, Paul declared, "For the grace of God that brings salvation has appeared to all men," and then speaks of "our great God and Savior Jesus Christ" (Tit 2:11). Pardington gives three scriptural reasons why Christ is the Savior of all men:

1. His atonement acts as a stay in the execution of the sentence against sin, securing for all men a space for repentance, and the enjoyment of the common blessings of life, forfeited by transgression: 2 Pet 3:9; Mt 5:45; Acts 14:17

2. His atonement has made objective provision for the salvation of all, by removing from the divine mind every obstacle to the pardon and restoration of sinner, except their willful opposition to God and refusal to turn to Him: Rom 5:8-10; 2 Cor 5:18-20.

3. His atonement has procured for all men the powerful incentive to repentance presented in the cross, together with the combined agency of the Christian Church and the Holy Spirit: Rom 2:4; John 16:8; 2 Cor 5:18-20."[7]

EXCURSUS ON ETERNAL TORMENT VS ANNIHILATIONISM

Torrey for WCFA and Pardington for the Alliance demonstrate exegetically Scriptures that support eternal torment vs. annihilation. For the Alliance, annihilationism is not an open question option. Scriptures are given describing heaven as a state of everlasting joy and bliss. This doctrine became a part of the Great Fundamentals as well as the Statement of Faith of The Alliance. Pardington quotes Torrey saying, "[Spiritual or eternal] death, then, is not mere non-existence, but wrong, wretched, debased, devilish existence."[8] Regarding the eternality of the torment, some have argued that the phrase translated "forever"—*eis tous aionas ton aionon*, 'unto the ages of the ages'—really means that punishment is a long duration, not forever. Pardington dealt with this question exegetically, quoting Farr.[9]

". . . AND THOSE WHO REPENT AND BELIEVE IN HIM ARE BORN AGAIN OF THE HOLY SPIRIT, RECEIVE THE GIFT OF ETERNAL LIFE, AND BECOME THE CHILDREN OF GOD."

These points are based on a straightforward reading of several segments of Scripture: The new birth; the gift of eternal life—we are justified by his grace to be made heirs according to the hope of eternal life; faith leads to birth into the family of God.

EXCURSUS ON INCLUSIVE PLURALISM

Inclusive pluralism by people today who claim to be evangelicals makes salvation available through various religions. Hermeneutical dances are done around these primary texts, especially John 14:6 and Acts 4:12, to dodge what they plainly say, that salvation is exclusively available through repentance and faith in Christ. The views of Clark Pinnock and John Sanders are discussed and refuted as skirting around a straightforward reading of these key texts, demonstrating violation of sound grammatical-historical principles of interpretation by those who espouse inclusivism. The *principles of plain intent, literal priority, grammar and syntax, context and Scripture comparison* all confirm, as Simpson makes clear, "To be without Christ is to be without God."[10]

9

CHURCH ESSENTIALS (ECCLESIOLOGY)

THE DOCTRINE OF THE CHURCH

Article 9 of the Statement of Faith presents "The Doctrine of the Church. This chapter in the proposed full systematic theological book will examine this article more fully. The US and Canadian Statements of Faith read:

US: *The Church consists of all those who believe on the Lord Jesus Christ, are redeemed through His blood, and are born again of the Holy Spirit. Christ is the Head of the Body, the Church, which has been commissioned by Him to go into all the world as a witness, preaching the gospel to all nations.*

The local church is a body of believers in Christ who are joined together for the worship of God, edification through the Word of God, prayer, fellowship, the proclamation of the gospel, and observance of the ordinances of baptism and the Lord's Supper.

Canadian: *The universal Church, of which Christ is the Head, consists of all those who believe on the Lord Jesus Christ, are redeemed through His blood, regenerated by the Holy Spirit, and commissioned by Christ to go into all the world as a witness, preaching the Gospel to all nations. The local church, the visible expression of the universal Church, is a body of believers in Christ who are joined together to worship God, to observe the ordinances of Baptism*

and the Lord's Supper, to pray, to be edified through the Word of God, to
fellowship, and to testify in word and deed to the good news of salvation both
locally and globally. The local church enters into relationships with other
like-minded churches for accountability, encouragement, and mission.

Article 9 was not a part of the WCFA Doctrinal Statement but was added by the C&MA in 1928, evidently seeing a need in the developing organization for a theology of the Church.[1] It does show evidence of being a summary of Bishop John Ryle, writing for the Fundamentals,[2] and based on a collection of verses descriptive of the Church, using the grammatical-historical principles. The 1965 article is a condensed version of the 1928 C&MA Statement of Faith for Schools. The Canadian version includes updated language and a fuller explanation of the nature and mission of the church. Changes to the US statement have been proposed to General Council.

The full book will explain the doctrine of redemption through the blood of Christ as stated in 1 Peter 1:1-2 and is founded on the *historical and cultural context* of the Jewish rites of purification based (see Ex 24:3-8; Num 19: 9, 13, 20, 21), and fulfilled in Jesus Christ. Other related and relevant Scriptures compared together demonstrate this truth as well. The belief in Christ as the Head of the Church as His body is a literal paraphrase of several verses of Scripture: (Eph 1:22-23; Col 1:18; Mt 28:18-20; Mk 16:15; Acts 1:8. Pardington observes from these Scriptures that evangelization and edification as the two-fold mission of the Church.[3]

Article 9 recognizes the intent of Paul's metaphor of the Church as a Body according to Ephesians 4, Romans 12:3-4; 1 Corinthians 12. It also observes the priorities and essential activities of the Church in the book of Acts, especially in Acts 2:42-47, which include worship, teaching, fellowship, prayer, the breaking of the bread, and baptism. Speaking at the WCFA Conference in 1919, William Riley emphasized baptism and the Lord's Supper as the essential ceremonies of the church because they are commands of Jesus.[4] Likewise, in The Alliance, baptism and the Lord's Supper are essential 1st tier ceremonies, not to be neglected. Note, however, that beliefs and practices regarding baptism and communion are not regarded as 1st tier doctrines and practices.

10

END-TIME ESSENTIALS
(ESCHATOLOGY)

REALITY OF HEAVEN AND HELL (ARTICLE 10)

Article 10 reads the same for both the US and the Canadian Faith Statements:

There shall be a bodily resurrection of the just and of the unjust; for the former, a resurrection unto life; for the latter, a resurrection unto judgment.

Affirming the Great Fundamentals of 1910, Pardington affirmed in 1912 that The Alliance regarded as essential belief the reality of heaven and hell and the visible, physical second coming of Christ:

The Alliance . . . is in substantial accord with evangelical truth and in common with the various denominations accepts the great body of Protestant theology. By this we mean such *fundamental* doctrines as . . . the second coming of the Lord, the eternal salvation of those who believe in Christ and the everlasting punishment of those who reject Him.[1]

Article 10 of The Alliance Statement of Faith on "Resurrection and

Judgment" is based on Article 9 of the 1919 WCFA Doctrinal Statement, and exegesis of numerous Scriptures. The fact of a bodily resurrection is found in 1 Corinthians 15:21-22. This is not just a spiritual transformation, but a physical resuscitation according to Revelation 20:13, as Simpson and Pardington explain, also citing Romans 8:23 regarding the redemption of the body.[2] This will be discussed more fully in the proposed full systematic theological book.

VISIBLE PHYSICAL SECOND COMING OF CHRIST (ARTICLE 11)

Article 11 reads as follows:

> US: *The second coming of the Lord Jesus Christ is imminent and will be personal, visible, and premillennial. This is the believer's blessed hope and is a vital truth which is an incentive to holy living and faithful service.* (Councils 1965, 1966, 1974).
>
> Canadian: *The second coming of the Lord Jesus Christ is imminent and will be personal and visible. As the believer's blessed hope, this vital truth is an incentive for holy living and sacrificial service toward the completion of Christ's commission.*

Apart from the notable omission of the word "premillennial" the Canadian statement, the US and Canadian Faith Statements are almost the same, with a little more description and clarity in the Canadian Statement. The issue of premillennialism will be dealt with under Alliance Distinctives in Chapter 17, not as an essential of the faith confessed by all evangelical Christians. Note also that the issue of premillennialism will be up for discussion in the US 2023 General Council.

Article 11 on the Second Coming of Christ is based on Alliance teaching from its founding and coincides with the Fundamentals. Pardington's 1912 statement affirmed "such *fundamental* doctrines as . . . the second coming of the Lord." According to Princeton Theological Seminary professor Charles R. Erdman, writing for *The Fundamentals* on "The Coming of Christ": "The return of Christ is a fundamental doctrine of the Christian faith."[3] Erdman emphasized that the second coming of Christ is personal, visible, and imminent, as did The Alliance.

". . . IS IMMINENT AND WILL BE PERSONAL, VISIBLE . . ."

Even though the word "imminent" is in the 1919 Fundamentals statement, interestingly, it does not occur in the 1928 C&MA statement of faith. It was re-added in the 1965 statement of faith, when some insisted on the term "imminent" to specify a pre-tribulation rapture. However, others recognized that in believing in the imminency of Christ Coming, Simpson did not narrow the meaning of "imminent" to mean any moment, but rather that Jesus could come very soon—taking the text of Matthew 24 at face value, as in this very generation, if the gospel is preached to all people. Writing for *The Fundamentals*, Erdman explains the writers' understanding of imminence:

> It is an event which may occur in any lifetime. Whatever difficulties the fact involves, there is no doubt that all the Biblical writers and their fellow Christians believes that Christ might return in their generation. . . . However, "imminent" does not mean "immediate." . . . "Imminence" as related to our Lord's return indicates uncertainty as to time, but possibility of nearness.[4]

Although he expressed support for the premillennial view, Erdman's presentation of imminence could be accepted more broadly by other millennial views as well.

By declaring that the Second Coming is personal and visible, the Alliance regards literally the words of the angel of the Lord in Acts 1:10-11: He shall return just has He went up into the cloud, and "all eyes shall see him." This is not merely a vision, but a real appearance. The context indicates a physical ascension into heaven by Jesus, thus by implication as physical descension to earth."[5] Basing the doctrine of a personal, visible Second Coming of Christ on literal grammatical/historical hermeneutics, The Alliance and *The Fundamentals* give further exegesis of other Scriptures to build stronger support.

Based on a straightforward reading of Titus 2:11-14, years before the publication of *The Fundamentals*, Simpson listed four biblical reasons why the Second Coming of Christ is a blessed hope: 1) It is a supernatural literal and visible revelation of Christ. 2) Believers will be supernaturally transformed. 3) The material world will have a supernatural transformation. 4) It will transform the government of the world.[6]

Premillennial:
A 2ND Tier Doctrine of the Faith, Not 1ST Tier Essential

Premillennialism is not dealt with here, but under the Alliance Distinctives, for neither the original Fundamentals of 1910 nor The Alliance regarded it as a 1st tier essential doctrine. Notably, although the Alliance was premillennial in orientation, Pardington affirmed a more generic view of the second coming in his 1912 statement, not mentioning premillennial. This shows that premillennialism was not a 1st tier essential of the Alliance, but rather a 2nd tier distinctive with 3rd tier liberty, as we will see.

PART III

TIER 2: ALLIANCE DISTINCTIVES

11

THE ALLIANCE AND THE SUPERNATURAL

"THE ALLIANCE STANDS PREEMINENTLY FOR THE SUPERNATURAL."—A. B. SIMPSON

When I put this manuscript together as a PDF, I listed this chapter as the last of the Alliance distinctives—Chapter 17—after the Fourfold Gospel. However, when I was revising and preparing this manuscript to be published as a book, I realized that I had done A.B. Simpson and the Alliance a disservice. I assumed (wrongly) that when Simpson wrote of the "distinctives" of the Alliance that he would begin with the Fourfold Gospel. I was wrong.

I came across this quote of Simpson, declared at a Nyack convention in 1899 of the principles and "distinctive doctrines of the Alliance": "First, it stands for an absolute faith in supernatural things and a supernatural God."[1] He did not say, "First, the Fourfold Gospel," but rather, "*First, absolute faith in the supernatural*." So, I have switched the order of presentation to be in sync with Simpson's priorities of emphasis—first the supernatural, then the Fourfold Gospel flows from the supernatural. Mind you, this is before the Pentecostal movement.

Implicit in the Alliance distinctives of Christ Our Sanctifier (the sanctifying filling of the Spirit), Christ our Healer, and Christ our Coming King is the doctrine of Christological continuism, as Simpson expressed it, "If the Christ of Christianity is the same yesterday, today and forever, the Christianity of Christ ought also to be the same yesterday, today, and forever."[2] The Alliance, from the start, with miraculous healings confirming its founding at Old Orchard Camp in 1887, has believed in all of the gifts of the Spirit for today.

Some have questioned whether this should be a 2nd-tier distinctive of The Alliance or downgraded to a 3rd-tier open question. In practice, this may have sometimes been the case, as there appear to be some soft cessationists in the C&MA who have slipped through the cracks. However, there was no question in the mind of early Alliance leaders. Simpson made it clear even 23 years after the founding of the Alliance, "This [C&MA] movement stands preeminently for the supernatural"[3]—a compelling reason to put this first among the Alliance distinctives. If it was paramount to the founder, we would not only be cracking the foundations, but breaking the foundations to downgrade the primacy of this distinctive. This was not a new stance, nor a hyperbole, but standard Alliance teaching since its founding, and would continue to be. See this repeated pattern and emphasis:

- 1899—"The Alliance stands for an absolute faith in supernatural things and a supernatural God."—A. B. Simpson[4]
- 1900—"We are a supernatural people born again by a supernatural birth, kept by a supernatural power, sustained on supernatural food, taught by a supernatural Teacher from a supernatural Book. We are led by a supernatural Captain in right paths to assured victories."—J. Hudson Taylor, quoted in the C&MA Weekly[5]
- 1908—"The Alliance has a distinct testimony and message. . . . It is a message of supernatural power."—A. B. Simpson[6]
- 1907—"Christianity is supernatural or nothing. . . ."—A. B. Simpson[7]
- 1916—"The Alliance is supernatural, or it is nothing."—William T. MacArthur[8]
- 1923—"The Alliance is 'supernaturally natural.'"—H. W. Shuman[9]

- 1934—"Ours should be a day of constant miracles, the mighty Acts of the Holy Spirit."—Robert Jaffray[10]
- 1950s—"All that is worthwhile in Christianity is a miracle! I believe that supernatural grace has been the teaching and the experience of the Christian church from Pentecost to the present hour!"—A. W. Tozer[11]

THE ALLIANCE HERMENEUTIC IS UNAMBIGUOUSLY CONTINUIST; IT NOT DISPENSATIONAL/CESSATIONIST.

Simpson affirmed, "The Alliance Movement stands for all the scriptural manifestations of the Holy Spirit since Pentecost."[12] Continuism was taught by Simpson as a matter of consistent biblical hermeneutical logic as early as 1884, and it has continued to be taught throughout Alliance history:

> A common objection is observed in this way—Christ's last promise in Mark embraces much more than healing; but if you claim one, you must claim all. If you expect healing of the sick, you must include the gift of tongues and the power to overcome malignant poisons; and if the gift of tongues has ceased, so in the same way has the power over disease. We cheerfully accept the severe logic; we cannot afford to give up one of the promises. We admit our belief in the presence of the Healer in all the charismata of the Pentecostal church.[13]

Gifts Have Ceased Because of Unbelief, Not God's Will.

"An unbelieving church has said, 'They belong to the apostolic age; they are no longer necessary; they were only for the establishing of the church; miracles are not to be expected in these days.' The true answer lies in the saying, 'According to your faith be it unto you.'"—**William C. Stevens, 1891**[14]

A Dispensational Hermeneutic "Kills the Deep Spirit of Prayer and Revival."

- **Armin Gesswein, C&MA evangelist, 1941:** "Those who taught us the combination key [of dispensationalism] say, 'God doesn't do those things now. God doesn't work like that anymore.'. . . Dispensationalism does not open the book of Acts and the power of God; it closes them. . . . it is arbitrarily superimposed by man. . . . Wherever dispensationalism gets in, it kills the deep spirit of prayer and revival. . . . But how bracing in this day of need to know that we are still in the dispensation of the Holy Spirit just as in the Acts, and that God can baptize and fill believers with His Spirit, set churches on fire, and through them bring sinner to repentance and to Christ. . . . For neither the promise of the Holy Spirit nor the promised Holy Spirit has been withdrawn, except where men no longer want Him as the first Christians did."[15]

- **A.W. Tozer, 1950s:** "In view of much of today's dispensational teaching about Bible interpretation, the apostles, miracles of God, and the fullness of the Spirit, I must remind you that the Lord Jesus Christ is the same yesterday, today and forever. . . . There is nothing that Jesus has ever done for any of His disciples that He will not do for any other of His disciples! Where did the 'dividers-of-the-Word-of-Truth' get their teaching that all the gifts of the Spirit ended when the last apostle died? . . . When some men beat the cover off their Bible to demonstrate how they stand by the Word of God, they should be reminded that they are only standing by their own interpretation of the Word."[16]

The Alliance Hermeneutic Affirms Power Evangelism.

From the very beginning Simpson and The Alliance have affirmed that supernatural signs and wonders are vital for evangelism, and throughout Alliance history.

1884—A.B. Simpson: "What right have we to go to the unbelieving world and demand their acceptance of our message without these signs following? . . . No, Christ did give them, and they did follow as long as Christians continued to 'believe' and expect them. . . . The signs shall correspond to the extent of their faith."[17]

1908—A. B. Simpson: "We are not to go abroad to preach the signs, nor to begin with the signs, nor to produce the signs ourselves. Our business is not to work miracles and wait until we can do so before telling the story of Jesus. Our work is to tell the simple story of His life and death and resurrection, and to preach the Gospel in its purity. But we are to do it expecting the Lord to prove the reality of His power, and to give the signs which His has promised."—[18]

1913—E.O. Jago, Field Director of C&MA Missions, Palestine, speaking in a Pentecostal church: "I care not what society a man belongs to. I simply want to know if he is filled with the Holy Spirit and has sufficient ability to master a foreign language. . . . In these days the supernatural must take place in the foreign field, especially among the Mohammedans, and we need men filled with the Holy Spirit."[19]

1924—William C. Stevens: "An unmutilated gospel ministry is two-fold —the supernatural in word and deed, preaching and teaching and healing through the power of the Holy Spirit. Supernatural works were the handmaid of preaching and teaching with Jesus. There is no better advertisement today. People can generally be reached quickest on the side of physical need; and the ministry to this need is as divine and spiritual as the ministry of the Word. But Jesus healed not as an advertisement, but as an essential ministry."[20]

1934—Robert Jaffray, C&MA missionary statesman: "We have come to feel so strongly that we need such 'signs and wonders' in the name of the Lord Jesus to attest the Message of the Gospel here in Makassar. It seems as though in no other way can we demonstrate to hardhearted

Moslems . . . that Jesus Christ is verily the Son of God, and that He alone has power on earth to forgive sin, and to save their souls."[21]

1953—Paris Reidhead, Sudan Interior Mission missionary & Alliance pastor: "For five long years my Islamic friend's question, 'What can your living Jesus do that my dead Mohammed can't?', has been a sword behind me driving me to the Bible to read, study search and believe God's Word. . . . Can we blame the Moslem if he asks for a sign before submitting to baptism, when he knows full well that such a step means almost inevitable death? Can we blame the Chinese coolie if he demands a miracle before burning his idols, when he remembers that the last man in his village thus to declare war on the demons was smitten with blindness on the second day?[22]

ALLIANCE LEADERS ENCOURAGED FULL HARMONIOUS EXERCISE OF ALL GIFTS IN EVERY CHURCH

Despite the Pentecostal excesses and departures, the Alliance continued to encourage practices of all of the gifts of the Spirit, including tongues:

- **1914--J. Hudson Ballard:** "Alliance leaders are quite agreed in believing that speaking with tongues . . . should have a place in every Spirit-controlled church."[23]
- **1917—A. B Simpson:** "Why may we not have all the gifts and all the graces of the Apostolic Church blended in one harmonious whole. . . . even the tongues of Pentecost, without making them subjects of controversy?"[24]
- **1928—Dr. Ira David, Ph.D.,** Toccoa Falls Professor, Board of Managers: "An ideal New Testament church would have all of the spiritual gifts of 1 Corinthians 12 effective among the believers." [25]
- **1940—John A. MacMillan,** Board of Managers: "Love's divine overflow . . . is God's ideal. . . . The Holy Spirit, ungrieved by carnality, would be manifest in such power

that His gifts would once again be in full exercise in the assembly, to the glory of God."—John MacMillan[26]

- **1948—R. S. Roseberry**, Chairman, French West Africa C&MA Mission: "a crying need for the full manifestation of the Spirit in the Church? . . . The gifts are given for the perfection of the body. Should they not be manifest in every assembly if the body is to perform her function fully?"[27]
- **1950s—A. W. Tozer:** "Missing gifts—a tragedy in the church."

THE ALLIANCE CONTINUIST HERMENEUTIC HAS SUBSTANTIAL BIBLICAL BASIS.

In addition to Hebrews 13:8 and Mark 16:17-20 cited above, Alliance leaders cited several additional Scriptures in support of supernatural gifts and manifestations continuing today.

1 Corinthians 12—Gifts Are Needed to Edify the Church—Missing Gifts Are a Tragedy.

A tragedy in the church—the missing gifts. . . . Much of the religious activity we see in the churches is not the eternal working of the Eternal Spirit, but the mortal working of man's mortal mind—and that is a raw tragedy! . . . About ninety percent of the religious work carried on in the churches is being done by ungifted members. . . . There has never been a time in the history of the Christian church that some of the gifts were not present and effective. Sometimes they functioned among those who did not understand or perhaps did not believe in the same way that we think Christians should believe.—A. W. Tozer[28]

John 14:12—The Church Will Do Greater Works.

The Alliance is supernatural or it is nothing. . . . One thing that is certain as regards the work of the Alliance, modern innovations accomplish no permanent good, and I do not believe that anything but the Master's methods can advance the interests of our work. . . . It is not so much a matter of method as of the underlying principle or rule of action—doing what He saw the Father doing and adopting the method best suited to the occasion or the task.—William T. MacArthur[29]

John 5:19—We Do What We See the Father Doing.

It is not so much a matter of method as of the underlying principle or rule of action—doing what He saw the Father doing and adopting the method best suited to the occasion or the task.—William T. MacArthur[30]

Ephesians 4:11-13—All Gifts Are Still Needed Until Christ's Coming.

Were these [supernatural gifts] meant merely to be transitory and special and temporary signs in connection with the introduction of Christianity into the world? Or were they part of the permanent enduement of the church? Does not the apostle tell us that these gifts and ministries were bestowed 'till we all come into the unity of the faith and the knowledge of the Son of God unto a perfect man, unto the measure of the stature of the fulness of Christ'? Certainly, the church has not yet reached that maturity and if these gifts were need then they are needed still.—A. B. Simpson[31]

The Church Needs the Fivefold Ministry Gifts of Ephesians 4:11-13 for Full Maturity.

"Does not the apostle tell us that these gifts and ministries were bestowed 'till we all come into the unity of the faith and the knowledge of the Son of God unto a perfect man, unto the measure of the stature of the fulness of Christ'? Certainly, the church has not yet reached that maturity and if these gifts were need then they are needed still."—A. B. Simpson[32]

"Until the Body, the Church, is complete, these gifts [Ephesians 4:11] will continue."—A. E. Thompson[33]

"Some are called to be apostles, some prophets, some evangelists, some pastors and teachers, some workers of miracles."—A. B. Simpson[34]

"It is true that God has ordained that some in the church should be apostles, some prophets, some evangelists, some pastors and some teachers, and He has, furthermore, invested these with certain limited authority in the congregation of the saints; but the notion that they constitute a superior or privileged class is wholly wrong. They do not, but the exercise of their proper offices within the church easily leads to the idea that they do and this makes for division."—A.W. Tozer[35]

1 Corinthians 12:18—God Appointed These Gifts Permanently in the Church.

"In 1 Corinthians 12:18 we read, 'But now God has set the members, each one of them, in the body just as He pleased.' In verse 28 we read, 'And God has appointed [set] these in the church: first apostles, second prophets, third teachers, after that miracles, then gifts of healings, helps, administrations, varieties of tongues.' The word *set* [appointed] is in both cases the same in Greek (*etheto*), and signifies to place, establish, ordain, with the idea of permanency." —William C. Stevens [36]

Acts 1:8—The Need for Supernatural Power, Not Our Own.

- *Most Needed.* "A supernatural gospel is meant to accomplish supernatural results and needs a supernatural power behind it and its messengers."—A. T. Pierson, friend and associate of A. B. Simpson, published by the C&MA[37]

- *Most Lacking.* "Power, supernatural power. This is perhaps the most unique and impressive feature of the Gospel and is the element most lacking in the average life of the Christian and the Church."—A. B. Simpson[38]

Note: For a full description of 25 Scripture passages affirming continuism, see my book *Is It of God? A Biblical Guidebook for Spiritual Discernment*, Volume 1, Chapter 12.

DISCERNMENT—THE SIGNATURE THEME OF THE ALLIANCE

What sets The Alliance apart from Pentecostals and charismatics is the emphasis upon the need for discerning what is of the Spirit, what is of the flesh, and what is demonic. The C&MA welcomes all the gifts and manifestations of the Spirit but recognizes that not all that appears supernatural is from God. A. B. Simpson counseled:

> The Alliance Movement stands for all the scriptural manifestations of the Holy Spirit since Pentecost. Its peculiar testimony has ever been for the supernatural. Because we seek to guard against wild-fire and fanaticism, and against handing over our meetings to leaders of doubtful character and scenes of disorder and confusion, is no evidence of antagonism to any and all the operations of the Spirit of Pentecost. That Spirit Himself has bidden us "try the spirits whether they be of God," and has given us as tests of His true working, decency, order, self-control, soberness, edification, and above all else, love. Give us these and then welcome to all the dynamite of God.[39]

Simpson and The Alliance thus advocated discerning acceptance of revival phenomena and movements. There is a tendency either to reject all unusual revival phenomena (swooning, falling, trembling, holy laughter, drunkenness in the Spirit, etc.) or to accept all such phenomena undiscerningly. Simpson and Alliance leaders advocated that the wise biblical approach is to seek discernment and try the spirits. The Alliance motto was: "Be watchful, not fearful."

SECOND TIER DISTINCTIVE: TONGUES NOT THE EVIDENCE.

The Alliance has always affirmed that speaking in tongues is a genuine and real gift of the Spirit for today. Yet The Alliance has also always maintained that speaking in tongues is not the necessary evidence of the baptism in the Spirit.[40] This is where the split occurred about 1912 and the Assemblies of God was formed about two years later. Prominent evangelist F. F. Bosworth had been involved in the C&MA but became a charter member of the Assemblies of God. When the Assemblies firmed up the "evidence doctrine" in 1918, Bosworth left and rejoined the C&MA, along with several others.

By the late 1930s, an informal motto began to circulate around The Alliance: "Seek Not, Forbid Not," meaning, "Don't seek after tongues, but don't forbid speaking in tongues either." In 1963, the motto was codified into C&MA policy (1963-2005). Although it was originally intended to discourage intensive seeking after tongues, not discouraging tongues altogether, it began to be understood that tongues should be avoided. So, the motto became humorously (or not so humorously) known as "Seek Not; Forbid Not; Hope Not." By 2005, the C&MA Board of Directors felt that the policy was too negative, focusing on what we don't believe rather than what we do believe. A new policy statement was drafted along with a new motto: "Expectation Without Agenda." This more accurately summarizes the intent of Simpson and the early Alliance leaders.

CONTINUISM AS A 2ND-TIER DISTINCTIVE WITH SOME 3RD-TIER LIBERTY

This continuist distinctive allowed 3rd tier liberty for a variety of beliefs and practices within continuism. Some would be "considerably charismatic"; others would be "cautiously charismatic," but if all gifts were affirmed and discernment was exercised, both were welcomed in the Alliance. Simpson affirmed two years before his death, "Why may we not have all the gifts and all the graces of the Apostolic Church blended in one harmonious whole . . . without controversy?"[41] In essence, 3rd tier liberty regarding continuism meant:

"Don't be too wary; don't be too wild; be watchful and wise."

ADDITIONAL RESOURCES

FOR MORE ON the biblical basis of continuism, see Paul L. King, *Is It of God*, Chapters 11 and 12.

Deere, Jack. *Surprised by the Power of the Spirit*. Grand Rapids: Zondervan, 1993. Although not an Alliance source, Jack Deere affirms the continuing operation of the supernatural today like the C&MA. Deere, a former professor at Dallas Theological Seminary tells his theological and spiritual discovery of the reality of the supernatural today.

King, Paul L. *Genuine Gold: The Cautiously Charismatic Story of the Early Christian and Missionary Alliance*. Tulsa, OK: Word & Spirit Press, 2006.

Ruthven, Jon Mark. *On the Cessation of the Charismata*. Tulsa, OK: Word & Spirit Press, 2007.

Simpson, A. B. *The Supernatural*. Camp Hill, PA: Wingspread.

"Spiritual Gifts: Expectation without Agenda," C&MA position paper, C&MA website, (See https://www.cmalliance.org/about/beliefs/perspectives/spiritual-gifts).

12

"THE RALLYING POINT"

THE FOURFOLD GOSPEL

FORMULATION OF THE CORE OF ALLIANCE DISTINCTIVES

The formulation and arrangement of Fourfold Gospel originated with A.B. Simpson in 1887, with the founding of the Christian Alliance and the Evangelical Missionary Alliance, which merged to become the Christian and Missionary Alliance. Simpson declared that the "rallying point" of the Alliance was the fourfold gospel and "all differences that are non-essential will be forgotten in the unity of Jesus and His precious life."[1] That rallying cry was expressed as "Jesus Christ Our Savior, Sanctifier, Healer, and Coming King."

Why Four? Occasionally someone will criticize the "fourfold-ness" of the Alliance message, saying, "Why just these four? There are many other elements to the gospel." Simpson would, in fact, agree: "In one sense it is a manifold gospel with countless blessings and ever higher and higher stages of spiritual privileges and attainment. . . . There are four messages in the gospel that sum up in a very complete way the blessings which Christ has to offer us."[2]

In other words, most of the many other elements that make up the gospel of Jesus Christ can be sub-categorized under these four emphases. Soon after the founding of The Alliance, George Mueller, the great aged apostle of faith, came to visit Simpson in New York City and "told Dr. Simpson that this arrangement of truth was most evidently 'of the Lord' and suggested that he never change its mold."[3]

FOURFOLD CHRIST-CENTEREDNESS

The Alliance at our core is Christocentric—"Jesus only is our message." Each of the four "folds" is about Jesus Christ—as Savior, Sanctifier, Healer, and Coming King. It is all about Jesus. Dr. Franklin Pyles, former president of The Alliance in Canada, explains the uniqueness of Jesus as God's Son, as the agent of God's work, and in Christian spirituality. He emphasizes:

> This is not a doctrinal affirmation; this is an invitation to enter into the divine life and experience God's fullness. It is a reflection on the possibilities of living in relationship with God through Jesus Christ. It is a spirituality that centers on Jesus and affirms that through him all the possibilities of knowing God's presence and power are ours. When we affirm the idea of "Jesus Only," we are embracing God's ultimate self-manifestation in Christ as an essential element of entering into the fullness of life that God has made available through relationship with his one and only Son. This is the provision that he has made for us, and the invitation that we are given to know God in all of his living reality.[4]

Fourfold Unity Is Essential

Simpson repeatedly stressed a need for presentation of these four essentials of the Gospel: "All of our Branches need to remember to keep the four points of testimony upon which we are united."[5]

The Distinctiveness of the Fourfold Gospel. William T. MacArthur, close Simpson associate, wrote: "It is not Simpson; it is the fourfold Gospel that has attracted the people. . . . In those days, the four points of the message were held in perfect balance. . . . When this is the case in any assembly, the "flavor" will be both unmistakable and inevitable.[6] Canadian Alliance theologian Dr. Bernie Van de Walle aptly calls it "The Heart of the Gospel."

Fourfold Unity with Diversity. In 1891, Simpson described the beauty of united diversity in the Alliance:

> We have among us the rich and cultivated, we have also the poor and illiterate. . . . We have in our meetings the conservative Churchman, the staid Presbyterian, and the plain quiet Quaker; and we have also the fervid Methodist and the demonstrative Free-Methodist; and sometimes, the shouting and emotional brother whose full heart runs over with a joy and freedom which the ordinary Christian cannot understand. We must not try to reduce all Christian life to one set form. We must be content to have unity of spirit.[7]

Diversity, no set form, but unity of spirit—that is the Alliance!

Fourfold Unity with Balance. Early on Simpson maintained a need for a balanced presentation of the Fourfold Gospel: "Let there always be solid teaching and ample time for testimony. Keep from all side issues and mere phases of truth. Don't let it be purely a Divine healing meeting, or a Holiness meeting. Avoid criticisms or mere phases of holiness, or other truth. Keep all error out . . . and separate them from the true centre."[8] Simpson likened the Fourfold Gospel to the four-part musical harmony of soprano, alto, tenor, and bass, that "completes the whole effect, and swells the chorus to the very heights of triumph."[9]

Four Wheels on Simpson's Chariot. John Alexander Dowie, an Australian with a healing ministry in America, wanted Simpson to go on the road with him to do healing crusades. It would have greatly expanded Simpson's ministry. However, Simpson replied that he had four wheels on his chariot, and he could not go with just one. Simpson kept all four together in balance.

2nd Tier Fourfold Unity with 3rd Tier Flexibility and Freedom. Simpson maintained that each of the four folds of the Gospel are essential, but they are not a strait jacket.[10]

Limits to Liberty. It wasn't just "Anything goes." The "big tent" had walls. Simpson encouraged liberty on some aspects or varied details of belief within the four essential distinctives, but also set limits:

- Avoid side issues.[11]
- Don't make minor points into major points.[12]
- Don't drift from these standards.[13]
- Avoid antagonism and attack.[14]

THE FOURFOLD IMPACT

Many Other Groups Have Adopted or Adapted the Fourfold Gospel.

While the Fourfold Gospel originated with Simpson and The Alliance, it is not uniquely Alliance alone. Several denominations and ministries have followed suit by embracing or adapting in some way Simpson's Fourfold Gospel:

- *The Missionary Church* (German immigrant-oriented church founded by Alliance-related leaders; founded Ft. Wayne Bible College, and almost merged with The Alliance in the 1960s).
- *Pilgrim Holiness Church*, founded by Seth Rees (associated with The Alliance from its earliest days) and Martin Wells Knapp in 1897. Originally known as the International Holiness Union and Prayer League) in 1897, not as a church but as an interdenominational organization, in 1905 it was renamed *International Apostolic Holiness Church* with Charles and Lettie Cowman as General Superintendents.
- *Charles and Lettie Cowman* and Oriental Mission Society (OMS), as well as in Lettie's classic devotionals, *Streams in the Desert* and *Springs in the Valley*. The Cowman's were touched by the Holy Spirit through A. B. Simpson's ministry when he laid hands on them. Lettie's devotionals feature many quotes from Simpson and other Alliance leaders.

- The Cowman's work in South Korea produced *the Korean Holiness Church*, which uses the Fourfold Gospel, as a ministry of the International Apostolic Holiness Church/Pilgrim Holiness Church.
- *David Yonggi Cho*, pastor of the largest church in the world, located in South Korea, added a fifth gospel of prosperity of the soul, based on 3 John 2.[15]
- *Numerous Pentecostal groups* emerged out of the Alliance, carrying the Fourfold Gospel message with them.
- *Aimee Semple MacPherson founded the Foursquare Church* with her own inspiration and insight from the Holy Spirit, replacing Christ as Sanctifier with Christ Our Baptizer in the Holy Spirit (whereas Simpson included the baptism in the Spirit in Christ as Sanctifier).
- *Holiness Pentecostals*, on the other hand, distinguished between Christ as Sanctifier and Christ as Baptizer in the Spirit, expanding it to a Fivefold Gospel.

Not Doctrines to Believe, But Spirituality to Be Practiced.

The real impact of the Fourfold Gospel is not on a set of beliefs, but living truths actualized in and through our lives. Franklin Pyles gives clear summary:

> The fourfold gospel is not a series of doctrines to believe in, but it is rather a spirituality that is to be practiced. It is a way of life that is rooted in the person of Jesus and our ongoing relationship with him. As we begin to understand our Alliance heritage as a spirituality that centers us in Jesus rather than a series of doctrinal affirmations, it opens us to receive all that Christ has for us as a result of his life, death, and resurrection on our behalf.[16]

13

FOUNDATIONS OF THE FOURFOLD GOSPEL

COVENANT THEOLOGY AND HIGHER LIFE

W hat makes the Alliance "Alliance"? You would probably answer "The Fourfold Gospel" and you would be partially correct. However, there would be no Fourfold Gospel without Covenant Theology and Higher Life foundations, which are the roots and heritage of The Alliance.

COVENANT THEOLOGY ROOTS IN THE ALLIANCE

As mentioned in Chapter 1, Covenant Theology provides the theological-historical foundation for the Alliance Distinctives. Even though Simpson was not a five-point Calvinist, he and other early Alliance leaders were steeped in Reformed Covenant Theology. Simpson's writings are filled with teaching on "redemption rights," inheriting the promises of the Covenant today through the covenant of redemption or covenant of grace,[1] as are those of other prominent early Alliance scholars.[2] Simpson and other Alliance leaders related fourfold gospel themes of Christ Our Sanctifier and Christ Our Healer to the promises of the covenants, specifically identifying sanctification, the baptism in the Spirit, and healing as covenant rights of the covenants of redemption and grace.[3]

WHAT IS THE HIGHER LIFE AND HOW DID IT ORIGINATE?

The Higher Life movement was launched by Presbyterian minister William Boardman through his book *The Higher Christian Life* in 1858. This book greatly impacted A.B. Simpson and is one of the main foundations of the Fourfold Gospel of the Alliance.[4] Calling it the "full gospel" like Boardman, Simpson described this fourfold gospel as "a manifold gospel with countless blessings and *ever higher and higher* stages of spiritual privileges and attainment."[5] Some important features of this Higher Life movement to note include:

- It spans theological labels.
- It has roots in Scripture, the early church fathers, the Reformation, the Pietists, and Puritans.
- It is a Reformed alternative to Wesleyan sanctification —something more.
- It is not synonymous with Keswick. The Higher Life movement predates and is much broader than the Keswick movement.
- The Higher Life is the "full gospel"—the language of fullness. Boardman appears to be the earliest person I can find who used the terms "the higher Christian life" and "full gospel," as well as "full salvation," "full trust," "full surrender," and "filled my soul." Simpson also used these phrases frequently.
- The Higher Life involves a second experience of the Spirit —the baptism in the Spirit. Boardman also described it as "deeper work of grace, a fuller apprehension of Christ, a more complete and abiding union with him than at the first."[6] Simpson, Pardington, and other Alliance leaders also use this language.
- The Higher Life movement has its critics—as is true of all holiness movements. Reformed cessationist theologian B. B. Warfield, who was critical of Simpson and healing as well, called the Higher life teaching a heresy.

THE FULL GOSPEL/HIGHER LIFE IS THE MESSAGE AND MINISTRY OF THE ALLIANCE.

Simpson's Writings on the Higher Life

Simpson wrote numerous books involving redemption rights and the Higher Christian Life, including *The Highest Christian Life*, an exposition on Ephesians; *In Heavenly Places*; *A Larger Christian Life*; *Land of Promise*; *The Life of Prayer*; and a devotional, *Days of Heaven on Earth*, among others. Simpson described the message of the early Alliance:

> We believe it is in God's great heart of love to make the Christian Alliance a mighty and world-wide movement for Christ and the *fullness of the gospel* . . . the Alliance has a broader basis, . . . it also aims to accomplish an equally important work for the promotion *of a higher Christian life* and *full salvation for both soul and body*.[7]

The four phrases of the Fourfold Gospel were not new, not coined by Simpson, but uniting the four together was unique to Simpson. Drawing upon Boardman's language of fullness and the full gospel, Christ as Sanctifier and as Healer, in 1887 Simpson summarized all this in the fourfold full gospel:

> There are four messages in the gospel that sum up in a very complete way the blessings which Christ has to offer us: Jesus Christ as Savior, Sanctifier, Healer, and Coming King. . . . Is not this great blessing of the *full gospel* worth believing, receiving, and telling?[8]

BIBLICAL AND THEOLOGICAL THEMES OF THE HIGHER LIFE MOVEMENT: IMPACT ON THE ALLIANCE AND THE FORMULATION OF THE FOURFOLD GOSPEL

Simply speaking, the Higher Life is the belief, based on Philippians 3:10-14; Ephesians 1:15-23; 2:5-6; Colossians 3:1-3; and other Scriptures, that there is more to be experienced in the heights of the

Christian life than conversion. These include, but not limited to, covenant or redemption rights, privileges, and inheritance as a believer, being seating in the heavenly places in Christ, life on wings —soaring in the heights, a higher plane of living, enjoying the heavenly life now, believers as royalty—reigning in life, believers are the head and not the tail, the authority of the believer, healing and the baptism in the Spirit as covenant rights, claiming our inheritance and confessions of faith based on our redemption, among many others. (See my book *Come Up Higher* for in-depth study). Alliance distinctives and theology are saturated with these Higher Life theological themes:

Higher Life Christology (Doctrine of Christ) is strongly *Christocentric.*

Higher Life Soteriology (Doctrine of Salvation) Is *"Full Salvation,"*

- Not only salvation from sin and hell, but so much more.
- Salvation of the whole person—spirit, soul, and body.
- Redemption involves rights and privileges of the New Covenant.
- Atonement involves Christ both as Our Savior and our Healer—the effects of the atonement on the whole person.
- Healing is a provision of the atonement as a dimension of the Higher Life.

Higher Life Pneumatology (Doctrine of the Holy Spirit): Christ Our Sanctifier and the Baptism in the Holy Spirit.

Higher Life Anthropology (Doctrine of Man) and Ecclesiology (Doctrine of the Church): Seated in Heavenly Places (Eph 2:6).

In The Alliance, this identification with Christ, raised and seated with Him in the heavenly places became known as "Throne Life."

Higher Life Eschatology (Doctrine of the End Times): *Christ Our Coming King—A Foretaste of the Millennial Life Now*

"Reigning in life" (Rom 5:17) through "the authority of the believer" (John 1:12; Lk 10:19).

RESOURCES ON COVENANT/REDEMPTION RIGHTS AND THE HIGHER LIFE

- Boardman, William E. *The Higher Christian Life.*
- King Paul L., *Come Up Higher! Rediscovering Throne Life-The Highest Christian Life for the 21ˢᵗ Century.*
- MacMillan, John A. *The Authority of the Believer.*
- Murray, Andrew. *Holiest of All.*
- Murray, Andrew. *The Two Covenants.*
- Simpson, A. B. *Days of Heaven on Earth*
- Simpson, A. B. *The Land of Promise*, newly modernized by Marv Nelson.
- Simpson, A. B. *A Larger Christian Life.*
- Simpson, A. B. *The Highest Christian Life.*
- Simpson, A. B. *In Heavenly Places.*

14

JESUS CHRIST OUR SAVIOR—THE GOSPEL OF FULL SALVATION

We may have a tendency to gloss over The Alliance distinctive of Jesus Christ Our Savior. Many often have the attitude, "we get this," "everyone knows this," so let's move on. However, beyond this, the distinctive of the Alliance testimony of Christ as Savior is a full gospel of full salvation. As Simpson put it, "This glorious gospel of full salvation. . . . Jesus, a complete Savior for body, soul and spirit."[1] It is the whole gospel for the whole person to the whole world. For Simpson and The Alliance, the Gospel is not merely getting people saved, although that is where it begins with the impetus for the Great Commission. The Gospel is a multi-faceted Gospel. Jesus Christ Our Savior encompasses so much more.

- *A Supernatural Salvation with a Supernatural Savior.*
  Simpson quoted J. Hudson Taylor: ""We are a supernatural people born again by a supernatural birth, kept by a supernatural power, sustained on supernatural food, taught by a supernatural Teacher from a supernatural Book. We are led by a supernatural Captain in right paths to assured victories." [2]

- *"A Person, Not a Doctrine"*—to cite William T. MacArthur.[3] Bernie Van de Walle summarizes Simpson's elevated view of Christ Our Savior: "For Simpson, salvation is more than restoration to some pre-fall condition, for some degree of divinization accompanies this indwelling of Christ. His indwelling lifts humanity to a higher nature than it could ever have acquired on its own."[4]

- *A "Whole" Gospel, Not a Merely a "Holistic" Gospel*—to quote Dr. Arnold Cook.[5] Dr. Franklin Pyles explains the Alliance perspective of a holistic gospel: "God saves us so that we can experience intimacy with him, just as he originally intended; he saves us so that we can participate in authentic relationship with others, and he saves us so that the whole of creation can be restored to its original intention, as a place of peace, harmony, and intimacy."[6]

This whole gospel for the whole person for the whole world through a supernatural Savior and a supernatural salvation will be explained more fully in the full systematic theological book.

A DISTINCTIVE WITHIN A DISTINCTIVE: FULL SALVATION EXPERIENCED THROUGH BELIEVERS' BAPTISM BY IMMERSION.

Believer's baptism by immersion for Simpson was a part of his personal "full gospel." By Simpson's own testimony, he wrote an award-winning paper in seminary defending infant baptism, yet he encountered Christ in such a personal revelation that baptism in water and baptism in the Spirit were identified together as a "double baptism," which resulted in his own believer's baptism by immersion. This was part of "full salvation" for Simpson.

The Alliance does not believe in baptismal regeneration, the belief that baptism saves a person from hell, but The Alliance believes and practices believer's baptism. Yet baptism often is not required for membership. This reflects Simpson's spiritual journey. (Note: Canadian C&MA required believer's baptism for membership then moved back to requiring just baptism.)

A 2nd Tier Distinctive With 3rd Tier Liberty—A Case of "We Believe This, But We Allow That."

Simpson's biographer and Alliance historian A. E. Thompson recorded that "No one was excluded from membership whose conscience was satisfied with their infant baptism."[7]

NOTE: **For Simpson's fascinating baptismal journey, see Appendix 5, Part A: "Simpson's Triple Vision of the Double Baptism of Believer's Baptism by Immersion and Baptism in the Spirit."**

15

JESUS CHRIST OUR SANCTIFIER
THE SANCTIFYING BAPTISM IN THE SPIRIT

This chapter briefly examines and explains the biblical, historical, hermeneutical, and exegetical basis for Article 7 of both the US and Canadian Statements of Faith on the second fold of the Fourfold Gospel—Jesus Christ as our Sanctifier, and its main tenet, the sanctifying baptism or filling with the Holy Spirit. The Canadian Statement of Faith revised the 1965 statement, not to change the doctrine, but to clarify the doctrine in current theological language, while maintaining historic Alliance meaning. The full systematic theological book will examine this more thoroughly,

THE ESSENCE OF CHRIST OUR SANCTIFIER

Our doctrine of Christ as Sanctifier covers the entire life of the believer from conversion to glorification. Yet the essence of the doctrine of Christ Our Sanctifier, according to early Alliance leaders, is the sanctifying baptism or filling with the Spirit and the progressive work of the Spirit following that "crisis" experience. C&MA president Frederick N. Senft wrote in his 1924 annual report:

> The message [of the Alliance] is the fulness of Jesus through the indwelling Holy Spirit to meet & satisfy every need of spirit, soul & body. . . . It is not an ecstasy, not merely an experience, not a cold doctrine, but the living, victorious Christ. It is "Christ our Sanctifier." This simple phrase expresses at once the mightiest fact and the profoundest philosophy of holiness. It includes the definite baptism with the Holy Spirit, making Christ "unto us sanctification."

This article is one of the C&MA distinctives that was added in 1928 to the basic doctrinal statement adapted from the WCFA.[1] It is based on the 1906 "Conference for Prayer and Counsel Regarding Uniformity in the Testimony and Teaching of the Alliance." Out of this conference came the following doctrinal guidelines for belief in the sanctifying filling of the Spirit based on the emphasis of Christ as Sanctifier:

- 1. a definite second blessing, distinct in nature, though not necessarily far removed in time, from the experience of conversion.
- 2. the baptism of the Holy Ghost as a distinct experience, nor merely for power for service, but for personal holiness over the world and sin.
- 3. the indwelling Christ in the heart of the believer as a distinct experience.
- 4. sanctification by faith as a distinct gift of God's grace to every open and surrendered soul
- 5. growth in grace and the deeper filling of the Holy Spirit as distinct from and the result of the definite experience of sanctification.

This was reaffirmed by the Board of Managers in 1922 with just a few word description changes and an added sentence on spiritual gifts. These guidelines were eventually capsulized in the 1928 statement of faith to be used by Alliance schools, which reads almost word-for-word as the 1965 Statement of Faith. The Canadian Statement maintains the same meaning but clarifies some of the language and emphasis for 21st century believers.

2nd Tier Doctrine with 3rd Tier Liberty of Expression.

THE 1906 STATEMENT ended with this word of guidance (italics mine):

> It is understood that all our Alliance officers and teachers *are at liberty to present the truth of sanctification in such phases and phrases as his own convictions warrant,* in general accordance with the above specifications, but with the understanding that such extreme views as are sometimes taught under the name of "eradication" or "suppression" *shall not be presented in an aggressive or controversial spirit toward those who differ.*

Yet Firmly a 2nd Tier Alliance Distinctive.

Simpson periodically and adamantly warned about watering down this Alliance distinctive, which he held as a 2nd tier essential, not a 3rd tier optional belief for the Alliance:

- 1909: "Loose views about sanctification, the baptism of the Holy Spirit, the definite experience of union and fellowship with Christ . . . are out of place on such a platform."[2]

- 1913: "the doctrine of a second work of grace, a spiritual crisis after conversion followed by entire consecration and the baptism of the Holy Spirit, is also becoming obsolete even in evangelical religious circles. . . . The importance of this transaction I cannot emphasize too strongly."[3]

- 1914: "The great body of Christians united in this movement believe most firmly a definite experience of personal sanctification distinct from the experience of conversion. . . .

We should deeply deplore any drift from this high and established standard."[4]

THE CURRENT C&MA STATEMENTS OF FAITH

Note: This statement is in the process of being updated and revised in the US C&MA General Councils. As mentioned earlier, this statement is based almost verbatim on a 1928 Statement of Faith for Alliance schools. The intent of the updated and revised language is not to change the doctrine, but rather to update 100-year-old language for 21st century understanding. The Canadian C&MA has already done this, revising the 1965 statement, not changing the doctrine, but clarifying the doctrine in current theological language:

US: *"It is the will of God that each believer should be filled with the Holy Spirit and be sanctified wholly, being separated from sin and the world and fully dedicated to the will of God, thereby receiving power for holy living and effective service. This is both a crisis and a progressive experience wrought in the life of the believer subsequent to conversion."*

Canadian: *"It is the will of God that in union with Christ each believer should be sanctified thoroughly thereby being separated from sin and the world and fully dedicated to God, receiving power for holy living and sacrificial and effective service toward the completion of Christ's commission. This is accomplished through being filled with the Holy Spirit which is both a distinct event and progressive experience in the life of the believer."*

"... A CRISIS AND A PROGRESSIVE EXPERIENCE ..."

Both Instantaneous and Gradual—Crisis and Progressive.

Simpson explains how this experience of the Spirit is both: "There is an instantaneous and there is a gradual work of the Holy Spirit. There is an act by which He baptizes us into Himself forever. And there is a process in which He sits down beside the crucible and watches the molten silver until it perfectly reflects His image."[5] Chinese writer Watchman Nee, who was a C&MA pastor's son-in-law, illustrates in his classic book *The Normal Christian Life*, both crisis and process with a wicket gate and a narrow path:

> Such experience usually takes the two-fold form of a crisis leading to a continuous process. . . . in terms of John Bunyan's "wicket gate" through which Christian entered upon a "narrow path": (a) A wicket gate (Crisis). (b) A narrow path (Process). . . . There may be a crisis that, once reached and passed, can transform our whole life and service for God. It is a wicket gate by which we may enter upon an entirely new pathway. Such a crisis occurred in the life of Jacob at Peniel.[6]

The Crisis of the Language of "Crisis."

During the eight years I served on our district's Licensing, Ordination, and Consecration Council (LOCC), the Alliance distinctive of Christ Our Sanctifier was the muddiest for candidates to understand and articulate. Responses were all over the map. Consequently, not only in doctrine but also in experience responses have been all over the map. After all, some have opined, "Yes, I have had a crisis experience— but what Christian hasn't? Everyone has had a crisis experience of some sort."

Lack of a True Crisis of the Spirit Encounter. The theological meaning of "crisis" is lost in today's jargon. Everyone has had a crisis, but not the crisis of the deeper life or sanctification. "Crisis" was the typical jargon of the holiness movements of the 19th and early 20th centuries for the subsequent event of sanctification, and it is vital to our theology, but today's Christians don't usually have a clue. The language of "the crisis of sanctification" is off most people's radar, and the language of "filling" and "baptism in the Spirit" mean so many different things to many people. **See Appendix 6, Part A for The Alliance and Historic Views on Spirit Baptism.**

Consequently, confusion is common, and the true Alliance doctrine and experience as originally understood is often lost or watered down, and people have many times been licensed with a defective comprehension of what the crisis experience of the Spirit is in the Alliance. Many who have claimed a crisis experience or filling of the Spirit, may not have experienced that true filling or baptism in the Spirit as Simpson experienced and taught it.

For this reason, I will be taking extra time and care to explain this Alliance distinctive clearly, as well as providing a historical and biblical exegetical basis, primarily in Appendices 6-8.

What, Then, Does The Alliance Mean by a "Crisis" Experience?

Early Alliance theologian George Pardington wrote an entire book on this entitled *The Crisis of the Deeper Life*. He defined it as "a second definite work of grace—a *crisis* as radical and revolutionary as the crisis of conversion."[134] The language of "crisis," though foreign to 21st century Christian culture, was used in a variety of holiness movements and denominations to describe this experience of sanctification.

So, what is this crisis in Alliance understanding? It is a critical point of realization that we cannot live the Christian life in our own power but only in the power of the Holy Spirit, resulting in full surrender to Christ and being filled with the Holy Spirit to overflowing—a baptism, if you will.

Simpson, Pardington, and other Alliance leaders explain it in a variety of ways: a definite line of demarcation; a decisive act—an event at a point in time; total surrender and victorious filling, as radical and revolutionary as conversion; a death-to-resurrection experience; the cross life or crucified life followed by the higher life or resurrection life; turning on a power switch; second blessing/second work of grace; sealing of the Spirit; baptism in the Spirit.[7]

Many other terms are used in Scripture to describe the same biblical experience: baptism in the Spirit, receiving the Spirit, receiving or clothed with power, filled with the Spirit, sealed with the Spirit, Spirit fell upon, overflowing with rivers of living water, etc. Andrew Murray called it "absolute surrender." J. Hudson Taylor called it "the exchanged life." The Puritans called it the "sealing of the Spirit" and the "witness of the Spirit."

This distinctive of The Alliance is that sanctification begins at conversion but also involves a post-conversion crisis or life-changing event of the Spirit followed by a more intensified progressive experience of ongoing sanctification. This might be pictured like this:

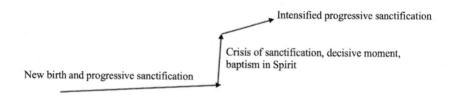

When we are born again, we are sanctified positionally and begin to be sanctified gradually in our experience. The baptism in the Spirit (filling of the Spirit, crisis of the deeper life) is, in Simpson's words, an elevator lifting us to the higher life in Christ. Church revival historian Richard Lovelace describes it as "a large leap forward in progressive sanctification." Simpson stresses that progressive sanctification continues at an intensified level.[8]

A DISTINCT-SUBSEQUENT-SANCTIFYING EXPERIENCE

Both the U.S. and Canadian statements are saying the same thing, just with different wording. and the terms of "crisis," "subsequent," and "distinct" are all used interchangeably in early Alliance documents.

A Distinct Event

The Canadian Statement of Faith states that this sanctifying filling of the Spirit is "a distinct event." It is distinct in two ways:

Distinct from Conversion. The term "distinct" appears five times in the 1906 document. A.B. Simpson understood that it could occasionally occur at almost the same time as conversion, but that it is distinct from conversion.[9] Alliance theologian George Pardington similarly explains:

In the experience of the Apostolic Church, as recorded in the book of Acts, there were three things that were closely connected, namely: conversion, baptism, and the reception of the Holy Spirit. . . . [They] are three separate and *distinct* things. . . . These three things, while separate and *distinct*, are yet closely related both as doctrines and experiences.[10]

Distinct as Distinguished from Other Holiness Views of Sanctification. The Higher Life and holiness movements understood that the baptism with the Spirit is in some way a sanctifying experience, based on mainly on Luke 3:16-17, as well as other texts. Some called it the "crisis of sanctification" or the "crisis of the deeper life."

- Wesleyans taught it is the eradication of the old man of sin.
- Early Keswick leaders taught that it is suppression of the old man.
- Later Keswick leaders taught that it is counteracting the old man.
- Still others, notably, the Oberlin school, taught a form of perfectionism.

A. B. Simpson and the C&MA taught that it is the "law of lift," lifting us to a higher plane of living above the old life of sin through habitation by Christ—Christ in you, the hope of glory. A.B. Simpson called the baptism in the Spirit "God's elevator to the higher planes of the Christian life." Simpson's close associate William T. MacArthur explains Simpson's views:

A. B. Simpson . . . found two opposing schools, known as Eradications and Suppressionists—the former contending that in the crisis of sanctification, sin is eradicated, root and branch, leaving the subject free to love and serve God unhindered; the latter contending that sin with all its possibilities is always present, demanding constant suppression. Mr. Simpson's reply to these was characteristic. He would say, 'It is neither suppression nor eradication; it is Christ in you, the hope of glory.' It was this persistent exaltation of Christ above human experiences that distinguished the Alliance from other bodies of holiness people.[11]

So, sanctification is not eradication or suppression, but transformation by Christ in you (Col 1:29). This is the distinct Higher Life perspective of the Alliance. There is much more to understanding the Alliance doctrine of Christ as Sanctifier that will be contained in the full-length systematic theological book.

An Event Subsequent to Conversion

Simpson, along with hosts of evangelical leaders, especially from both the Higher Life Reformed and the Wesleyan holiness camps, taught that a crisis of sanctification and/or empowerment, whether called the baptism in the Spirit or another terminology occurs subsequent to conversion. As mentioned above, some, like Simpson, acknowledged that the two could occur virtually simultaneously, yet be distinct events:

> The difference is one in the nature of things rather than in the order of time. The early Christians were expected to pass quickly into the baptism of the Holy Spirit and the fulness of their life in Christ.[12]

> We are willing . . . to concede that the baptism of the Holy Spirit may be received at the very same time a soul is converted. We have known a sinner to be converted, sanctified, and saved all within a single hour, and yet each experience was different in its nature and was received in proper order and by a definite faith for that particular blessing, and this involves the crisis: a full surrender and an explicit preparation of the promise of God by faith."[13]

Opposition to a post-conversion experience of the Spirit usually comes from some in Baptistic, Fundamental, Reformed, or cessationist theological camps. For instance, John MacArthur erroneously calls it the "charismatic doctrine of subsequence," apparently not aware of the rich history of belief and practice of the baptism in the Spirit outside of and millennia prior to the Pentecostal and charismatic movements.

Distinctives of the Fourfold Gospel, including the sanctifying baptism in the Spirit, were supported by grammatical-historical exegesis by A. B. Simpson, Dr. George P. Pardington, Dr. T. J. McCrossan, Dr. Bob Willoughby, Dr. Samuel Stoesz, Dr. Gerald McGraw, Dr. Keith Bailey, Dr. Bernie Van de Walle, Dr. Rob Reimer, Dr. David Schroeder, Dr. Richard Gilbertson, Dr. Randy Harrison, myself, and other Alliance leaders and scholars. What follows is a summary of some of the exegetical basis for a post-conversion experience of the Holy Spirit. **See Appendices 6 and 8 for more on the historical and exegetical bases for the subsequent baptism in the Spirit.**

KEY SCRIPTURES FOR HISTORIC ALLIANCE INTERPRETATION AS A SANCTIFYING EXPERIENCE

Certain Scriptures were key to the Alliance interpreting this post-conversion experience as a "sanctifying" experience.[14]

Luke 3:16-17—The Phrase "Baptism with the Holy Spirit <u>and Fire</u>" Signifies a Sanctifying Experience.

> *As for me, I baptize you with water; but He is coming who is mightier than I, and I am not fit to untie the straps of His sandals; He will baptize you with the Holy Spirit and fire. His winnowing fork is in His hand to thoroughly clear His threshing floor, and to gather the wheat into His barn; but He will burn up the chaff with unquenchable fire (Lk 3:16-17).*

This is a key Scripture in historic holiness and Alliance circles to support biblically a crisis of sanctification, or what Alliance leaders called "The Sanctifying Baptism in the Spirit." Some commentators interpret "and fire" and the following verse about burning up the chaff as eschatological judgment, while early Alliance and holiness leaders, as well as most of the church fathers and commentators throughout church history, interpreted it as God's sanctifying work, or as both. I believe both are right. Scripture is filled with double entendre. Throughout the Old Testament, fire relates to holiness and purifying by fire (Isaiah 6:1-9; Job 23:10. Simpson especially used this image for the *fire of intensified sanctification:*

> This does not mean that the Holy Spirit and fire are different, or that the baptism of fire is something distinct from that of the Spirit, but simply that the figure of fire expresses more fully the intensity and power of this divine baptism. It means that the person who is baptized with God is a soul on fire.... penetrating, ... purifying, ... consuming, ... refining, ... melting, ...[15]

> Christ's baptism was by fire and went to the roots of conduct. The purity He required included motives, aims, and 'the thoughts and intents of the heart,' and He not only requires but He gives the purity that springs from the depths of our being. Like a flame that consumes the dross and leaves the molten metal pure and unalloyed, so the Holy Spirit separates us from our old sinful and self-life and burns into us the nature and the life of Christ.[16]

Other Alliance leaders used similar imagery to describe the sanctifying baptism with the Spirit as burning away sin and self, or as transformation and consuming all that is not of God.[17]

Acts 1:4, 5, 8—Power to Be a Witness

One of the core values of the Alliance is that without the power of the Holy Spirit we can do nothing. Dr. John Stumbo, president of the US Alliance, has emphasized that the Alliance is an Acts 1:8 family. Jesus identifies the baptism in the Spirit that He gives (Acts 1:4-5) is the Holy Spirit coming upon people for the purpose of power to be a witness—a threefold power:

- *Power to **speak** a witness* with boldness, wisdom,

effectiveness, and anointing from the Holy Spirit (Acts 2:14-37; 4:31).

- *Power to **live** a witness* through transformed holy living, overcoming sin and the devil (Acts 4:13).
- *Power to **demonstrate** a witness **supernaturally*** through the gifts and manifestations of the Holy Spirit (Acts 2:4ff; Acts 3; Acts 8:14-17; Acts 19:6).

Romans 12:1-2—The Point of Presentation as a Living Sacrifice

Romans 12:1-2 describes the crisis. William T. MacArthur explains the position of Simpson and the Alliance:

> There was a marked difference of opinion among those who taught sanctification. One party taught that the work of sanctification I the life of the believer was completed in one *crisis*; the other contending for a lifelong *process*. Mr. Simpson wisely met this issue by accepting both positions as Scriptural and combining them in one experience— a *crisis* followed by a *process*. St. Paul in Romans 12:1 describes the *crisis*: "I beseech you therefore, brethren by the mercies of God, that ye present your bodies a living sacrifice, holy acceptable unto God which is your reasonable service." And in 1 Thessalonians 5:16-24 he describes the *process*.[18]

1 Thessalonians 5:23—Sanctification of the Whole Person

This filling of the Spirit is often linked with sanctification. Based on the plain intent, literal priority, grammar, and syntax of 1 Thessalonians 5:23, Simpson taught that to be sanctified wholly means that every part of a person's being—spirit, soul and body—is to be sanctified, that is, separated, dedicated, and filled.[19] In addition, this statement is based upon Scripture comparison with Romans 12:1-2 and 2 Corinthians 6:14-7:1, as well as several other Scriptures. Simpson considered it a transfusion of the life of God within.[20]

"... AND A PROGRESSIVE EXPERIENCE ..."

The last point of the 1906 Statement on Christ as Sanctifier reads, "growth in grace and the deeper filling of the Holy Spirit as distinct from and the result of the definite experience of sanctification.[21] This explains the uniqueness of the Alliance understanding of sanctification, especially how it differs from a Reformed view of sanctification as well as how it differs from Wesleyan entire sanctification/eradication and Keswick suppressionism. The Alliance view is not perfectionistic, nor is it static (thus, Gerald McGraw calls it "dynamic sanctification"),[22] but rather, after the encounter of the sanctifying baptism in the Spirit, the Spirit-baptized believer can grow in grace and receive deeper fillings.

Fullness After Baptism

George Pardington expressed it as after baptism comes fullness:

> Glorious, however, as is the reception of the Spirit, it is not the climax of spiritual life. It is only a unique crisis, which marks a new beginning in Christian experience. After the baptism comes the fullness of the Spirit. . . . The fullness of the Spirit marks an advance upon the baptism of the Spirit. . . . It is not an act, but a process. It is not a transaction, but a habit. Having received Christ (act), we grow up into Him in all things (process). Having received the Holy Spirit (transaction), we drink, and keep drinking of His fullness (habit).[23]

Second Pentecosts

Simpson acknowledged that there are second Pentecosts lifting us to a higher plane: "It is not so much a perpetual fullness as a perpetual filling. There are periodic experiences of spiritual elevation that are part of God's plan for our life in Christ and are designed, no doubt, to lift us to a higher plane of abiding in Him. There are the Pentecosts and the second Pentecosts."[24]

Deeper and Fuller Baptisms

There is no resting on our laurels, no place to say, "We have been there and done that." Simpson himself prayed for deeper and higher baptisms in the Spirit:

> I pressed upon Him a new claim for a Mighty Baptism of the Holy Spirit in His complete Pentecostal fullness embracing all the gifts and graces of the Spirit. . . . I knew that I had been baptized with the Holy Spirit before, but I was made to understand that God had a deeper and fuller baptism for me."—A. B. Simpson, Diary, August 9, 1907

Fulfilling Incomplete Effusions

On the other hand, William C. Stevens suggests that some may receive "incomplete effusions of the Spirit," due to ignoring or even "deploring" gifts and manifestations of the Spirit.[25] So a deeper, fuller experience of the Spirit may be needed to complete to overflowing the baptism in the Spirit.

Enlarging and Expanding-- Larger Capacities and Dormant Powers

Simpson emphasized that God is always enlarging us and our capacities: "We need a larger baptism of the Holy Spirit. . . . There are capacities in the human spirit none of us has ever yet begun to realize! . . . New baptisms awaken the dormant powers that we did not know we possessed."[26]

Multiple Baptisms as an Alternative Explanation for Pentecostal Experiences.

People from a Wesleyan background who had experienced a crisis of sanctification sometimes had called it the baptism in the Spirit, but when they later experienced an outpouring of the Spirit with speaking in tongues, they called the earlier experience the crisis of sanctification and the latter experience the baptism in the Spirit evidenced by speaking in tongues—thus a five-fold gospel.

Don't Discredit Your Prior Experiences. In contrast, A. B. Simpson emphasized, "We do not need to discredit our past spiritual experiences because we have not yet entered into God's deeper revelations and manifestations." Rather, the latter experience is a deeper or fuller or larger baptism:

> In a very important sense, it is simply the enlarging, expanding, and completing of that which has already begun. The later experience may be called an enduement, or clothing upon, with divine power. The Spirit on us describes the yet higher manifestation of God in clothing us with power from on high for special ministry in the kingdom.[27]

So, in the Alliance view, one baptism in the Spirit may not involve speaking in tongues, but a later baptism in the Spirit could be accompanied by speaking in tongues, but not be a necessary evidence.

WHY USE THE LANGUAGE OF "BAPTISM" IN THE SPIRIT?

Why use the term "baptism in the Spirit"? This question was asked of me at my licensing interview with the District Licensing and Ordination Council. I responded with three basic reasons:

1. Baptism Means Immersion—Overwhelming.

The word "baptize" means to "immerse, saturate, overwhelm." That accurately describes this subsequent experience of the Spirit. "Filling" can describe the experience as well, but it is not as strong a word. A person can be filled to a degree, even to the brim, but not necessarily to "overwhelming." To be baptized with the Spirit is something more—it is to be filled to overflowing—beyond the brim. Before my baptism in the Spirit, I had been "filled," but not FILLED!

2. It Was the Terminology of Simpson and Early Alliance Leaders

Although the Alliance used a wide variety of terms to express this experience, as did the New Testament writers as well, the term "baptism of the Spirit"[28] was used frequently by Simpson, as well as in official Alliance documents.

The Licensing Council Didn't Know. When I interviewed before the Licensing Council, they were aware, at least, that Simpson had used the language of baptism in the Spirit. However, to most of those on the Council, they were unaware that this had been official C&MA language. They were also unaware of the exegetical basis for the language. I told them that one of my earliest mentors, Rev. Roland Gray, Sr. had told me, "The Alliance does not teach the baptism in the Spirit like it once did." In the very first Alliance church I pastored, both an Alliance pastor's widow and the mother of Alliance missionaries told me the same thing.

So, as I began to research, I discovered that not only did A. B. Simpson use that term frequently, emphasizing its importance, many other early Alliance leaders and Alliance documents did as well. Although the Alliance used a wide variety of terms to express this experience, as they did in the New Testament as well, the term "baptism of the Spirit" was used frequently by Simpson, as well as in official Alliance documents. Here is a sampling (italics mine):

- 1906 Board of Managers Statement: "a definite second blessing, distinct in nature, though not necessarily far removed in time from the experience of conversion; ... The *baptism of the Holy Spirit* as a distinct experience not merely for power for service, but for personal holiness and victory over the world and sin."
- 1912—George Pardington: "it is the *baptism of the Holy Ghost* which brings to our hearts the revelation of the indwelling Christ."[29]
- 1924—F. N. Senft, 3rd C&MA president: "'Christ our Sanctifier.' This simple phrase expresses at once the

mightiest fact and the profoundest philosophy of holiness. It includes the definite *baptism with the Holy Spirit*, making Christ 'unto us sanctification.'"[30]

- 1927, 1932—Board of Managers, *Alliance Weekly*: "The Alliance accepts without question . . . The *Sanctifying Baptism with the Holy Spirit.*"[31]
- 1927—H. M. Shuman, 4th president of the C&MA: "There is special need in this hour of a strong Scriptural presentation of the *truths of sanctification and the baptism of the Holy Spirit.*"
- 1929—Shuman: "The *truths of sanctification and the baptism of the Spirit* are points in our message that *are of paramount importance.*"[32]
- 1930s—J. H. Cable, history of Nyack Missionary Training Institute, one of the doctrines of the institute was *"the Baptism of the Holy Spirit for life and witnessing."*
- 1937—Armin Gesswein, *Alliance Weekly*: "they were "endued with Power from on high," or "baptized" with the Holy Spirit. In other words, an experience subsequent to conversion is clearly spoken of.... This baptism (Acts 1:5) seems to be a functional rather than a regenerative baptism. Regeneration is not spoken of...."[33]

To Simpson, the baptism in the Spirit is vital, not optional: Every believer needs it; human self-sufficiency is not enough; we become more in touch with God's thoughts.[34] Nothing can take its place;[35] it is God's elevator to the higher life.[36] *It is a double baptism along with baptism in water.*[37] **See Appendix 5, Part B, on "Simpson's 'Double Baptism' of Water and Spirit in Church History."**

Evidence for a Sanctifying Spirit Baptism Throughout Church History. A post-conversion experience of sanctification in some way is found in many theological backgrounds throughout church history, sometimes clearly identified as the baptism in the Spirit. These experiences are not nuanced theologically, but clearly demonstrate a special event of heightened or intensified impartation of holiness. **See Appendix 6, Part B, for a sampling.**

3. There Is Good Exegetical Evidence for Using the Terminology.

My third response to the L&O Council was that there were good scriptural reasons for using the terminology "baptism in the Spirit." Some leaders in the Alliance, including L&C Council members, had moved away from the language of "baptism in the Spirit" and instead re-interpreted the phrase to mean a conversion experience, using the language of "filling with the Spirit," similar to that of the Third Wave movement. **(See Appendix 7 for the "History of the Decline and Recovery of Baptism in the Spirit Language in the Alliance").**

So, I shared with the committee just briefly the trinity of baptisms or 3-in-1 baptism as I present in the charts on Appendix 8. Even though I heard this teaching growing up in the Alliance in the 1960s, some of these L & O members had never heard this explanation before. Years later I was speaking at a conference where a district superintendent questioned my use of the term "baptism in the Spirit." When I told him the same thing, he said he had never heard this before either.

HOW CAN THIS BE?

This has been due to four main reasons. Alliance leaders, pastors, professors, and even district superintendents have had:

- lack of knowledge of and teaching on the historic Alliance doctrine and interpretation of the baptism in the Spirit in Alliance circles.
- desire to distance the Alliance from Pentecostal teaching on the baptism in the Spirit evidenced by speaking in tongues.
- influence and infiltration of non-Alliance hermeneutics, mainly from Baptistic and Reformed interpretations of the baptism in the Spirit.
- the new Keswick influence promoted by Anglican John Stott. A survey in the 1970s found that a third of Alliance pastors had been influenced by Stott.
- The third wave/Baptistic influence of Wayne Grudem's

Systematic Theology and others link Paul's phrase "baptized by/in one Spirit" (1 Cor 12:13) to being "baptized with the Holy Spirit and fire" (Mt 3:11).

SIMPSON'S WARNINGS ABOUT COMPROMISING ALLIANCE TEACHING ON THE BAPTISM IN THE SPIRIT

In the spirit of being interdenominational and providing a measure of 3rd tier liberty, the Alliance allowed for and respected other terminology for this subsequent experience of the Spirit, However, the classic Alliance position has been that the baptism in/with/of the Spirit is subsequent to conversion. Simpson warned against compromising this position:

- 1909: "Loose views about sanctification, the baptism of the Holy Spirit . . . are out of place on such a platform."[38]

- 1913: "the doctrine of a second work of grace, a spiritual crisis after conversion followed by entire consecration and the baptism of the Holy Spirit, is also becoming obsolete even in evangelical religious circles."[39]

In light of Simpson's warnings, we can use the more ecumenical term "filled with the Spirit" for those who do not understand and/or do not accept the language of baptized with the Spirit, but let's not capitulate to a non-Alliance hermeneutic. Since a comprehensive academic exegesis is lengthy and at times complex and detailed, Appendix 8 provides a brief overview of the exegetical basis for the subsequent baptism in the Spirit.

Additional Resources: For More on the C&MA Doctrine of Christ Our Sanctifier, see Appendix 8.

16

JESUS CHRIST OUR HEALER

This chapter examines and explains historically, biblically, hermeneutically, the third fold of the Fourfold Gospel, Jesus Christ Our Healer, and Article 8 of the Alliance Statement of Faith on "The Redemptive Work of Healing." Key Scriptures exegeted included Isaiah 53:3-5; Matthew 8:16-17; 1 Peter 2:24; Psalm 103:1-5; James 5:13-17; Exodus 15:26, among others. Also included as part of Alliance healing ministry is deliverance from demons.

JESUS CHRIST OUR HEALER MEANS WHOLE PERSON HEALING

For the C&MA, as a part of the "Full Gospel" and the "Higher Life" Jesus Christ Our Healer means healing the whole person. Intertwining the Alliance distinctives of Christ as Sanctifier and Christ as Healer, Simpson was fond of saying, "Holiness is wholeness." The body, mind, and spirit were all a part of the full gospel of the Alliance.[1]

Article 8 of the U.S. C&MA Statement of Faith, 1965, "The Redemptive Work of Healing," reads as follows:

Provision is made in the redemptive work of the Lord Jesus Christ for the healing of the mortal body. Prayer for the sick and anointing with oil are taught in the Scriptures and are privileges for the Church in this present age.

The Canadian Statement of Faith is virtually almost the same, with only a minor change of wording.[2] It is significant that in 1928 the C&MA added this article of doctrine to the Nine Fundamentals. As mentioned earlier, the Fundamentals Association in 1928 renounced the doctrine of divine healing along with speaking in tongues, identifying them negatively with Pentecostalism. By explicitly and intentionally making healing a part of the Statement of Faith at this critical moment, the C&MA was taking a stand against and parting company with the Fundamentals Association. The Fundamentals Association thus alienated itself against some of its original supporters, such as R. A. Torrey, who believed in healing (and died in 1928), and Paul Rader, who believed both in healing and in tongues.

This Alliance statement was developed out of the 1906 guidelines formulated by Simpson and Alliance leaders and revised in 1965.[3] The 1906 statement read as follows:

It is understood the Alliance holds and teaches:

1. The will of God to heal bodies of those who trust and obey Him by His own direct power without means.

2. The atonement of Christ for the body.

3. The life of the risen Christ for our mortal frame received by faith.

4. The ordinance of anointing and laying on of hands with proper recognition of the necessity of faith on the part of the individual anointed.

5. Power over evil spirits through the name of Jesus.

6. The disclaiming of merit or individual power on the part of the worker, and the constant recognition of the name of Jesus as the source of all supernatural power.[4]

While not all the doctrinal details of the 1906 document are contained in the Statement of Faith, the basic concepts of divine healing through the atonement are included in this statement.

"Provision is made in the redemptive work of the Lord Jesus Christ for the healing of the mortal body. . ."

The Alliance Hermeneutic: Christological Exegesis

The Alliance recognizes the prophetic and exegetical connection between the Christological passage of Jesus' atonement in Isaiah 53:4-5 with Matthew 8:16-17:

Now when evening came, they brought to Him many who were demon-possessed; and He cast out the spirits with a word and healed all who were ill. This happened so that what was spoken through Isaiah the prophet would be fulfilled: "He Himself took our illnesses and carried away our diseases."

Using the hermeneutical principles of literal priority and Scripture comparison, Simpson noted, "There is no doubt about the literal reference of this passage to the redemption of our bodies. The word translated 'infirmities' literally means sicknesses and is so translated in scores of other parallel passages in the Old Testament."[5]

Further, the historical and cultural context of these passages of Scripture involves the holistic nature of Hebrew thought. For the Hebrews, the physical and the spiritual go hand-in-hand. Applying Scripture comparison and the principle of genre through Hebrew poetic parallelism, this concept is evident:

> *Praise the Lord, O my soul.*
> *and forget not all his benefits—*
> *Who forgives all your sins*
> *and heals all your diseases (Ps 103:2-3).*

The Hebrew parallelism demonstrates the close connection

between forgiveness of sins with healing, as Jesus also demonstrated in His healing ministry as well.

Alliance pastor and classical languages scholar Dr. T. J. McCrossan, while serving as interim president of Simpson College and pastor of Seattle Gospel Tabernacle (C&MA), wrote his book *Bodily Healing and the Atonement*. In it he extensively exegeted these and many other passages of Scripture, thoroughly demonstrating that healing is a part of the work of the atonement. For example, he notes via the hermeneutical principle of context:

> We all admit that this verb (*nasa*) in Isaiah 53:12 teaches us that Christ bore our sins vicariously. . . . The very same verb (*nasa*) . . . is used in Isaiah 53:4 of bearing our sicknesses. The clear teaching therefore is that Christ bore our sicknesses in the very same way that He bore our sins.[6]

A Covenantal Redemption Right

Thus, Simpson concluded that healing is one of the covenantal "redemption rights" of the atonement. He and other Alliance leaders followed the exegesis of evangelical scholars like the German academic Franz Delitzsch, considered a world class Old Testament and Hebrew scholar. Exegeting the passage from the Hebrew, Delitzsch had explained,

> Freely but faithfully does the Gospel of Matthew translate this text, "Himself took our infirmities and carried our sicknesses.'" The help which Jesus rendered in all kinds of bodily sickness is taken in Matthew to be a fulfillment of what in Isaiah is prophesied of the Servant of Yahweh.[7]

First Peter 2:24 is also cited as support for healing in the atonement: "He Himself bore our sins in his body on the tree, so that we might die to sins and live for righteousness; by his wounds you have been healed." Some scholars claim that this Scripture refers only to sin and the atonement. However, McCrossan, using the principles of grammar, syntax, and Scripture comparison, demonstrates that the Greek word for healing here is not *sozo*, which can refer to physical healing as well as salvation, but rather *iaomai*, which is used only of physical healing.[8]

"PRAYER FOR THE SICK AND ANOINTING WITH OIL ARE TAUGHT IN THE SCRIPTURES."

This is based on a literal understanding of James 5:14-16:

> Is any one of you sick? He should call the elders of the church to pray over him and anoint him with oil in the name of the Lord. And the prayer offered in faith will make the sick person well; the Lord will raise him up. If he has sinned, he will be forgiven. Therefore, confess your sins to each other and pray for each other so that you may be healed.

Both the principles of plain intent and literal priority apply to this passage. The Alliance does not try to water this down to say that anointing with oil is rubbing medicine on the afflicted area. Using the hermeneutical principle of context demonstrates that, first of all, the setting gives no indication of medical treatment, and secondly that such medicinal external application would not help for internal ailments. Simpson thus comments on distorted hermeneutics of the passage:

> Nothing but the most strained and specious and plausible reasoning can turn aside the plain meaning of the passage and construe it as a medical prescription. To attempt this is to handle the Word of God deceitfully and find an excuse for our unbelief and failure.[9]

". . . AND ARE PRIVILEGES FOR THE CHURCH IN THIS PRESENT AGE."

Christological Continuism

Christ continues to work His supernatural power in healing. The

Christocentric hermeneutic of the C&MA includes the Christological consistency of continuism from Hebrews 13:8—that Christ is the same yesterday, today, forever. Jesus' purposes are the same—He still heals. This is based on the covenant nature of God as a Healer—*Yahweh Rophe*--just as God was Israel's Divine Healer in Exodus 15:26, so Simpson explains, "He reveals Himself throughout the ages as a Living Presence, who can sustain our entire being from His own life."[10]

A Covenant Redemption Right

As above, Simpson stressed that healing is a covenant redemption right of the believer, saying, "It is not some extra privilege of the favored few, but it is the common heritage of the children of faith."[11] If it is a provision of the atonement, it applies to our lives today, not merely in heaven.

A 2ND TIER DOCTRINE WITH SOME 3RD TIER ALLOWANCES

The Alliance taught healing in the atonement as a 2nd tier distinctive but allowed some 3rd tier variations or nuances of interpretation.[12] Thus, some in Alliance ranks discouraged use of doctors and medicine, others allowed and even encouraged them (and some even switched positions, like Russell Kelso Carter who had been anti-medicine and doctors, but himself became a medical doctor). Some would only anoint with oil if abandoning medicine (such as future C&MA president Frederick Senft); others would allow anointing of all (which seemed to be Simpson's position). Some would allow only elders to anoint with oil; on the other hand, Simpson would allow a woman to "act as an elder" if a suitable elder was not present, and even welcomed women to anoint and pray for the sick together with him.

ATTACKS AGAINST THE ALLIANCE DOCTRINE OF HEALING IN THE ATONEMENT

Attacks in the Early Alliance. The doctrine of healing in the atonement was attacked in Simpson's day by cessationist theologian B. B. Warfield. Greek and Hebrew scholar T. J. McCrossan, in his book *Bodily Healing and the Atonement* ([1930] 1982), presented an in-depth study of the Greek and Hebrew passages in defense of the doctrine of healing in the atonement. In addition to Delitzsch, he cited additional scholars in support of the interpretation, including Young, Leeser, MacLaren, Gaebelein, and Calvin.[13]

Attacks Today. It has come under attack in Alliance circles again today by those influenced by popular non-Alliance teachers such as Hank Hanegraaff, and cessationists John MacArthur and R. C. Sproul. John MacArthur in *Charismatic Chaos* and Hank Hanegraaff in *Christianity in Crisis* write against the doctrine of healing in the atonement as if it is a cultic misinterpretation of Scripture by charismatic faith teachers.[14] I knew of an Alliance church that was taken in by Hanegraaff's propaganda because the Alliance teaching seemed too much like Word of Faith. Thankfully, after the church had seriously declined, a new pastor retaught historic Alliance doctrines of healing and the gifts of the of the Spirit, the church recovered and blossomed in Holy Spirit revival and healing. MacArthur and Sproul have taught cessationism, that healing in atonement is only in heaven after 2nd Coming. These leaders believe that the Alliance position is a twisting of interpretation.

Criticism of *The Gospel of Healing*. Further, even though Simpson's *The Gospel of Healing* has been standard fare for ordination studies, there has been some criticism for some of its more radical-seeming pronouncements, especially statements that sounded like Simpson was opposed to medicine and doctors.

First, to be fair, Simpson has been misunderstood and taken out of context. Simpson never opposed the use of medicine. He cautioned never to abandon medicine unless God has made it clear to you to do so. Second, we need to distinguish between "early Simpson" and "later Simpson." it should be recognized that *The Gospel of Healing* was early Simpson. He honed, refined, and moderated some of his views over times, just as he did with other issues such as church government, end times, and women in ministry. Later Simpson did not abandon these teachings but refined and modified them. Third, Simpson allowed for variations in views regarding the doctrine of healing.

ALLIANCE RESPONSES AND DEFENSE OF HEALING IN THE ATONEMENT

Dr. Keith Bailey, in his book *Healing: The Children's Bread*, documents that this doctrine is not uniquely charismatic or word of faith teaching but was also held by non-charismatic evangelical leaders of various denominations such as Presbyterian/C&MA Simpson, German Lutheran Stockmayer, Baptist A. J. Gordon; and Congregationalist R. A. Torrey. He also cites Princeton scholars A. A. Hodge and J. A. Alexander, as well as Franz Delitzsch, Hebrew professor at the University of Leipzig, Germany, as supporters of the doctrine.[15] To these can be added Andrew Murray and Oswald Chambers.[16]

For instance, contrary to Hanegraaff, Andrew Murray (whose view on healing was almost identical to Simpson's) asserted on the basis of Reformed Covenant theology:

> It is His Word which promises us healing. The promise of James 5 is so absolute that it is impossible to deny it. This promise only confirms other passages, equally strong, which tell us that Jesus Christ has obtained for us the healing of our diseases, because He has borne our sicknesses. According to this promise, we have right to healing, because it is a part of the salvation which we have in Christ.[17]

While it is true that some Word of Faith teaching takes the meaning of healing in the atonement too far, there is much historical and exegetical evidence by sound biblical scholars that healing is in the atonement for today. The Alliance teaching would be considered "Classic Word of Faith," as opposed to "Modern Word of Faith." When reading *The Gospel of Healing* by Simpson, some may think this sounds like Word of Faith, and it is true that Word of Faith people read A. B. Simpson's works, probably more than Alliance people do. The books on healing by Alliance leaders T. J. McCrossan (*Bodily Healing and the*

Atonement), F. F. Bosworth (*Christ the Healer*), John MacMillan (*The Authority of the Believer*), and A. B. Simpson (*The Gospel of Healing*) are popular with Word of Faith leaders, and their books are found in Kenneth Hagin's Rhema Bible Training Center bookstore and are used as textbooks in their schools.

Where Alliance Teaching Differs from Modern Word of Faith

Although modern Word of Faith teaching is similar—because they got a lot of their teaching from Alliance writers—there are significant differences.

Healing in the atonement not an absolute. Russell Kelso Carter's early teaching in *The Atonement for Sin and Sickness* took a more radical viewpoint opposed to doctors and medicine, similar to some of the criticized contemporary faith teaching and practice. However, his later book, *Faith Healing Reviewed After 20 Years*, moderated his earlier position, disavowing that the doctrine means that all will be healed, and that medicine and doctors should not be used. In fact, he actually trained to become a medical doctor.

Healing in the atonement is not a guarantee of healing. While Alliance leaders believed in healing as a provision of the atonement, in contrast to contemporary faith teachers, they did not consider it a given in all circumstances. Carter explained the emerging view of Simpson and the Alliance: "Mr. Simpson has always allowed that one's time may come, and the faith not be given, but the point here is that practically the position [of the C&MA] has been one of special answers in the will of God, not a broad atonement for all at any time."[18]

Don't abandon medicine to prove your faith, but only if God has given you faith. Some Word of Faith people have erroneously believed that if you are sick or cannot be healed, you must have lack of faith or sin. While Alliance teaching would recognize that sin or lack of faith can be hindrances to healing, this is not a legalistic hard-and-fast rule, and we must not put a guilt trip on people.

Not all diseases are caused by demons. Some Word of Faith people tend to demonize every disease. Simpson and early Alliance leaders recognized that some diseases are indeed caused by demons, but not all.

Binding and loosing of demons and disease is often misunderstood and misused in Word of Faith circles. As Neill Foster and I emphasized in the book we co-authored, *Binding and Loosing: Exercising Authority Over the Dark Powers*, we can only bind what God has bound; we can only loose what God has loosed, not vice versa, as some Word of Faith teachers have claimed.

God gives strength until our life's work is done. Simpson and Alliance leaders held to the ideal of healing in the atonement, but they also believed that not all are automatically healed, as some Word of Faith teachers would claim. Alliance theologian George Pardington declared some who have not received divine healing but receive strength in their infirmities.[19] Simpson echoed the words of Spurgeon and Cromwell, "A man is immortal until his work is done." When Simpson was nearing death himself, several leaders gathered around him, including Robert Jaffray, to claim life for him. Simpson responded that he could not go that far with them, that he knew his time was near.

Leave room for the sovereignty of God. Some Word of Faith people tend not to believe in the sovereignty of God. It is generally God's will to heal, but there may be exceptions. God's sovereignty rules over all His promises and provisions. We can pray expectantly for healing, but leave room for God's greater purposes, which are higher and greater than our understanding.

The kingdom is here now, but not fully here yet. Therefore, kingdom healing is here now, but not fully here yet. Some modern Word of Faith people tend to believe that the kingdom of God is fully here now.

ALTHOUGH IN SIMPSON'S earliest days, he might have sounded more like modern Word of Faith, he and The Alliance developed a more balanced approach over time, understanding that healing is provided for in the atonement, and we can claim healing as a redemption right, but not all receive the fullness of healing in this life. Many times, it is a partial healing, or a supernatural enabling in the midst of weakness that is imparted from God.

For more on a theological analysis of what is sound and and what is not sound in the modern Word of Faith movement, as well as more similarities and differences between the C&MA and Word of Faith, see Paul L. King, *Only Believe: Examining the Origin and Roots of Classic and Contemporary Word of Faith Movments.*

HISTORICAL SUMMARY OF THE DEVELOPMENT OF CHRIST OUR HEALER

- 1870s—The influence of Boardman, Covenant Theology, and the Higher Life teaching.
- 1881—Simpson's own experience of healing.
- 1883—Simpson's development of healing rooms, healing homes, and meetings.
- 1884—Simpson's *Gospel of Healing* was published.
- 1887—The Alliance was founded with the Fourfold Gospel motto. A crippled woman was miraculously healed at the founding of The Alliance, resulting in her two sisters being converted, and confirming the calling, mission, and message of The Alliance.
- 1906—Board of Managers statement on Christ Our Healer.
- 1922—The Board of Managers reaffirmed the 1906 Statement of Distinctives.
- 1924—Alliance evangelist F. F. Bosworth's book *Christ Our Healer* was published, containing testimonies of miraculous healings in Alliance meetings. The book was required in C&MA ordination studies for a period of time.
- 1928—Statement of Faith for Alliance Schools was produced, from which the 1965 Statement of Faith was formulated.[20]

DELIVERANCE MINISTRY AS AN INTEGRAL PART OF ALLIANCE HEALING MINISTRY

In the 1906 and 1922 statements the following point is listed under the section on Divine Healing: "**Power over evil spirits through the name of Jesus.**" A part of the Alliance distinctive of Christ as Healer is Christ as Deliverer. The healing that is provided in the atonement included deliverance from demons as part of the believer's redemption rights to claim. Simpson himself had declared: "Deliverance from demons stands right alongside divine healing and stands or falls with it."[21] Deliverance from demons and healing go hand-in hand. Likewise, Simpson's associate William C. Stevens affirmed, "This intimate association of the exorcism of evil spirits and of the healing of sicknesses is likewise the outstanding feature of apostolic ministry."[22]

Ethan O. Allen—Pioneer of Alliance Deliverance Ministry

Ethan O Allen, called by Simpson as the father of healing in American, was also the father of deliverance ministry in America. This elder statesman was known for his ministry of casting out demons as well as healing. Referring to Genesis 3:15 and Luke 10:19, Allen wrote a tract entitled "Satan Under Your Feet." He operated in the gift of discernment of spirits, and often practiced rebuking, binding the strong man, or "words of castin' out" evil spirits before praying for the sick. A.B. Simpson held him in high respect and called him the "Father of Divine Healing" in America.[23] In one humorous incident, he followed Jesus' example of casting a demon into a pig. His wife was upset because she wanted to butcher the pig.

William MacArthur and A. B. Simpson Mentored by Allen

Allen mentored leaders in healing and deliverance, especially William T. MacArthur and A. B. Simpson, and was a speaker at Alliance conventions, revered as "Father Allen." Allen prophesied to MacArthur in the 1890s, "Young man, you look like somebody the Lord could use in castin' out devils."[24] His prophecy came true, as MacArthur did indeed engage in deliverance ministry through the years, on at least one occasion teaming up with Simpson in 1912.[25]

Alliance Leaders Who Have Led Deliverance of Believers from Demons.

While some in the Alliance who do not know Alliance history and theology might question whether a Christian can have a demon, there was no doubt in the mind of Simpson and his colleagues and successors. Some of the prominent ministers of deliverance in the earlier Alliance included: Ethan O. Allen, A. B. Simpson, Carrie Judd Montgomery, William T. MacArthur, George Peck, Robert Jaffray, Minnie Draper, William C. Stevens, Paul Rader, Dr. T. J. McCrossan, F. F. Bosworth, John MacMillan, and many of the older missionaries, such as Dr. Thomas Moseley, who became president of Nyack Missionary Training Institute. MacMillan himself mentored dozens of students in deliverance ministry when he was a professor at Nyack.

Later 20th Century and 21st Century Alliance Spiritual Warfare Ministries.

In more recent decades, prominent leaders who have been involved in casting out demons have included Dr. Keith Bailey and Dr. Gerald McGraw (both mentored by MacMillan); Dr. K. Neill Foster; Dr. John and Helen Ellenberger; several women evangelists; Florence Gray, wife of Southwestern District Superintendent R. Mills Gray; Jim and Delores Sunda (who served as ministers of deliverance at Dr. Fred Hartley's Lilburn Alliance Church after they retired from the mission field); many of the more recent missionaries; Dr. Ron Walborn; Dr. Chuck Davis; Dr. Rob Reimer; Dr. Paul King; Dr. David Chotka; Dick LaFountain; Dr. Michael Plunkett; and the list goes on. Chuck Davis at Alliance Theological Seminary and Gerald McGraw at Tocoa Falls College have taught Power Encounter courses. Myriads of Alliance leaders have used Dr. Neil T. Anderson's Truth Encounter approach, and some have combined both Truth Encounter and Power Encounter approaches. I have taught a course on Spiritual Warfare online through Crown College using both approaches.

ALLIANCE THEOLOGY AND PRACTICE OF DELIVERANCE FROM DEMONS

I hope to put together a Manual on Alliance theology and practice of spiritual warfare. Here is a brief summary of some of the features of Alliance theology and practice of deliverance:

Christians Cannot Be "Possessed," i.e., "Owned" by Demons.

"It is a serious mistake to say that Satan possesses any child of God."—William T. MacArthur[26]

Note: Some early Alliance leaders used the ancient and archaic language of "possession" as used in the King James Version of the Bible, but they did not mean that a Christian can be owned by a demon, only controlled by a demon.

Soul or Body May Be Occupied by Demons—But Not a Believer's Human Spirit.

Dr. V. Raymond Edman, editor of *The Alliance Witness* following Tozer, president of Wheaton College, and Alliance missionary to South America, probably best sums up Alliance theology and practice regarding demonization of Christians:

Being born again of the Spirit means that the Holy Spirit dwells in the human spirit. This does not guarantee that a child of God may not be attacked and indwelt by an evil spirit in soul or body. . . . According to Scripture the believer is the temple of the Holy Spirit (2 Cor. 6:16). The Holy Spirit inhabits the holy of holies, which no evil spirit can enter. The holy place, which corresponds to the soul, and the outer court, to the body, are subject to occupation by a foreign spirit.[27]

Sources of Demonization of Believers Include:

Involvement with the occult; transmission of unclean spirits; generational bondages and curses; counterfeit supernatural manifestations; passive, non-discerning acceptance of demonic forces.

Varying Degrees of Demon Presence and Power May Be Discerned.

Demon presence and power in a person's life and being is by no means confined to the actual and entire surrender of the inmost personality to the demon's abode and sway. . . . More generally demonism in a life does not preclude salvation, although sometimes exorcism is necessary before salvation can take place, and often demonism is found in the experiences of saved one without the loss of fellowship with Christ. There is a very wide range of demon presence and power which, in manifold ways and degrees, involves the brain, the senses, and the bodily members and functions. Very many conditions commonly viewed as disease are not such and cannot be dealt with as such, at least without first casting out the spirit directly producing and lodged in those symptoms.[28]—Simpson associate William C. Stevens:

We Have the Authority of the Believer.

This was taught by Ethan O. Allen, A.B. Simpson, William T. MacArthur, Robert Jaffray, many other Alliance leaders, and especially John Macmillan, in his classic book *The Authority of the Believer*.

Satan Is Not Currently Bound on Earth (Rev 20:1-3); Believers Are Thus Called to Bind and Loose.

This was taught and practiced by those mentioned above and others, and especially by John MacMillan, but without the errors of the

Word of Faith movement. The 1998 book *Binding and Loosing: Exercising Authority Over the Dark Powers* by Dr. K. Neill Foster and Dr. Paul King, provides balanced teaching and practical real-life examples from missionaries, pastors, and lay people.

Some Use Both the Truth Encounter Approach, Based on Dr Neil T. Anderson's Freedom in Christ, and Power Encounter.

In his endorsement of my book *A Believer with Authority: The Life and Message of John A. MacMillan*, Neil Anderson credits MacMillan impacting his thought and ministry: "John MacMillan's published work on the authority of the believer greatly influenced the development of my own thinking.".His teaching on our identity in Christ and the authority of the believer is based on MacMillan's writing, which was, in turn, based on A. B. Simpson's teaching. Although Anderson uses only the truth encounter approach, typically many Alliance leaders will use both approaches when deemed appropriate.

∾

Overall, A. W. Tozer counsels us to be be Christ-conscious, not devil-conscious.[29]

ADDITIONAL RESOURCES FOR HEALING AND DELIVERANCE

THESE ARE books from Alliance sources, Alliance-related sources, and Alliance-compatible sources. This is not a complete list. Books with an asterisk (*) are out of print.

Spiritual Warfare Resources

- Anderson, Neil T. *The Bondage Breaker.*
- Anderson, Neil T. *Steps to Freedom in Christ.*
- Anderson, Neil T. *Victory Over the Darkness.*
- Arnold, Clinton E. *3 Crucial Questions about Spiritual Warfare.*

- Davis, Chuck. *The Bold Christian.*
- Foster K. Neill, and Paul L. King. *Binding and Loosing: Exercising Authority Over the Dark Powers.*
- *Freligh, Harold M. *Say to This Mountain.* (Freligh, a Nyack professor, like his colleague John MacMillan, wrote about authoritative praying and binding and loosing.)
- King, Paul L. *A Believer with Authority: The Life and Message of John A. MacMillan.*
- *MacArthur, William T. *Ethan O. Allen.*
- MacMillan, John A. *The Authority of the Believer.*

Healing Resources

- Bailey, Keith M. *Divine Healing: The Children's Bread.*
- Bosworth, F. F. *Christ the Healer.*
- *McCrossan, T. J. *Bodily Healing and the Atonement.*
- Murray, Andrew; A. J. Gordon; A. B. Simpson. *Healing: The Three Classics.*
- Reimer, Rob. *Soul Care: Seven Transformational Principles for a Healthy Soul.*
- Simpson, A. B. *The Gospel of Healing.*
- Simpson, A. B. *The Lord for the Body,*
- Sipley, Richard. *Understanding Divine Healing.*
- Smith, David J. *How Can I Ask God for Physical Healing? A Biblical Guide.*
- Travis, Drake. *Healing Power, Voice Activated.*

17

JESUS CHRIST OUR COMING KING

A 2ND TIER DISTINCTIVE WITH 3RD TIER LIBERTY

THE US AND CANADIAN STATEMENTS OF FAITH

The US Statement of Faith, based on the 1965 Faith Statement, includes "premillennial"; the Canadian Statement of Faith removed it. The US Alliance is discussing the issue to be brought to the US 2023 General Council. The current Faith Statements read as follows:

US: *The second coming of the Lord Jesus Christ is imminent and will be personal, visible, and premillennial. This is the believer's blessed hope and is a vital truth which is an incentive to holy living and faithful service.* (Councils 1965, 1966, 1974).

Canadian: *The second coming of the Lord Jesus Christ is imminent and will be personal and visible. As the believer's blessed hope, this vital truth is an incentive for holy living and sacrificial service toward the completion of Christ's commission.*

As discussed in Chapter 10 on "End-time/Eschatological Essentials," belief in the Second Coming of Christ is a first-tier non-negotiable doctrine of The Alliance, which is accepted by all orthodox, evangelical Christians and churches. As cited in Chapter 3, as a 2nd tier distinctive, premillennialism was included in the founding Constitutional Statement of The Alliance, August 1887, with a caveat, providing 3rd tier liberty.

Throughout his life, Simpson did stress that the Alliance was premillennial but did not make it a condition for fellowship or doctrine. His attitude and teaching were more like, "this is a great truth and here are good reasons for believing it."

THE HISTORY OF PREMILLENNIALISM IN THE ALLIANCE

The history of premillennialism in The Alliance can be summarized briefly as follows:

August 1887—The founding Constitutional Statement of The Alliance included premillennialism as one of the four folds of the Fourfold Gospel, but with a caveat, providing 3rd tier liberty:

> Inasmuch as many persons who desire to become members of this Alliance and are in full accord with its principles in other points, cannot yet fully accept the doctrine of Christ's Pre-millennial Coming, it is agreed that such persons may be received into full membership provided they receive the first three points of testimony, and are willing to give this subject their candid and prayerful consideration.[1]

By taking a stance that the Second Coming is premillennial, the original Alliance interpreted Revelation 20 literally, asserting the grammatical/historical hermeneutical principle of plain intent.[2] This continued to be maintained flexibly in The Alliance throughout Simpson's life.

1896—H. Grattan Guiness, wrote supporting premillennialism in *The Christian Alliance* magazine, yet also wrote with Simpson's approval: "I for one would treat this point as an open question."[3]

1906—The Board of Managers, chaired by Simpson, met to discuss essentials, distinctives, and open questions, affirming that the Alliance believed in premillennialism, but "Liberty is accorded to our teachers in connection with the various opinions held" about end times events, timing, order, peoples, interpretation of apocalyptic literature of Daniel and Revelation, including such things as the Anti-Christ, The Tribulation, the Last Week of Daniel, Rapture, etc. The key caveat is that such views must be expressed "with the understanding that any spirit of antagonism and toward those who may hold different opinions is discountenanced."[4] Simpson continued to maintain that no one had a corner on the truth:

> In regard also to the Lord's return there is room for much variety of opinion and expression concerning details, and yet all may be one in the great principles involved in this blessed life. . . . Perhaps none of our individual views and opinions express the whole circle of truth, and the whole mind of Christ. Let us therefore not judge one another anymore, but rather this, that no man put a stumbling block in his brother's way. Whatever our opinions may be, let us at least be one in heart in life and personal intimacy with Jesus, and in lives of practical righteousness and love.[5]

Recognizing various interpretations of the Scriptures regarding the Second Coming, Simpson and The Alliance did not choose or narrow down to one particular interpretation. They recognized that even grammatical-historical exegesis cannot pinpoint a narrow understanding. There is enough ambiguity so as not to become dogmatic. Throughout Simpson's life, he continued to stress that The Alliance was premillennial but did not make it a condition for fellowship or doctrine. His attitude and teaching were more like, "this is a great truth and here are good reasons for believing it."

1910—The original Fundamentals of 1910, which The Alliance affirmed, included the 2nd Coming of Christ, but not premillennialism as an essential to the faith.

1912—George Pardington's public summary of Alliance beliefs in 1912 in the *Alliance Weekly* included the 2nd Coming, but with no mention of premillennialism, continuing to demonstrate 3rd tier liberty.

1919—The year that Simpson died, WCFA expanded the fundamental beliefs in 1919 to include the premillennial coming of Christ: "We believe in 'that blessed hope,' the personal, premillennial, and imminent return of our Lord and Savior Jesus Christ." (Article VII of the Fundamentals). Alliance leaders Paul Rader and Charles Blanchard were a part of those drafting the documents.

1922—After Simpson's passing, a stronger premillennial stance was emerging, swept into the wave of the expanded Fundamentals of 1919. In 1922, the Niagara Creed (see Appendix 1), which included premillennialism, was referenced for the first time by the Board of Managers as part of the Statement of Faith.

1928—By 1928 when the Statement of Faith was created for Alliance schools, the word "premillennial" was included. After Simpson's death, premillennialism became more established in The Alliance as a 2nd tier doctrine without as much 3rd tier liberty, at least for leaders and students at Alliance schools.

1965—The US Statement of Faith of 1965, based on the 1928 Statement of Faith, included "premillennial."

2000—The Canadian Statement of Faith removed the word "premillennial."

2021-2023—In the US C&MA, it is currently being reconsidered, discussed, and debated, both at the district levels, in special meetings, and at US General Council 2021 and 2023

THE ALLIANCE RATIONALE FOR PREMILLENNIALISM

Apart from premillennialism becoming the most popular end-times theology of the late 19th century and the early 20th century evangelical movement, what was the biblical rationale of Simpson and the early Alliance for teaching and encouraging premillennialism?

The Failure of Idealist Post-Millennial Hermeneutical Expectations.

The interpretations and expectations of Bible-believing Puritans were that God was going to establish the kingdom of God on earth through the Church. The interpretations and expectations of the liberal church influenced by the Enlightenment were that humankind would better itself through the Church's moral influence. Both had dismally failed. The world appeared only worse.

The Expectations of Literal Pre-Millennial Realism.

After rehearsing 1800 years of "worldliness and wickedness" throughout the world, Simpson opined, "Yet there is no real progress to millennial righteousness in our land." A literal biblical scenario of end-time events made more logical sense: "The spiritual application of these promises and prophecies of the Scripture respecting Israel, in accordance with which post-millennialists constantly refer these pages to the New Testament church, is contrary to all true principles of inter-pretation."[6]

The Hermeneutical Principle of Plain Intent.

The historic Alliance grammatical-historical hermeneutic sought to interpret the "plain meaning" of the text by discovering the writer's original intent.[7] In other words, if the plain sense makes sense, don't look for some other sense. Regarding this text, Simpson asserts this principle: "Why should we doubt the simple meaning of His Word?"[8]

The Hermeneutical Principle of Literal Priority.

Naturally following from above, this principle asserts that the plain meaning is usually the literal meaning: Accept the plain literal meaning unless there is good evidence to interpret as figurative or alle-gorical. Simpson and the early Alliance accepted Revelation 20 at face value on the basis of the *principle of literal priority,* without trying to read into the Scriptures a preconceived eschatology: "Undoubtedly, if we are to believe the literal meaning of the twentieth chapter of Revela-tion, which must mean just what it says if the Bible is to mean anything."[9] By identifying the Second Coming as premillennial, the

Alliance did not spiritualize or allegorize Revelation 20, but viewed the thousand years as a real period of time following the return of Christ.

Premillennial 2nd Coming Is a Greater Catalyst for Evangelism and Missions.

According to George Pardington, "Contrary to the post-millennial view, we are not to bring the world to Christ, but to bring Christ to the world."[10]

Premillennial 2nd Coming Is a Greater Incentive to Holiness.

Both the U.S. and Canadian Statements affirm that the 2nd Coming is an Incentive for Holy Living.

US: "*. . . and is a vital truth which is an incentive to holy living and faithful service.*

Canadian: "*this vital truth is an incentive for holy living and sacrificial service toward the completion of Christ's commission.*"

The C&MA emphasis on holiness was added to the World Christian Fundamentals Doctrinal Statement. This is based on Simpson's understanding of the plain intent of 2 Peter 3:10-14,[11] further corroborated by Scripture comparison with Jesus' statements in Matthew 24 and 25 regarding faithfulness and obedience. Citing 1 Thessalonians 5:23-24, Simpson comments, "The coming of the Lord is a powerful incentive to holiness."[12]

Simpson, of course, meant that a premillennial coming is a powerful incentive to holiness. In his view, it would be a more powerful incentive to holiness than other millennial views. H. Grattan Guiness, writing in the *Christian Alliance Weekly* for Simpson in 1896 gave numerous reasons for supporting premillennialism, especially evangelism and missions as already cited above. Another was that it calls "the dead Church" and the "slumbering and indifferent" to rise up.[13]

Restoration of Early Church Doctrine: The Earliest Church Fathers Viewed the 2ⁿᵈ Coming as Premillennial.

Guiness, cited above, and William Riley, speaking on the Great Fundamentals (as do many other scholars), pointed out that virtually all of the earliest church fathers viewed the Second Coming as premillennial. I presented a fuller overview and citations of these church fathers as well in the first chapter of the book *Essays on Premillennialism*, used for a period of time in C&MA ordination studies.[14] I

t was only after Origen's allegorical approach to hermeneutics in the mid- 3ʳᵈ century that other millennial views became popular in the 4ᵗʰ century and following, replacing and discarding the teaching of the earliest church fathers, which was too literal and too physical for Greek thought that viewed the physical as evil and to be avoided.

A. B. SIMPSON—AN AMILLENNIAL PREMILLENNIALIST

It might seem to be an oxymoron, but while believing in a literal millennium for the church following the rapture and Christ's return, Simpson also believed in a symbolic spiritual millennium for believers in the here and now, similar to the amillennial view, yet maintaining a literal millennium as well. Decades before Oscar Cullman and George Eldon Ladd taught the principle of the "kingdom here now, but not yet," A. B. Simpson was teaching virtually the same concept, calling it "the overlapping of the ages":

> As in the past God was always *overlapping the coming age*, so is He *today overlapping the next age*. . . . The coming of the Lord is to bring the resurrection of these mortal bodies. Surely, we may expect some earnests in the last days. . . . Healing of the body is an actual earnest and firstfruit of the future resurrection. . . . a new emphasis upon the baptism of the Holy Spirit. All this is the overlapping of the millennial day. . . . We shall find nothing awaiting us yonder that we have not begun to find in our experience here.[15]

Just as these ancient saints looked forward and overlapped and got into the age to come in some measure by their faith, so God permits us to live under the powers of the age to come, and come into the border zone, where our feet are yet on earth, and our heads, our eyes, and our hearts are in the coming kingdom. Divine healing is one of the *overlappings of this coming age.*[16]

Even clearer and to the point, Simpson believed in a *dual* millennium—both now and future. Scholars note that others preceding Simpson appeared in some form to be dual millennialists—Albert Bengel and John Wesley, as examples, and perhaps Spurgeon (who seemed to waffle between pre-mil and a-mil, depending on his sermon). To Simpson, this dual millennium meant the beginning of a personal spiritual millennium for the believer now and a physical millennium for the church in the future:

There is a sense in which His coming to each heart will bring a millennial blessing to that heart. There is a millennium for the soul as well as for the Church. There is a kingdom of peace and righteousness and glory into which, in a limited sense, we can enter with Him here. There is a Kingdom of God which is within us.[17]

Further, Simpson repeatedly exhorted to begin living the millennial life now:

We may press forward to His coming . . . by anticipating already in some measure the millennial life. Even here and now we may receive a foretaste of the coming kingdom.[18]

Let us begin the millennial life here if we expect to enjoy it by and by.[19]

To each of us, like Esther, God has given a kingdom of influence and power. . . . Our king has given to each of us a trust to occupy. . . . Have you claimed all your kingdom?[20]

In Simpson's framework, a person can be both an amillennialist and a premillennialist—an "amillennial premillennialist," if you will, like Simpson, making room for both in Scripture without sacrificing a literal interpretation of Scripture.

THE ALLIANCE HERMENEUTIC OF END TIME LATTER RAIN REVIVAL

Restoration and Increase of Apostolic Church Power

A particular emphasis of the early Alliance connected both the 2nd coming and contiinuist restoration of gifts of the Spirit, believing that an end-time supernatural revival would usher in the Second Coming with increased evangelism and worldwide missions. The Alliance taught a hermeneutic based on Peter's quotation and application of Joel's prophecy to the outpouring of the Holy Spirit on Pentecost (Joel 2:23, 28-32; Acts 2:16-21).

> "He has poured down for you the rain, The early and the latter rain as before
> . . . . I will pour out My Spirit on all mankind . . ." (Joel 2:23, 28)

As did many evangelical leaders of that day, The Alliance extended the application to the former and latter rains mentioned in the preceding verses in Joel 2:23-27, as a further fulfillment of the New Testament church age. Simpson, W. C. Stevens, G. P. Pardington, D. W. Myland, May Mabette Anderson, and a host of other Alliance leaders taught a form of "Latter Rain" theology, that God was pouring out a greater latter rain before the Second Coming of Christ.[21]

The Alliance teaching on the latter rain predated and overlapped with the Pentecostal latter rain teaching, thus actually influencing Pentecostal belief in the Latter Rain. Especially about 1907 and following, The Alliance affirmed that the Latter Rain indeed was falling, testifying, "These are the days of the latter rain." However, they did not accept all Latter Rain teaching, which they believed sometimes went beyond the clear teaching of Scripture.

Simpson envisioned that The Alliance is meant to be a restoring of the New Testament Church today, declaring that The Alliance is to be "an attested copy of the Church of apostolic times." [22] Simpson declared that the church needs to return to a primitive piety—back to Christ and Pentecost.[23] Irrespective of Simpson's premillennial and partial rapture views, Simpson's end time perspective includes the following insights:

- There will be a latter rain reappearance of mighty miraculous manifestations.[24]
- We should expect a greater outpouring to usher in the 2nd coming of Christ.[25]
- Expect an increasing supernatural presence.[26]
- We will be drawn like a magnet toward His coming.[27]
- God is preparing the end-time army and bride of Christ.[28]

Each of these viewpoints of Simpson warrant more in-depth study and evaluation beyond this survey and summary. What can be observed is that Simpson had some concept of what today is sometimes called "victorious eschatology"—while the world is getting worse approaching the Second Coming of Christ, the Church is becoming prepared as a purified Bride and a victorious Army of the Lord.

THE ALLIANCE END-TIME HERMENEUTIC: A 2ND TIER DOCTRINE WITH 3RD TIER LIBERTY

As cited in Chapter 10, Charles R. Erdman drafted one of the papers of the Great Fundamentals regarding the 2nd Coming. Although Erdman supported the premillennial view, like Pardington and The Alliance, he and the originators of the Fundamentals did not make the premillennial view a 1st tier essential, but rather uniting in evangelization of the world regardless of details and order of end time events. Erdman affirmed:

The great body of believers are united in expecting both an age of glory and a personal return of Christ. As to many related events they differ; but as to the one great precedent condition of that coming age or that promised return of the Lord there is absolute harmony of conviction: the Gospel must first be preached to all nations (Matthew 24:14). The Church must continue to "make disciples of all the nations ... even unto the end of the age" (Matthew 28:19, 20).

This is therefore a time, not for unkindly criticism of fellow Christians, but for friendly conference; not for disputing over divergent views, but for united action; not for dogmatic assertion of prophetic programs, but for the humble acknowledgment that "we know in part;" not for idle dreaming, but for the immediate task of evangelizing a lost world.

For such effort, no one truth is more inspiring, than that of the return of Christ. None other can make us sit more lightly by the things of time, none other is more familiar as a Scriptural motive to purity, holiness, patience, vigilance, love. Strengthened by this blessed hope let us press forward with passionate zeal to the task that awaits us.[29]

This reads very much like the ecumenical Alliance hermeneutic. Basically, like Erdman, the Alliance affirmed, we believe in the premillennial second coming of Christ, but we will not let that separate us from those who do not—"We believe this, but we allow that." As mentioned earlier, recognizing various interpretations of the Scriptures regarding the Second Coming, the C&MA did not insist on choosing or narrowing down to one particular interpretation. It recognized that even grammatical-historical exegesis cannot pinpoint a narrow understanding. There is enough ambiguity so as not to become dogmatic.

PART IV

TIER 3: ALLIANCE NON-ESSENTIALS/OPEN QUESTIONS

18

THIRD TIER PRINCIPLES FOR OPEN QUESTIONS

Certain matters of teaching and testimony shall be recognized as open questions, and all teachers shall hold in mutual charity without any spirit of controversy their individual convictions concerning them, endeavoring to keep the unity of the Spirit in the bonds of peace till we all come into the unity of the faith and of the knowledge of the Son of God (Eph 4:3, 13)."
—1922 C&MA Board of Managers

With a hermeneutic of "unity in loving liberty," the early Alliance was as inclusive as Scripture allows (based on Romans 14) and as exclusive as Scripture mandates, building bridges of interdenominational cooperation in what Board of Managers member John MacMillan called "harmonized diversity."

Note: As we approach our study of this third tier, please keep in mind that the issues considered as non-essentials, open questions, or side issues, are not my own invention or opinions. Rather, Simpson and other Alliance leaders used this terminology and these classifications, as discovered through extensive research. If anyone has additional information, please let me know.

WHAT WERE NOT CONSIDERED OPEN QUESTIONS

Basically, the Essentials discussed in Part II and the Distinctives discussed in Part III were off limits to being open questions. To summarize:

- **The Essentials of the Faith.** Any belief that watered down the Trinity; the sovereignty of God; God as Creator (vs. evolution); the authority, infallibility, and inerrancy of Scripture; the person, work, and deity of the Holy Spirit; the lostness of man; the deity, humanity, incarnation, virgin birth, death, vicarious atonement, physical resurrection, ascension, and second coming of Christ.

- *The Alliance Distinctives.* Any belief that watered down or compromised the Alliance distinctives of Christ-centeredness, supernatural continuism, Christ as Savior, Sanctifier (the sanctifying baptism/filling with the Spirit), Healer, and Coming King.

- *Anything That Would Disrupt Unity on the Points Above.*

Some 3rd tier flexibility was allowed in terminology and under-standing of "phases and phrases" of the Distinctives, but no laxity or excessive latitude that would compromise any of these points.

How Big a Tent?—The Problem of "Big Tent" Language.

In more recent decades, leaders in The Alliance have used the term "big tent" to describe our openness and flexibility. It has served us well for most of that time, but the ambiguity of what comprises the big tent has caused big problems. Some have assumed that because we are a big tent, apart from out-and-out heresy, anything goes. As a result, non-Alliance, and even anti-Alliance theology has crept into The Alliance. Sometimes LOCCs (Licensing, Ordination, and Consecration Councils) have let issues slide or looked the other way because, after all, we are a big tent. Especially our distinctives of the sanctifying baptism in the Spirit and divine healing have taken a big hit.

PRINCIPLES FOR OPEN QUESTIONS

Simpson and Alliance leaders affirmed these, among other principles, for what were considered open questions, secondary or side issues:

The Principle of Broad Platform and Bridge-Building: "A platform broad and deep enough for any child of God."[1] In more recent years, we have used the term "big tent."

The Principle of Flexibility, Not Rigidity: "God's methods allow for exceptions and adjustments."[2]

The Principle of Family over Religious Formality. Increasingly, Simpson described the Alliance as "fraternal" vs. "ecclesiastical."[3] We are family, after all, not a corporation. Simpson himself, having come out Reformed ecclesiology and tradition, gradually moved away from his own ecclesiasticism, which was shown in his growing flexibility regarding various church worship practices and various forms of church government, including and especially in regard to women's roles in ministry, as will be seen below.

The Principle of Maintaining Biblical Expression When Possible. Simpson advised, "Keep close to Bible terms as much as possible. We shall find it very safe to keep close to Bible terms. If we meet God on His own very Word, we shall find that He will meet us in blessing."[4] Obviously, some terms are not found in the Bible, such as Trinity, rapture, theology, etc., but where possible to maintain phraseology. Articulate beliefs in terms of biblical concepts. Even then, Simpson counseled, "The finest theories and the most Scriptural phrases do not constitute the divine life. Let us learn to recognize the Christ life behind every variety of temperament and theological expression.

The Principle of "We Believe This But We Allow That."[5] How was this practiced in The Alliance? Here are four examples:

- The Alliance historically has believed in *the sanctifying baptism in the Spirit* and *divine healing in the atonement* but has allowed nuanced variations about "phases and phrases" theologically and practically, agreeing to disagree without antagonism.
- The Alliance has promoted belief in *a premillennial second coming of Christ*, but has welcomed membership for those who do not, but are willing to give "their candid and prayerful consideration."
- The Alliance believes in and practices *believer's baptism by immersion* but does not require it of those who do not: As cited earlier, "No one was excluded from membership whose conscience was satisfied with their infant baptism."
- The Alliance believed that men are usually elders and pastors but allowed for women to be pastors and elders if the local church so desired and the woman was under authority and had an anointing from God.

The Principle of Balance: "Overstress the minors, and you have chaos; overlook the majors, and you have death."—A.W. Tozer.[6]

Principles of Harmony.
Following Paul's counsel, "Live in harmony with one another" (Rom 12:16, NIV), one term Alliance leaders used repeatedly was "harmony." Not always easy to maintain, it was still the goal:

- *The Principle of Harmonious Disagreement.* Agreeing to disagree in mutual love and respect.[7]

- *The Principle of "Harmonized Diversity"*—John MacMillan, Board of Managers member, coined this phrase to allow for diversity of belief and practice on these 3rd tier issues.[8]

- *The Principle of Harmonious Liberty,*[9] allowing for freedom of belief and practice *within that diversity.* The 1906 "Conference for Prayer and Counsel Regarding Uniformity in the Testimony and Teaching of the Alliance"[10] "accorded liberty" in beliefs for what they considered *"open questions* about which our brethren agree to differ and hold in mutual charity their individual convictions."[11]

- *The Principle of Harmonious Whole Without Controversy.* Simpson's desire for the operation of the gifts of the Spirit in the Alliance was "blended in one harmonious whole. . . . without controversy."[12]

HOW ARE DISAGREEMENTS OVER OPEN QUESTIONS TO BE HANDLED?

Disagreements over these debatable doctrines, practices, and policies are inevitable. How did the early Alliance handle such issues? Here are some of the practical principles from A. B. Simpson:

- Let there be no controversy or argument on these issues—agree to differ, not divide.
- Don't make a major over a minor even if it is a major in your eyes.
- Don't become dogmatic and warlike over your position.
- Do not judge one another—be one in heart.
- Do not be aggressive or pressure others with your viewpoint.
- Avoid any spirit of antagonism.
- Avoid attacking those who differ.
- Don't let a narrow, sectarian spirit divide us.

- Don't speak a reckless word against another believer—don't speak unkindly, don't slander, don't be bitter.
- Have an attitude of humility. None of us have the whole truth.
- Don't force your opinions or interpretations of Scripture on others.
- Even if separation is necessary, as with Paul and Barnabas, separate in a spirit of mutual love.[13]

ISSUES CONSIDERED "OPEN QUESTIONS" FOR THE ALLIANCE

Without knowing the Alliance three-tier hermeneutic, a survey of what people in the Alliance think are open question non-essentials might yield very different and contradictory responses. I know people in the Alliance for whom Calvinism or Arminianism is not an open question. I know people in the Alliance for whom women in ministry is not an open question. Yet in the historic Alliance hermeneutic, they *are* open questions. A.W. Tozer, in his wisdom, sadly but truly observed,

> I have seen the motto, "In essentials unity; in nonessentials charity," and I have looked for its incarnation in men and churches without finding it, one reason being that Christians cannot agree on what is and what is not essential. Each one believes that his fragment of truth is essential and his neighbor's unessential, and that brings us right back where we started.[14]

I have scoured through Alliance magazines and other documents to find what are considered open questions, secondary or side issues, non-essentials to Simpson and early Alliance leaders. The open questions or non-essentials would not be limited to these, but these are specific issues mentioned by Simpson and other Alliance leaders from time to time, some of them repeatedly. These historically have represented the theology, hermeneutic, and practice of The Alliance.

Variously called open questions, side issues, secondary issues, minor issues, or non-essentials, they include the following views and practices to varying degrees regarding:

- *Church government* (polity, ordination, women in ministry).
- *Calvinism and Arminianism* (election, falling from grace, etc.)
- *Various worship practices*
- *Water baptism*—2nd tier with 3rd tier liberty
- *Views regarding communion*
- *Dedication of children*
- *Modern hymns and tunes* (use of musical instruments, etc.)
- *When to worship* (sabbath, etc.)
- *fasting*
- *foot washing*
- *Roles of the ministry of women*
- *Catholicism vs Protestantism*
- *Varying views on Creation* (except Darwinian evolutionary theory)
- *Varying views, "phases and phrases" of sanctification*[15]
- *End-times, 2nd Coming and rapture:* The C&MA held a pre-millennial eschatology, but did not require belief it in for membership when Simpson was living, and gave liberty to teachers in presenting various opinions about the end-times[16]
- *Views on Israel*[17] (such as Zionism and the Anglo-Israel theory, but not the view that the church replaced Israel).
- *Various views on speaking in tongues permitted except*: 1) insistence on tongues as the initial evidence of the baptism in the Spirit and 2) tongues are not for the church today.

In the following chapters, we will look at how these were practically applied.

19

THE OPEN QUESTION HERMENEUTIC APPLIED TO THEOLOGICAL ISSUES

CREATION, CALVINISM AND ARMINIANISM, END TIMES

D octrinal controversies abound regarding the beginning of time (creation); the theology of salvation (Calvinism and Arminianism—TULIP), and the end times, as well as many other issues. These are three particular open question doctrinal areas mentioned in Alliance documents, though there may be more. This chapter examines the Alliance open question hermeneutic as applied to these three areas.

VARIOUS VIEWS OF CREATION

Various views on creation are considered in the Alliance as 3rd tier open questions, except where a certain view might compromise 1st tier doctrines such as direct creation by God and historicity of Genesis.

Simpson himself believed in the "gap theory" or "re-creation" of creation.

This interpretation was popular among many evangelicals of his day. This view proposes that there is a gap of time between the original creation in Genesis 1:1 and the re-creation which followed, aa Simpson explains in his *Christ in the Bible* series.[1]

Simpson's explanation leaves room for both old earth and young earth theories of different types.

The revelations of geology bear ample witness to the existence of a primitive condition of convulsions and desolation. During this period of whose length we are not informed, there was ample time for geological formations which science has traced to the pre-historic period.[2]

Simpson and the early Alliance accepted that the "days" of Genesis 1 need not necessarily be 24-hour periods.

There is no necessity in the record itself to limit the word to the natural day of 24 hours. The ordinary scriptural usage of the word day is much varied. In the present passage, even, it is employed in several senses. In the fifth verse it means half a day, or the period of light that came in alternation with darkness. In the end of the same verse, it means a whole day, including both morning and evening. And in the fourth verse of the second chapter, it means the whole period of six days, while in other Scriptures, again and again, it denotes a general period of indefinite duration.[3]

Simpson and the Alliance did not insist that the Bible is a science textbook.

They believed that rue science will not contradict Scripture, but Scripture may not express the natural world and universe scientifically.[4]

Views of Creation That Are Not Open to Question

- ***Views That Contradict Creation by Direct Power of God.***
  Simpson and the Alliance did not accept any view that did

not involve creation. This would seem to eliminate the theory of theistic evolution and macro evolution (but not micro-evolution within species) from open question options.[5]

- **Views That Dispute Historicity of the Genesis Account.**
  George Pardington, a Semitic scholar, discusses the meaning of various terms relating to creation, and asserts of The Alliance, "We accept without question the historicity of the early chapters of Genesis."[6] The Alliance affirms there was a real creation, a real Adam and Eve, a real Fall, a real flood. These were not merely symbolic stories, legends, or myths.

CALVINISM AND ARMINIANISM

The Alliance was formed primarily out of the Reformed/Presbyterian camp out of which A.B. Simpson came, and thus naturally leaned in its earlier days toward more Reformed theology and practice. People coming into the Alliance, as they are made aware of this background, may mistakenly think that the Alliance is Reformed in its theology.

However, Simpson and early Alliance leaders determined that the Alliance would not be exclusively Reformed in doctrine and would not allow it to be an issue. Simpson himself moved away from five-point Calvinism. He gave leadership positions and pulpit time to people of both Wesleyan and Reformed persuasions, as well as a variety of theological backgrounds—Episcopalian, Baptist, Salvation Army, Quaker, Lutheran, etc.

The Alliance thus recognized that believers have various opinions regarding Calvinism vs. Arminianism. They considered these as secondary issues and did not take a firm position on these issues. They allowed people to agree to disagree harmoniously, not making an issue of either position. Occasionally, Simpson allowed opposing beliefs to be aired, then gave commentary balancing the viewpoints. Articles in the *C&MA Weekly* in 1906 presented both sides of the view of backsliding and losing salvation or being eternally secure.[7] In response, Simpson wrote:

> Having printed both sides of this controversy, to do no injustice, we wish now to say that *both articles are out of keeping with the purpose of the Christian and Missionary Alliance*, which regards the questions between Arminians and Calvinists, and the various theological controversies that divide the Churches, as open questions. Our testimony is distinct from that altogether, and has reference only to Christ our Saviour, Sanctifier, Healer, and coming Lord.[8] [italics mine]

As another example of dealing with this issue, in 1922 an instructor at Nyack was asked to resign, not because he held a strong-Calvinist point of view (as some other Alliance leaders held strong Calvinist views as well), but because he was adamant in his hyper-Calvinistic position. He apparently did not fit the Alliance hermeneutic of loving liberty by agreeing to disagree.[9]

The Alliance is not Reformed, but allows Reformed theology so long as not pushed aggressively or dogmatically; The Alliance is not Arminian, but allows Arminian theology so long as not pushed aggressively or dogmatically.[10] Applying that to our churches and pastors today, someone who is a Calvinist or an Arminian can share their beliefs with their congregations, but with the caveat, "This is my belief, not the theological position of The Alliance, which is that it is an open question and a non-essential."

The opposing views can be discussed and even debated in appropriate occasions and settings in a harmonious manner, but they should never be presented with an adamancy that negatively affects our fellowship and service together in The Alliance.

VARIOUS VIEWS OF END TIMES

From the founding of The Alliance in 1887, premillennialism was taught as an Alliance distinctive, but not dogmatically. It was the softest and most malleable of the Alliance distinctives. As cited in Chapter 3, the original constitution of The Alliance demonstrates that flexibility:

> Inasmuch as many persons who desire to become members of this Alliance and are in full accord with its principles in other points, cannot yet fully accept the doctrine of Christ's Pre-millennial Coming, it is agreed that such persons may be received into full membership, provided they receive the first three points of testimony, and are willing to give this subject their candid and prayerful consideration.

As stated earlier, belief in the premillennial second coming of Christ was a 2nd tier distinctive, but with 3rd tier open question liberty— "We believe this but allow that." As mentioned earlier in Chapters 3 and 17, this continued to be maintained flexibly.

Tribulation and Rapture Views

Regarding tribulation views, Simpson himself, along with several other Alliance and evangelical leaders of his time (especially in the holiness movements and later in the Pentecostal movement) held to a partial rapture tribulation view.[11] While preferring a partial-rapture doctrine of eschatology, Simpson also permitted those with a more classical post-tribulational view such as A. J. Gordon and William Oerter to teach their viewpoints as well.[12]

End Time Views of Israel

With belief in the pre-millennial second coming of Christ came a wide range of theories regarding the role of Israel in the end times, among them debates about Zionism, replacement theory, and Anglo-Israel views. Some of these theories were considered open questions; others were not.

Zionist Views. William Blackstone was an early Zionist who believed the Bible prophesied the restoration of Israel as a nation and worked actively throughout his life to make that happen. He was a friend of Simpson's and a speaker at Alliance gatherings. Simpson and The Alliance believed that Israel had a place in God's plan in the end times, although they did not specify how.

Replacement Theory. In much of the typical amillennial or post-millennial Covenant Theology thought, it was believed that the church as spiritual Israel replaced physical Israel. However, against replacement theory views, in the 1890s Simpson asserted, based on his understanding of Scripture, that God has an ongoing purpose for Israel, anticipating the restoration of Israel as a nation, followed by evangelization and conversion of Israel and Christ's return.[13] He did not specify or speculate what the nature of that plan was. Yet he affirmed clearly, that both physical and spiritual Israel have a place in God's end-time plans, and that hermeneutically the spiritual application does not negate the physical:

> The spiritual application of these promises and prophecies of the Scripture respecting Israel, in accordance with which post-millennialists constantly refer these pages to the New Testament church, is contrary to all true principles of interpretation. We admit, it is true, that the church does inherit the promise of Abraham spiritually, but this certainly does not displace the literal seed of Abraham from their own promises and covenants. . . . We share the privileges of Israel, but all their promises shall be literally fulfilled to them, for all the gifts and callings of God are without repentance. . . . We are ready to admit that there are spiritual and underlying references in the Scriptures which it is quite legitimate to apply, but the literal meaning must always first be satisfied. God's promises to Abraham and Israel have not been set aside, and yet, in perfect compatibility with this, He is able to extend the privileges of the gospel and the promises of His kingdom to the Gentile world. [14]

At the same time, even though the Alliance strongly supported Israel becoming a nation, Mideastern ministry was never just to the Jews, but to Palestinians and Arabs as well. The Alliance has balanced believing, on one hand, that Israel has a special place in God's plan, but, on the other hand, He also does for Palestinians and Arabs as well.

Dispensational Views. Simpson and The Alliance were a bit eclectic in end time views, accepting some elements of dispensational views, yet not all. Some people unfortunately identify premillennialism with dispensationalism or pre-tribulationism, which is not accurate.

Anglo-Israel Views. A popular teaching was circulating around the beginning of the 20th century that the Saxon peoples were originally Jewish in origin. Few people believe that today. Simpson asserted at the time that it was a "side issue." He assured that this teaching was not the position of the Alliance, but people who were part of the Alliance held this position. This was a side issue and not to be an issue of fellowship one way or the other.

However, decades later, one version of Anglo-Israelism, known as British-Israelism, became identified with a cult—The Worldwide Church of God, founded by Herbert W. Armstrong. It also became associated with racism and white superiority. These versions of the belief the Alliance considered as heresies, no longer as open questions. John MacMillan wrote a series of articles in the *Alliance Weekly* against the heresy in 1934.[15]

BALANCING 2ND TIER PREMILLENNIALISM WITH 3RD TIER LIBERTY.

As I shared above, Simpson believed in a dual millennium—a literal physical millennial kingdom for the church in the future and a spiritual kingdom for believers to begin to experience now.[16] So we see that some features of amillennialism and post-millennialism can be compatible with premillennialism and fit into a premillennial framework, and others do not. A premillennial framework can be malleable enough to encompass some amil and post-mil aspects.

Of course, some elements of post mil and a mil are not compatible with premillennialism or The Alliance. For instance,

- Some brands of amillennialism teach that Satan is currently bound on earth, according to their interpretation of

Revelation 20:1-3. The Alliance does not hold that Satan is currently bound and not deceiving the nations. Satan is very much active in harassing people's lives and deceiving. As mentioned earlier, Throughout Alliance history numerous Alliance leaders have stressed the need for binding Satan and his dark powers:

- Some brands of amillennialism stray far from The Alliance grammatical-historical hermeneutic of literal priority, and end up over-symbolizing and allegorizing more than is warranted by Scripture.
- Some brands of anillennialism in their allegorization teach that the church replaces Israel, and find no more place for physical Israel in God's plans.

20

THE OPEN QUESTION HERMENEUTIC APPLIED TO CHURCH GOVERNMENT ISSUES

CHURCH POLITY, ORDINATION AND ORDINANCES, WOMEN IN MINISTRY

W hile there are many theological and practical issues that fall under ecclesiology, the doctrine of the church, three of the main ones in Alliance thought and practice that were mostly considered non-essential open questions, with a few caveats, were church policy, ordination, and roles of women in ministry.

THE ALLIANCE OPEN QUESTION HERMENEUTIC APPLIED TO CHURCH POLITY

There are three main types of church polity or governmental styles: Episcopal (hierarchy of leadership), Presbyterial (elder-based leadership), Congregational (congregational-based leadership), and, of course, many variations within each of these. Coming from a Presbyterian background, Simpson naturally gravitated toward a presbyterial style, but gradually over time, given the nature of his ecumenical vison for The Alliance, he came to hold an open view to all church polities, recognizing biblical support for each:

There appears to have been no extremely rigid rule in the New Testament about church government further than that a certain body of spiritual overseers were appointed out of every church, and they were called elders or bishops. . . . It is a safe rule to recognize all these various forms of church government as sufficiently Scriptural to furnish a frame for the Gospel and the church of God, which is really the essential thing.[1]

Simpson gathered leaders from various theological and denominational backgrounds, which included all three church polities and their variations: episcopal (Methodist/Episcopal/Anglican/ Lutheran: E. D. Whiteside, George Peck, George Pardington; Kenneth MacKenzie, Kenneth Wilson); presbyterial (Reformed/Presbyterian: R. A. Forrest, Robert Jaffray; W. C. Stevens; J. Hudson Ballard; Robert Glover); congregational (Baptist/Brethren/Mennonite/Quaker: Carrie Judd Montgomery; Ethan O. Allen, Albert Funk, David Updegraff, Mary Mullen, John Salmon; Frederick Farr; William T. MacArthur; A. J. Gordon). Thus, styling the Alliance as a non-denominational parachurch organization, he designed great latitude in church polity styles, never intending for the Alliance to become a denomination—never intending to stipulate or implement only one church polity.

Eventually, The Alliance would develop into an organization that is mostly a blend of presbyterial and congregational styles, with just a little bit of episcopal hierarchy mixed in (President, Board of Directors, and District Superintendents), but some with some options and flexibility allowed for local church government. Former Canadian C&MA President Dr. Franklin Pyles expressed it this way: "a warm governance amalgam from both Methodist and Presbyterian sources."[2]

THE ALLIANCE OPEN QUESTION HERMENEUTIC APPLIED TO ORDINATION AND ORDINANCES

Ordination in general.

- For Simpson and the early alliance, ordination was not so much a theological issue as a practical one—for needs of travel, conducting weddings and funerals, access for professionally-recognized clergy.

- The view of ordination in the C&MA has been fueled mainly by Simpson's Reformed theology based upon a clergy/laity distinction, meaning a setting apart to be clergy.
- Other groups such as Brethren, Quakers, some Baptists, and other groups downplay the clergy/laity distinction and see ordination as confirming a call to ministry.
- Therefore, the Alliance has left the matter of different types of church government as an "open question," so while offering ordination, the emphasis in earlier days was more on certification for ministry.

Ordination of women:

- The Alliance did not ordain women since they did not find explicit biblical example or sanction of woman's ordination.
- However, women ordained by other organizations were welcomed and permitted to minister in The Alliance even before the end of the nineteenth century."[3]
- Kenneth MacKenzie, a close associate of Simpson for more than 30 years, when asked about ordination of women, he sidestepped the question, averring, ""We may not seek approval or disapproval on the Bible concerning matters that touch upon modern life and practices." [4]
- Thus, for nearly 100 years of its history and church polity, the C&MA did not outright say that they opposed ordination (for, in actuality, they accepted numerous women's ordination from other churches and organizations), but they did not "feel free" to ordain through the C&MA.[5]

Ordination and administering ordinances:

- Originally, administering ordinances was not limited to those licensed or ordained in the early Alliance. Lay people could administer, including women. The very year of the founding of the Alliance in 1887, Sara Musgrove instituted monthly Communion services and baptized 23 people, stirred out of meetings with A. B. Simpson. By 1889 her work as a lay evangelist was known as Fourfold Gospel Mission.[6]

- Over the vast majority of the 20th century, the U.S. policy was that administering ordinances was not forbidden to women. They could administer ordinances if accepted by the congregation and approval of the district superintendent.

- Writing to the IRS in 1964, C&MA President Dr. Nathan Bailey assured that women were permitted: "Women ministers are as fully qualified to perform sacerdotal functions as any male minister.... This is the historic position of the church for over seventy-five years."[7]

- After the Alliance became a denomination in 1975, women were increasingly restricted by some leadership in the United States, even though there was no General Council policy until 1999.

- Canadian policy: According to Canadian C&MA officials, "Canada was different. First, there were no rules, then, at Lavel 1998 General Assembly (GA), licensed women were allowed to do all pastoral functions including the sacraments. Then, at GA 2000 in Calgary they were allowed to become elders in the local church if the local church voted by 2/3 to allow it. This vote would then hold for that church's practice."[8]

THE ALLIANCE OPEN QUESTION HERMENEUTIC APPLIED TO MINISTRY OF WOMEN

Much of this can be found in my book *Anointed Women: The Rich Heritage of Women in Ministry in the Christian and Missionary Alliance,* so I will not duplicate it in this book. Women's roles in ministry was one of those issues relating church government as of 1906 that was considered an open question, in which differing beliefs could be held within the

Alliance without rancor or judgmentalism. The contemporary debate over complementarianism and egalitarianism was considered a side issue, not a 2nd or 1st tier doctrine. In fact, the terminology did not exist until the 1970s.

Regarding the issue of women in ministry, Tozer's two wings principle applied the two wings of complementarianism and egalitarianism —male headship, on one hand, and equality of ministry opportunity on the other hand. Rather than setting one against the other, early Alliance leaders embraced both viewpoints, amalgamating them into one—egalitarian-complementarianism. After weighing differing interpretations of pertinent biblical passages, Alliance leadership determined that there was sufficient uncertainty in the Scripture so as to have no clear example or sanction to ordain women, yet sufficient biblical evidence to allow practically complete latitude for women to serve in virtually any capacity of ministry as long as they were submitted to appropriate authority.

Alliance leaders interpreted these Scriptures to mean that it was God's ideal or usual intention for men to lead and exercise authority within the church. However, the need of the situation and God's special anointing and calling upon a woman by God trump His usual intention. With Simpson's good friend A. J. Gordon they concluded:

> How little authority there is in the Word for repressing the witness of women in the public assembly, or for forbidding her to herald the Gospel to the unsaved. . . . Beware, lest, in silencing the voice of consecrated women, they may be resisting the Holy Ghost.[9]

They did not want to be guilty of possibly resisting or quenching the Holy Spirit, so they did not silence the voice of consecrated women as pastors, evangelists, and Bible teachers. They heeded the admonition of Alliance Greek scholar T.J. McCrossan: "Let some of us beware how we condemn 'women pastors,' who are Spirit-filled," and gave women full liberty to minister under authority.

The Historic Alliance Position.

While the egalitarian vs. complementarian debate persists on in the 21st century, A. B. Simpson and The Alliance of the earlier 20th century forged an ecumenical middle path that was both intrinsically complementarian (affirming male headship) and at the same time granting virtually full freedom for women in ministry, including pastoral ministry and performance of all pastoral functions, providing latitude for both personal conscience and unity.[10]

This creative solution to a contentious practical-theological issue is just as timely in the 21st century to provide unity, tolerance, and liberty of conscience and practice. This position evolved more than a century ago through a decade or so of prayer, study of Scripture, and dialogue, but through historical drift and imbalanced tilt, the position was shifted from a 3rd tier open question to a 2nd tier doctrine and practice in the US C&MA in 1999. **For a history of the Alliance Position on women in ministry, see *Anointed Women*.**

THE ALLIANCE 3RD TIER OPEN QUESTION HERMENEUTIC APPLIED TO RELATED SCRIPTURES.

Again, much of this is found in *Anointed Women*, so just a brief summary is given here. The Alliance open question hermeneutic regarding biblical passages meant that the Alliance interpreted these passages, not in an absolutist sense, but in the sense of a general principles that can have exceptions. Alliance leaders affirmed that exegesis of these passages varied among evangelical scholars, so interpretations cannot be dogmatic and settled—thus open questions.

1 Timothy 2:12.

Early Alliance leaders recognized this as a pivotal passage, making this the primary text for interpretation by C&MA leaders. At the same time, they also recognized that its interpretation was thorny and not a sure thing. The interpretations were the generally accepted opinions among Alliance leaders, though various views were permitted.

The Passage Probably Refers to Husbands and Wives, Not the Church.—A. J. Gordon. *Alliance Weekly*, 1928.[11] Simpson associate Kenneth MacKenzie affirmed this view in 1929: "wife may be substituted for woman. . . . The word applied to Phebe (Rom. 16:1), *diakonos*, is a masculine noun, which may have the significance of the pastoral office in the Church. There should be no qualms whatever in our day as to placing consecrated and highly esteemed women in posts of Christian shepherdship." [12]

The Passage Is Cultural, Not Universally Binding for All Times. An *Alliance Weekly* article in 1898 with no byline, probably written by Simpson as was his custom, but certainly having his approval, asserts that the passage was in the context of the times, and not binding for all times:

> It is true that the Apostle Paul did not *at that time* suffer a woman to teach, or to usurp authority over the man. Doubtless *at that time* there were no women competent to act as teachers. . . . The Gospel of Christ lifts the yoke of burden from womanhood, rescues her from ignorance and degradation and introduces her to a new and better condition, where there is neither Jew nor Gentile, male nor female, but all are one in Jesus Christ. And woman thus enfranchised by the Gospel of Christ, has been a most successful worker in the cause and service of the Lord.[13]

Twice the phrase is used "at that time," indicating a reference to time constraints. Eleven years later, Board of Manager member Dr. J. Hudson Ballard paraphrased and reaffirmed the quote above in his pronouncement that a woman can pastor if a suitable man is not available. See below for his additional comments.

The Prohibition of This Passage Is a General Situational Principle Only in Certain Circumstances or Settings, Not an Absolute. Dr. J. Hudson Ballard adds additional commentary and support to the non-binding cultural interpretation above:

It will be noticed that this passage speaks particularly against a woman teaching or usurping authority "over the man." We may imply from this that the force of the prohibition is applicable only when there is a proper man around to do the teaching and have the authority. If there is such a man, it seems unscriptural for a woman to step in and usurp his place and prerogatives. In the absence of a man qualified for such work we do know that God has often chosen and anointed spiritual women for teaching and for leading on the work of the Lord Jesus Christ.[14]

Don't Cast Judgment—Weigh Local Factors. Kenneth MacKenzie, 1929: "We may not seek approval or disapproval on the Bible concerning matters that touch upon modern life and practices, without weighing the localisms, the orientalisms and the specifically individualistic features of the statements of the Bible which may bear upon such matters." [15]

Note: These founding Alliance leaders are not feminists or egalitarians, but what would be called today moderate or soft complementarians, believing in male headship, but granting full liberty for women under authority and anointed by the Spirit.

1 Timothy 3.

Alliance leaders, following A.J. Gordon, did not deny that this passage indicates that bishops (overseers or pastors) were *usually* male, but consistent with the open question hermeneutical approach toward the passage in 1 Timothy 2, since the prior passage is open to different interpretations by godly evangelical leaders, in order to be hermeneutically consistent, they did not view this passage as absolute either, but rather as an ideal.

- Male elder authority is the ideal, but this is not an absolute.
- "God has often chosen and anointed spiritual women for teaching and for leading on the work of the Lord."-J. Hudson Ballard, Ph.D.

- Women can thus serve as pastors or elders if needed and divinely appointed and anointed.
- C&MA published book in 1927 warned, "Let some of us beware how we condemn 'women pastors,' who are Spirit-filled."—Dr. T.J. McCrossan, Alliance pastor, Simpson Bible Institute professor, respected Greek scholar[16]

Romans 16:7—Junia the Apostle.

By 1903, Alliance leaders granted the possibility, even likelihood, that the feminine Greek name Junia (in some translations Junias) mentioned in Romans 16:7 may well have been a female apostle, acknowledging that the early church father Chrysostom also believed Junia was a female apostle. These are cited by Dr. Henry Wilson and Dr. A. J. Gordon in the *Alliance Weekly*.[17]

Joel 2/Acts 2:17-18—Pentecost Conveys "Equal Privileges Under the Outpoured Spirit" for Both Men and Women.

Gordon, as sanctioned in his *Alliance Weekly* articles, taught "equal privileges under the outpoured Spirit" for men and women according to the fulfillment of the prophecy of Joel fulfilled in Acts 2. Calling it the "Magna Carta of the Christian Church," he asserts, "It gives to woman a status in the Spirit hitherto unknown. . . . In Scripture we shall expect to find no text which denies to woman her divinely appointed rights in the new dispensation."

Likewise, Dr. T. J. McCrossan, an Alliance pastor, Simpson Bible Institute professor, and respected Greek scholar, wrote in a book approved and published by the C&MA, "God is now again pouring out His Spirit upon both His male and female servants, and when He says His female servants in the last days shall preach and expound Scripture publicly, let some of us beware how we condemn 'women pastors,' who are Spirit-filled." He and The Alliance interpreted the prophecy of Joel fulfilled through Pentecost as sanctioning women in pastoral leadership positions.[18]

~

These are the interpretations of Simpson, Simpson's associates, and Alliance leaders through the years regarding these texts. They recognized these were not the only valid interpretations, and so they gave liberty for other viewpoints as well, so long as people did not become hardliners for their position. Thus, the roles of women in ministry were left as an open question, a side issue, a non-essential.

Additional 3rd Tier Interpretative Principles Applied Here

Weigh the local cultural factors before expressing approval or disapproval.

Kenneth MacKenzie, a close associate of A. B. Simpson for 30 years (who knew both Simpson's early and later positions), presented this principle in regard to a question about ordination of women:

> We may not seek approval or disapproval on the Bible concerning matters that touch upon modern life and practices, without weighing the localisms, the orientalisms and the specifically individualistic features of the statements of the Bible which may bear upon such matters.[19]

MacKenzie, representing Alliance leadership, which did not by policy ordain, nonetheless could not approve or disapprove of ordination. In other words, Alliance leadership did not take a position on whether it was right or wrong to ordain, they just stayed out of the argument. After a discussion of various factors and Scripture exegesis, MacKenzie concludes, "There should be no qualms whatever in our day as to placing consecrated and highly esteemed women in posts of Christian shepherdship." Although The Alliance did not ordain women, they accepted women as pastors who had been ordained by other denominations.

The final exegesis not in the lexicon and grammar.—A.J. Gordon.[20]

When all is said and done, lexicons and grammars, as good and as important they may be, do not have all the answers. It comes back to the Holy Spirit.

Apply Tozer's two wings principle.

Regarding the issue of women in ministry, those two wings were complementarianism and egalitarianism—male headship on one hand, and equality of ministry opportunity on the other hand. Tozer considered this to be a side issue, and reportedly would walk out of the room if someone wanted to debate it.

Recognize God's intentional divine ambiguity.

A Greek scholar friend of mine has concluded that sometimes God intends divine ambiguities or mysteries in Scripture for us not to figure out this side of heaven. The Alliance acknowledged this in such issues as the events and timing surrounding the rapture, variations in church government, biblical support for Calvinism and Arminianism, and roles for women in ministry. Alliance leaders acknowledged this and left room for ambiguity in interpretation of Scriptures. There were strong points on both sides of a variety of issues, so rather than take sides as an organization or denomination, they left it an open question.

Where ambiguity exists, don't set absolutes.

While the Alliance affirmed a basic complementarian position, they regarded it as an ideal, not a firm absolute. God, in His sovereignty, makes exceptions to the ideal and chooses and anoints women.

Recognize the biblical principle of delegated authority—exercising authority under authority.

The Alliance recognized and practiced the principle of delegated authority (Mt 8:8-10) A woman who is submitted to appropriate authority is thus not usurping authority, so can exercise authority under authority appropriately.

SUMMARY: WHEN CAN A WOMAN PASTOR, LEAD, OR EXERCISE SPIRITUAL AUTHORITY?

After weighing differing interpretations of pertinent biblical passages, Alliance leadership determined that there was sufficient ambiguity in the Scripture so as to have no clear example or sanction to ordain women, yet sufficient biblical evidence to allow practically complete latitude for women to serve in virtually any capacity of ministry as long as they were submitted to appropriate authority. This had Simpson's approval. So, in Alliance 3rd Tier Hermeneutic, when could a woman lead, exercise authority or perform all the functions of the clergy?

- When a suitable man is not available.
- When a woman has been chosen and anointed.
- When a woman hears from heaven.
- When a woman is under proper authority, has been delegated authority, and does not usurp authority.
- Where her ministry is accepted.

What were the restrictions?

- Being under proper authority (males needed to be under authority too) and being delegated authority.
- Willingness to defer to male authority.
- Willingness to honor and defer to the wishes and policy of a local congregation regarding her role and title in that particular local church.
- Licensed, but not ordained in the Alliance (but could be ordained elsewhere and still serve in the Alliance).

CONSIDERED A SIDE ISSUE—AN OPEN QUESTION

The historic Alliance position was that the issue of women in ministry was an open question, with various viewpoints allowed, but without rancor and dissension. The ideal of male headship was maintained, but not rigidly or with dogmatism. Women were free to minister in all capacities so long as they were submitted to authority and anointed by the Lord. No church was required to have a woman pastor or elder. Women preachers were common throughout the history of The Alliance, beginning with A. B. Simpson. Women missionaries commonly spoke from the pulpit, unless a particular church did not want her to do so. In such cases, the woman "shared," rather than "preached," or spoke from the floor rather than the pulpit.

The historic C&MA was neither solely complementarian nor solely egalitarian, but a blend of both: egalitarian-complementarian. Egalitarians don't like the position because they want more; complementarians don't like the position because they want more. In the historic Alliance view, both sides are willing to give a little and honor each other's viewpoints, agreeing to disagree agreeably. **See endnote for resources for further study.**[21]

21

THE ALLIANCE OPEN QUESTION HERMENEUTIC APPLIED TO WORSHIP PRACTICES

Numerous worship practices are mentioned in Alliance documents as "open questions," "side issues" "secondary issues," "non-essentials. These will be briefly summarized.[1] As discussed under the Alliance Distinctive of Christ Our Savior, the subject and mode of water Baptism. ("The almost universal practice at home and in our mission field has come to be baptism of believers only by immersion," but not required for membership).

VIEWS REGARDING COMMUNION

Open or Closed Communion.

Most Alliance churches throughout Alliance history have maintained open communion, but the decision has been up to the individual congregation or national church to decide.

Methods of Administering Communion.

- Methods of intinction, common cup, separate cups, use of

wine vs. grape juice, etc. were considered 3rd tier non-essential open questions.

- Frequency of Communion was left open, whether weekly, monthly, quarterly, etc.

Who Can Administer Communion?

Some groups emphasized a clergy-laity distinction in which only clergy could administer Communion, whereas for those who did not emphasize a clergy-laity distinction, anyone—lay or clergy, male or female—could administer Communion. For the Alliance, this was a 3rd tier open question.

Theology of Communion

- The Catholic view of transubstantiation was not accepted.
- The various views—Reformed (sign of grace), Baptist (symbolic), Anglican/Episcopal/ Methodist (real presence), and Quaker/Salvation Army (spiritual, no physical elements present) views were all found with in Alliance fellowship and were accepted as 3rd tier open questions. There may have been some question about acceptance of the Lutheran view of consubstantiation—that Christ is physically present in the elements of Communion (but not all Lutherans hold this view).
- Simpson's personal view, which he taught openly in Alliance circles, seems to align very closely to a combination of Reformed and Anglican. He and other Alliance leaders saw a strong connection between Communion and healing. The combining of Communion with healing services at many District Conferences and General Councils seems to have emerged out of Simpson's eucharistic theology and practice.

OTHER NON-ESSENTIAL OPEN QUESTIONS ON ISSUES OF THE PRACTICES OF WORSHIP

- *Dedication of Children*: The early interdenominational Alliance included those who baptized infants and those who dedicated infants and children. Since this was considered in the Alliance as a 3rd tier non-essential, fellowship between them never became an issue. As the Alliance established churches of their own, since the Alliance practiced believer's baptism by immersion, most Alliance churches practiced dedication of children. Infant baptism was not practiced unless in rare cases it was considered infant dedication by sprinkling.
- *Music practices*—use of Psalter only or hymns and modern tunes, musical instruments, etc., according to Simpson "are simply non-essentials." [2]
- *When io Worship*—Sabbatarians (perhaps 7th Day Baptists and 7th Day Adventists) were apparently a part of this interdenominational Alliance, so arguments about which day of the week to worship were off the table and not to be an issue of fellowship.[3]
- *Fasting*—Some people were legalistically adhering to fasting. Simpson did not oppose fasting but insisted on balance. He observed extremes in which people thought they were hearing from God but were apparently disoriented because of food deprivation.
- *Foot Washing*—Some Alliance people practiced (especially Brethren and Mennonites), some did not—it was not made an issue of fellowship.
- *Regarding Dos and Don'ts,* Simpson advocated "operation of a principle rather than the application of a rule."[4]
- *Various views on the practice of speaking in tongues*—Belief in the reality of the gift of speaking in tongues was a part of the Alliance distinctive of continuism. Speaking in tongues was both embraced openly but not indiscriminately *and*

permitted with the exception of two views: 1) insistence on
tongues as the initial evidence of the baptism in the Spirit
and 2) tongues are not for the church today. Exercise of
tongues in public services was permitted if following the
guidelines of 1 Corinthians 14.

- *Catholicism vs Protestantism.* Even though Simpson had
  some negative things to say about what he called
  "Romanism," he also appreciated the Catholic mystics and
  cautioned about getting argumentative about Catholicism vs
  Protestantism.[5] Tozer had an even greater appreciation for
  Catholic mystics. The Alliance would not agree with Roman
  Catholic views such as communion as transubstantiation,
  relics, baptismal regeneration, purgatory, and salvation by
  works, but understood that some people had a real deep
  relationship and fellowship with God even with defective
  theology. Simpson and early Alliance leaders tried to avoid
  arguing over doctrines, but rather lead people to Christ.

22

SUMMARY OF THE ALLIANCE 3RD TIER HERMENEUTIC:

AN ECUMENICAL MIDDLE PATH

GUIDELINES FOR UNITY IN LOVING LIBERTY

For Simpson and the early Alliance, **the only essentials were the essential doctrines of the Christian faith,** to which all Bible-believing Christian can agree, **and the distinctives that were essential to the life of The Alliance**—those tenets that make The Alliance "Alliance. Everything else are non-essentials, open questions, side issues, minor points.These following principles summarized provide guidelines to maintain unity in loving liberty.

Counter-polarities are often found in truth. Each aspect of truth needs to be kept in balance. Apply the two wings principle.

Don't interpret the texts rigidly, but fluidly, leaving room for variations in interpretation. Recognize That the final exegesis is not in the lexicon and grammar, but through the Holy Spirit's interpretation.

Don't insist on absolutes. God does not reveal all the details or make everything crystal clear on the minor points. Everything is not always black and white on theological issues. Accept a divine ambiguity.

Agree to Disagree Harmoniously. Accept that there are good godly people on both sides of these issue. One can take a position on one of these issues without being argumentative, dogmatic, or hostile toward those taking an opposing view. In the Alliance 3rd Tier Ecumenical Hermeneutic, one can be

- a Calvinist without being argumentative, dogmatic, or hostile toward Arminians.
- an Arminian without being argumentative, dogmatic, or hostile toward Calvinists.
- premillennial without being argumentative, dogmatic, or hostile toward amillennialists.
- amillennial without being argumentative, dogmatic, or hostile toward premillennialists.
- complementarian without being argumentative, dogmatic, or hostile toward egalitarians.
- egalitarian without being argumentative, dogmatic, or hostile toward complementarians.
- young earth, 6 day-24-hour creationist without being argumentative, dogmatic, or hostile toward old earth, day-age, or other creationists.
- old earth, day-age, or other creationists without being argumentative, dogmatic, or hostile toward young earth, 6 day-24-hour creationists.
- fond of traditional hymns and worship without being argumentative, dogmatic, or hostile toward those who love contemporary worship music.
- fond of contemporary worship music without being argumentative, dogmatic, or hostile toward those who love traditional hymns and worship.
- And the list of applications goes on!

MOVING OPEN QUESTIONS TO CLOSED AND VICE VERSA

There have been and probably will continue to be some who say,

"That was then; this is now," wanting to move certain issues from open questions to closed questions; others wanting to move certain issues from closed questions to open questions. We should be very cautious about doing either—especially if the motives are relevancy or tilting a viewpoint one direction or another.

Moving Open to Closed

The first problem with making an open question a closed question is wanting to discard an Alliance position held for decades—making the wineskins more rigid and brittle, making The Alliance less Alliance, or "another" Alliance. Another problem is, who decides and how is it decided? When one side comes into power and tilts the balance? A third problem is, where does it stop? What open question is next to become a closed question? If the issue of women serving as elders and pastors was moved from open to closed question status, since it is based mainly on a Reformed hermeneutic, when does the issue of Calvinism vs Arminianism become a closed question? Already, there are groups within the Alliance trying to move in this direction.

Moving Closed to Open

What closed question is next to move to becoming an open question? What 1st tier doctrines are in danger of being moved to 2nd or 3rd tier? How loose do we allow the Alliance Distinctives become? What 2nd tier distinctives are being watered down or compromised? What needs to be changed to a different tier? If a 2nd tier distinctive with 3rd tier liberty crumbles to totally 3rd tier, does that create a slippery slope for another 2nd tier distinctive to slide into historical drift?

Perspectives from Alliance History

We see a little bit of this switching in Alliance history, especially after the death of A.B. Simpson:

- **Believer's baptism by immersion** moved from a more 3rd tier open question to a 2nd tier distinctive with some 3rd tier liberty in the 1920s. The C&MA Canada at first required believers' baptism for membership then moved back to requiring just baptism. This appears to have been maintained fairly flexibly, though there has been confusion at times on inconsistent application.

- **Premillennialism** moved from a 2nd tier distinctive with 3rd tier liberty for the first 35 years of Alliance history to more of a solid 2nd tier distinctive in 1922 and following until the Canadian Alliance dropped the word premillennial in 2000. Without some acknowledgment of the value of the premillennial heritage, this would seem to move the Fourfold Gospel to somewhat of a Threefold Gospel

- **The role of women in ministry** was a 3rd tier open question from about 1905 to 1999. In 1999, the US Alliance official policy shifted from a 3rd tier open question to a closed question as a 2nd tier complementarian distinctive. However, Canada and numerous other countries in the Alliance Worldwide Fellowship still maintain a type of 3rd tier open question stance, some even ordaining women. The US shift from the historical open question status to a more rigid 2nd tier complementarian distinctive shows both drift and a hardening of wineskins, as well as inconsistency in application worldwide.

- **Christ as Sanctifier—The sanctifying baptism in the Spirit.** Though there has not been a formal doctrinal change in the US Statement of Faith at this point, I hear rumblings from district discussions that our statement on sanctification is stirring desire on the part of some for significant change and watering down belief in the subsequence or crisis experience. The muddy water over recent decades is having its toll on this key distinctive. Simpson's warning against "loose views of sanctification" needs to be heeded at this time.

All of this discussion may create more questions than answers, but also much more food for thought, and most of all, for prayer. What of the original vision of Simpson and the early Alliance needs to be retained and maintained? What has become old rigid wineskins and needs to be replaced with new flexible wineskins to hold the effervescing new wine of the Holy Spirit? What can continue to be maintained with flexibility and liberty without discarding our founding fathers original intent? What would be quenching the moving of the Spirit in our midst in fresh revival?

LORD, CAUSE YOUR KINGDOM TO COME
AND YOUR WILL TO BE DONE IN AND THROUGH
THE CHRISTIAN AND MISSIONARY ALLIANCE
ON EARTH AS IT IS IN HEAVEN!

APPENDIX 1: THE NIAGARA CREED OF 1878

This 14-point creed, drafted by evangelical leaders at the 878 Niagara Bible Conference, was listed in 1922 as part of the statement of faith for C&MA schools.

- 1. The verbal, plenary inspiration of the Scriptures in the original manuscripts.
- 2. The Trinity.
- 3. The Creation of man, the Fall into sin, and total depravity.
- 4. The universal transmission of spiritual death from Adam.
- 5. The necessity of the new birth.
- 6. Redemption by the blood of Christ.
- 7. Salvation by faith alone in Christ.
- 8. The assurance of salvation.
- 9. The centrality of Jesus Christ in the Scriptures.
- 10. The constitution of the true church by genuine believers.
- 11. The personality of the Holy Spirit.
- 12. The believer's call to a holy life.
- 13. The immediate passing of the souls of believers to be with Christ at death.
- 14. The premillennial Second Coming of Christ. [1]

APPENDIX 2: US & CANADIAN C&MA STATEMENTS OF FAITH

1. **God:** There is one God, who is infinitely perfect, existing eternally in three persons: Father, Son, and Holy Spirit.

2. **Jesus:** Jesus Christ is true God and true man. He was conceived by the Holy Spirit and born of the Virgin Mary. He died upon the cross, the Just for the unjust, as a substitutionary sacrifice, and all who believe in Him are justified on the ground of His shed blood. He arose from the dead according to the Scriptures. He is now at the right hand of the Majesty on high as our great High Priest. He will come again to establish His kingdom of righteousness and peace.

3. **Holy Spirit:** The Holy Spirit is a divine Person, sent to indwell, guide, teach, and empower the believer, and to convince the world of sin, of righteousness and of judgment.

4. **Bible:** The Old and New Testaments, inerrant as originally given, were verbally inspired by God and are a complete revelation of His will for the salvation of people. They constitute the divine and only rule of Christian faith and practice.

5. **Sin:** Humankind, originally created in the image and likeness of God, fell through disobedience, incurring thereby both physical and

spiritual death. All people are born with a sinful nature, are separated from the life of God, and can be saved only through the atoning work of the Lord Jesus Christ. The destiny of the impenitent and unbelieving is existence forever in conscious torment, but that of the believer is everlasting joy and bliss.

6. **Freedom from Sin:** Salvation has been provided only through Jesus Christ. Those who repent and believe in Him are united with Christ through the Holy Spirit and are thereby regenerated (born again), justified, sanctified, and granted the gift of eternal life as adopted children of God.

7. **Christian Living:** It is the will of God that in union with Christ each believer should be sanctified thoroughly[16] thereby being separated from sin and the world and fully dedicated to God, receiving power for holy living and sacrificial and effective service toward the completion of Christ's commission.

This is accomplished through being filled with the Holy Spirit which is both a distinct event and progressive experience in the life of the believer.

8. **Healing:** Provision is made in the redemptive work of the Lord Jesus Christ for the healing of the mortal body. Prayer for the sick and anointing with oil as taught in the Scriptures are privileges for the Church in this present age.

9. **Church:** The universal Church, of which Christ is the Head, consists of all those who believe on the Lord Jesus Christ, are redeemed through His blood, regenerated by the Holy Spirit, and commissioned by Christ to go into all the world as a witness, preaching the Gospel to all nations. The local church, the visible expression of the universal Church, is a body of believers in Christ who are joined together to worship God, to observe the ordinances of Baptism and the Lord's Supper, to pray, to be edified through the Word of God, to fellowship, and to testify in word and deed to the good news of salvation both locally and globally. The local church enters into relationships with other like-minded churches for accountability, encouragement, and mission.

10. **Life after death:** There shall be a bodily resurrection of the just

and of the unjust; for the former, a resurrection unto life; for the latter, a resurrection unto judgment.

II. **Second Coming of Christ:** The second coming of the Lord Jesus Christ is imminent and will be personal and visible. As the believer's blessed hope, this vital truth is an incentive for holy living and sacrificial service toward the completion of Christ's commission.

U.S. C&MA STATEMENT OF FAITH--1965

Note: Changes of the US Statement of Faith are in the process of being discussed and proposed beginning with the 2019 US General Council. After all the dust settles, I will compile a full theological book with the changes, providing exegetical and theological background.

1 There is one God, who is infinitely perfect, existing eternally in three persons: Father, Son, and Holy Spirit.

2 Jesus Christ is true God and true man. He was conceived by the Holy Spirit and born of the Virgin Mary. He died upon the cross, the Just for the unjust, as a substitutionary sacrifice, and all who believe in Him are justified on the ground of His shed blood. He arose from the dead according to the Scriptures. He is now at the right hand of the Majesty on high as our great High Priest. He will come again to establish His kingdom of righteousness and peace.

3 The Holy Spirit is a divine person, sent to indwell, guide, teach, empower the believer, and to convince the world of sin, of righteousness, and of judgment.

4 The Old and New Testaments, inerrant as originally given, were verbally inspired by God and are a complete revelation of His will for the salvation of. men. They constitute the divine and only rule of Christian faith and practice.

5 Man was originally created in the image and likeness of God: he fell through disobedience, incurring thereby both physical and spiritual death. All men are born with a sinful nature, are separated from the life of God, and can be saved only through the atoning work of the Lord Jesus Christ. The prospect of the impenitent and unbelieving

person is existence forever in conscious torment, and that of the believer in Christ, is to have everlasting joy and bliss.

6 Salvation has been provided through Jesus Christ for all men; and those who repent and believe in Him are born again of the Holy Spirit, receive the gift of eternal life, and become the children of God.

7 It is the will of God that each believer should be filled with the Holy Spirit and be sanctified wholly, being separated from sin and the world, and fully dedicated to the will of God, thereby receiving power for holy living and effective service. This is both a crisis and a progressive experience wrought in the life of the believer subsequent to conversion.

8 Provision is made in the redemptive work of the Lord Jesus Christ for the healing of the mortal body. Prayer for the sick and anointing with oil are taught in the Scriptures and are privileges for the Church in this present age.

9 The Church consists of all those who believe on the Lord Jesus Christ, are redeemed through His blood, and are born again of the Holy Spirit. Christ is the Head of the Body, the Church, which has been commissioned by Him to go into all the world as a witness, preaching the gospel to all nations.

The local church is a body of believers in Christ who are joined together for the worship of God, edification through the Word of God, prayer, fellowship, the proclamation of the gospel, and observance of the ordinances of baptism and the Lord's Supper.

10 There shall be a bodily resurrection of the just and of the unjust; for the former, a resurrection unto life; for the latter, a resurrection unto judgment.

11 The second coming of the Lord Jesus Christ is imminent and will be personal, visible, and premillennial. This is the believer's blessed hope and is a vital truth which is an incentive to holy living and faithful service. (Councils 1965, 1966, 1974).

APPENDIX 3: TOZER'S ANSWERS TO OPEN THEISM QUESTIONS

A.W. Tozer lived and died before open theism ever emerged on the theological scene, but like the prophet he was, he spoke relevantly and prophetically to our times, anticipating decades in advance the arguments proposed by open theism. Due to fair use copyright laws, Tozer's answers to open theism's questions are too extensive to duplicate here, but you can investigate the sources on your own. See Tozer's answers by looking up the references in Tozer's books.

- **Can God Learn?** *The Knowledge of the Holy* (New York: Harper and Row, 1961), 61-63.
- **Does God know the future?** *The Knowledge of the Holy*, 66, 68, 71-72, 115, 116-119.
- **Is it the nature of truth that God has absolute knowledge?** *The Warfare of the Spirit*, 110; *Christ the Eternal Son*, 40, 43
- **Does God know your next move?** *We Travel an Appointed Way*, 3-4; *The Attributes of God*, 9, 62; *The Knowledge of the Holy*, 66, 68, 71-72, 115, 116-119.
- **Does God take a risk? Can God fail?** See *Born After Midnight*, 135; *Jesus, Our Man in Glory*, 88; *The Early Tozer: A*

Word in Season, 41; *Jesus Is Victor*, 14; *The Knowledge of the Holy*, 66, 68, 71-72, 115, 116-119.

- **Can God's will be thwarted?** *Jesus Is Victor*, 17.
- **Can God change? Can God grow or develop?** *The Pursuit of God*, 39; *Success and the Christian*, 39.
- **Is God limited in knowledge? Or does He know everything there is to know?** *The Attributes of God*, 131; *Echoes from Eden*, 36.
- **Does God allow suffering because He does not know what is going to happen?**
- *The Next Chapter After the Last*, 54.
- **Does God change His mind?** *The Early Tozer: A Word in Season*, 23-24.
- **If God knows all, are we truly free?** *The Knowledge of the Holy*, 66, 68, 71-72, 115, 116-119.; *Next Chapter After the Next*, 86; *The Attributes of God*, 48; *That Incredible Christian*, 29-31, 83.

APPENDIX 4: CHRIST'S HUMANITY, KENOTIC THEORIES AND THE ALLIANCE

Some kenotic theories are definitely unorthodox and heretical in nature (known as ontological kenotic theories). Others (known as functional kenotic theories or sub-kenotic theories) are in the range of evangelical orthodox beliefs and are not heretical. We need to exercise discernment to distinguish the nuances of orthodox and non-orthodox kenotic theories.

Evangelical theologian Donald G. Bloesch asserted, "One could legitimately argue that there is an orthodox form of kenoticism and a heretical form."[1] Church fathers throughout church history who are considered evangelical and orthodox have taught some form of orthodox kenotic theory, some perhaps in an embryonic and not fully explained form. They may vary from one another in just what ways and forms Jesus emptied Himself, but kenotic in nature in an orthodox manner, nonetheless.

Wayne House, in *Charts of Christian Theology and Doctrine*, summarizes the main orthodox and non-orthodox kenotic views.[2] Summarized below are the three main orthodox interpretations of kenosis cited by House and some representative people of those positions.

Sub-Kenotic (Functional Kenotic) Theories
(evangelical/orthodox)

Jesus was fully God and fully man on earth. Christ did not empty Himself of divinity or of the attributes of deity (omnipotence, omniscience, omnipresence) in the sense of not still being fully God on earth as well as fully man, but He "functionally limited" Himself in some way. Baptist theologian Millard Erickson explains, "By taking on human nature he accepted certain limitations upon the functioning of the divine attributes."[3] Presbyterian theologian J. Rodman Williams agrees, "There was a limitation in their use by Christ in His humanity."[4]

Christ Emptied Himself of the *Use of the Divine Attributes*

The Logos possessed the divine attributes but chose not to use them—voluntary temporary surrender or suspension or disuse of divine attributes.

- Lutheran view; J. R. Williams (Presbyterian); Baptists: A.J. Gordon, John Piper, Edgar Young Mullins (president, Southern Baptist Seminary); Andrew Murray (Dutch Reformed).
- **A. B. Simpson:** "voluntarily suspended the exercise of His rights and powers and placed Himself in the same attitude of dependence upon God and trust in God as He requires of us, His disciples."[5]
- **A. W. Tozer:** "Jesus veiled His deity and ministered as a man.... He limited Himself to the same power available to any one of us, the power of the Holy Spirit."[6]

Christ Emptied Himself of the *Independent Exercise of the Divine Attributes*

The Logos/incarnate Christ always possessed and could utilize the prerogatives of Deity but always in submission to and by the power of the Father (and the Holy Spirit), and never did anything independently by virtue of His own deity.

- Millard Erickson (Baptist), John MacArthur, Abraham Kuyper (Dutch Reformed), Augustus Strong, Reformed view.

Christ Emptied Himself of the *Insignia of Majesty, the Prerogatives of Deity*

The Logos emptied himself of the outward form of Deity.

- Bishop J. B. Lightfoot, Matthew Henry, John Piper

APPENDIX 5: UNDERSTANDING DOUBLE BAPTISM

Part A:
Simpson's Triple Vision of the Double Baptism: Believer's Baptism by Immersion and Baptism in the Spirit

A.B. Simpson's own testimony of his journey to embracing believer's baptism through three interrelated visions of the "double baptism" of water baptism and baptism in the Spirit. It was a revelation of interconnection of three events—the Israelites baptized in the cloud and the sea (1 Cor 10:2), Jesus' baptism at the Jordan, and Pentecost (Acts 2:38) as representing both water baptism and the baptism in the Spirit.

> It was in the autumn of 1881, while cherishing no thought of any change in my theological views, but very earnestly looking out upon the fields, and asking, "Lord, what wilt Thou have me to do?" I was giving a course of lectures to my [Presbyterian] congregation in the City of New York, and I had come to that passage describing the crossing of the Red Sea by the Israelites under Moses. Earnestly inquiring of the Spirit of God what the deeper meaning of the Red Sea was in our spiritual life, I saw

with great plainness that it represented our death to the old life of Egypt and the world.

Vision 1: There suddenly flashed into my mind that striking passage in 1 Corinthians 10:2: "And they were all baptized unto Moses in the cloud and in the sea," and like a vision there rose before me the picture of Israel's host passing through the flood, while at the same time the cloud, representing the Holy Spirit, fell upon them and covered them with its heavenly baptism. **Thus, there was a double baptism. They were baptized in the flood; they were baptized in the cloud. The water and the Spirit were both present.** Somehow there came with it such a vision of Christian baptism in its deeper and spiritual import, leading us down into the flood of death and burial, and at the same moment bringing to us the open heavens and the descending Holy Ghost, that it fairly startled me.

Vision 2: Christ entering the valley of Jordan in baptism, and as He passed through that sacred rite and came forth like Israel crossing the Sea, in like manner the Spirit descended also upon Him and abode, and **He received the double baptism of the water and the Spirit** at the same moment, and from that hour went forth, no longer the Man of Nazareth, but the Son of God, clothed with the power of the Holy Ghost.

Vision 3: The multitude of Pentecost, heart-stricken and convicted by the power of God, and crying out under Peter's sermon, "Men and brethren, what must we do?" And then came the answer of our text: "Repent and be baptized, every one of you in the name of Jesus Christ for the remission of sins, and ye shall receive the gift of the Holy Ghost." There again the water and the Spirit were inseparably linked. **The outward baptism was but a steppingstone to the higher baptism of the Holy Ghost,** and they were all expected to enter into both, **as though neither was complete without the other.**

As these visions flashed across my mind, there came to me such a restful and unalterable conviction that **baptism was much more than I**

had dreamed, much more than the rite of initiation into the Christian Church, much more than the sign and seal of a hereditary conviction on the part of parents to their children. . . . **The baptism of the Holy Spirit from that time had a new significance. And indeed, there was but one baptism, for the water and the Spirit were each but part of a greater whole.**"[1]

Note: This is just an excerpt from Simpson's testimony. The full-length book appendix will include Simpson's valuable full testimony, which few have read.

PART B:

SIMPSON'S "DOUBLE BAPTISM" OF WATER AND SPIRIT
IN CHURCH HISTORY

This was a new revelation to Simpson, but the concept of a double baptism of water and Spirit was not unknown in church history. Here is a brief summary. The full-length theological book will share more details.

- *Ambrose*: "The sacrament of baptism is *not complete until one is baptized in the Spirit.*" (Compare with Simpson: "The outward baptism was but a steppingstone to the higher baptism of the Holy Ghost, and they were all expected to enter into both, as though *neither was complete without the other*").

- *Philoxenus of Mabbug* (440-523), Syrian tradition, in John 3:5, "born of the Spirit" is *2nd baptism* (after water baptism) and 3rd birth (after natural birth and new birth)[2]

- *Joseph Hazzaya* (b. 710-713)—baptism in the Spirit as a *2nd baptism* and a 3rd birth.

- *Anglican Archbishop Jeremy Taylor* (17th century)—In John 3:5, born of water = water baptism; born of the Spirit = baptism in the Holy Spirit (Lk 3:16). "Born of water and of Spirit" is a *"double baptism,"* explaining, "We must pass through water and fire, before we enter into rest; that is, we must first be baptized with water, and then with the Holy Ghost."[3] One wonders if Simpson may have borrowed the term "double baptism" from Taylor.

APPENDIX 6: THE ALLIANCE AND HISTORIC VIEWS ON SPIRIT BAPTISM

Varying views on the baptism in the Spirit abound throughout church history. The early church fathers almost always believed in an experience of the Spirit subsequent to conversion, though closely tied to conversion. Some later Catholics made it a part of baptismal regeneration, while others retained a distinction, usually identifying it with confirmation; some considered it sanctifying. Often, it became institutionalized and ritualized, not necessarily experiential.

With the Reformation, as a carry-over from Catholicism, it was often viewed as received at conversion, but various movements began to continue or restore belief of a real subsequent experience. Post-Reformation revivals retained the language of baptism in the Spirit, or other terms such as sealing, anointing, charism, witness of the Spirit, assurance. By the 19th century, the terminology of a subsequent baptism in the Spirit became common once again in various theological traditions. Part A below identifies the major beliefs and groupings. Part B provides a sampling throughout church history of belief in a subsequent sanctifying experience.

PART A:

MAJOR BELIEFS AND GROUPS ON SPIRIT BAPTISM

I. Empowerment/Baptism in the Spirit Occurs at Conversion

Category 1: Baptismal Regeneration: Some Roman Catholics; Some Lutherans; Oneness Pentecostals (c. 1914ff. (Jesus Only, non-Trinitarian); Church of Christ/some Baptists

Category 2: Non-baptismal Regeneration: Reformed/Baptistic (Calvin, Presbyterian, some Baptist, and Anabaptist groups); New Keswick (1950s and following) (John Stott—1964); Third Wave (1980s and following) (C. Peter Wagner, Wayne Grudem, John Wimber)

II. Empowerment/Baptism in the Spirit Occurs Subsequent to Conversion

Category 1: Subsequent Empowerment Experience, Not Sanctification

- **Some Roman Catholics**
- **Puritan/Reformed Sealers** (18th-20th century)— Spirit baptism is subsequent sealing/ witness of the Spirit for power, not sanctification (Martyn Lloyd-Jones, John Owen, Thomas Goodwin, George Whitefield, Charles Hodge, John Flavel, Jonathan Edwards).
- **Higher Life/Empowerment** (19th-early 20th century)— empowerment for service, evidence is power (Moody, Torrey, Finney)
- **Baptistic/Finished Work Pentecostals**—subsequent Spirit baptism evidenced by tongues, not sanctification, which is a finished work in Christ at salvation. (Assemblies of God, Open Bible, Foursquare, Pentecostal Assemblies, Elim Pentecostal)
- **Charismatic** (1950s ff)—subsequent Spirit baptism may be accompanied by tongues and/or other gifts, but not

necessarily evidenced by tongues, though tongues may follow later. Sanctification does not play a part but may follow.

Category 2: Subsequent Crisis of Sanctification, But Separate Pentecostal Spirit Baptism

- **2nd Work or 3-Stage Wesleyan Pentecostals** (1906ff)—crisis experience of sanctification subsequent to salvation (like Wesleyans); baptism in the Spirit evidenced by tongues follows sanctification (Pentecostal Holiness, Fire Baptized Holiness, Church of God—Cleveland, Tennessee, Church of God in Christ, Charles Parham, William Seymour—early belief) (sometimes called a fivefold gospel of Christ as Savior, Sanctifier, Baptizer, Healer, and Coming King).

Category 3: Subsequent Sanctifying Empowerment Experience

- **Sanctifying Experience Through Laying on Hands/Rite of Confirmation** (3rd century ff)— Spirit baptism received through laying on of hands, which became known as confirmation--a sanctifying experience, defined in various ways (early church fathers, early Catholic church, Orthodox church, Anglican, Jeremy Taylor, some Puritans, Quakers, some Reformed Covenanters, some early Baptists, some Mennonites; some like Bernard of Clairvaux called it the "second operation" of the Spirit).
- **Wesleyan 2nd Work of Grace/Second Blessing** (18th-19th century ff)—crisis experience of sanctification subsequent to conversion, purifying the heart and eradicating the old man, possibility of living in heart purity of perfect love. (Wesley--witness of the Spirit; John Fletcher and Phoebe Palmer—baptism in the Spirit). (Church of Nazarene, Church of God —Anderson, Indiana, Wesleyan, Free Methodist)
- **Old Keswick** (late 19th-early 20th century)—subsequent crisis

of sanctification, suppressing old man, maintaining a victorious life (not sinless perfection). Reformed Holiness Revivalist response to Wesleyan belief in eradication (Oswald Chambers, C.T. Studd, Columbia International Seminary, Bill Bright—Campus Crusade)

- **Higher Life/Empowerment-Sanctification** (late 19th-20th century)—sanctifying subsequent Spirit baptism (not Wesleyan eradication or Keswick suppression, but transformation of old man by Christ within)—both a crisis and a progressive experience, may be multiple fillings or fuller baptisms. Tongues may be an evidence, but not *the* evidence. Primary evidence is power and a changed life, the fruit of the Spirit. (*A.B. Simpson, Christian and Missionary Alliance, A.W. Tozer;* Some other Higher Life groups; William Seymour (is closer to this view 1914ff); Richard Lovelace, professor of Church History, Gordon-Conwell Seminary)

Note: it is in this last category that A.B. Simpson and the C&MA are listed.

PART B:

SANCTIFYING SPIRIT BAPTISM THROUGHOUT CHURCH HISTORY

A post-conversion experience of sanctification in some way is found in many theological backgrounds throughout church history. A sampling of quotes follows from: Cyprian (3rd century); Augustine (4th century); Macarius (4th century); Philoxenus of Mabbug (6th century); Synod of Reims (c 624); Madame Jeanne Guyon (1648-1717); John Bunyan; Robert Barclay (Quaker theologian); Moravians & Count Nikolaus Zinzendorf; William Guthrie (Scottish theologian); Charles Simeon (Cambridge Anglican scholar); Puritan Jonathan Edwards; Baptists Charles Spurgeon and Oswald Chambers; Andrew Murray (Dutch Reformed). For more on this see the endnote below.[1]

APPENDIX 7: DECLINE AND RECOVERY OF C&MA SPIRIT BAPTISM EMPHASIS

GRADUAL ABANDONMENT OF "BAPTISM IN THE SPIRIT" LANGUAGE.

Simpson cautioned in 1909: "Loose views about sanctification, the baptism of the Holy Spirit ... are out of place."[1] Dr. Arnold Cook warned: "The failure of one generation to communicate effectively its faith to its children results in loss of personal experience with the living God."[2] Over time, historical drift did lead to loose views about the terminology and meaning of Spirit baptism in The Alliance.

Historical Drift From "Full Gospel" to "Gospel."

During the 1930s there were several signs that attitudes began to change. Ernest Wilson, who began his ministry in the C&MA in 1938, wrote a doctoral dissertation entitled *Modifications of Objectives in the Christian and Missionary Alliance*. He concluded through his research, "There has been to some degree a decline of emphasis in the CMA, upon the work of the Holy Spirit."[3] Wilson also cited indication of "historical drift" to indicate that one time the C&MA has been closer, not so much in its beliefs, as in its practices, to the Pentecostal camp.[4] He documented the trend "away from the strong emphasis (in its infancy) on the '*Full-gospel*,' to a concept more popular (in many evangelical circles) called simply *the 'Gospel.'*[5] Alliance publications did continue to use the term "full gospel" occasionally into the 1950s, but then seem to have abandoned the terminology altogether. As one old Alliance leader told me, "The Alliance got dignity."

Another doctoral dissertation involved an extensive academic study by Nguyen Vinh Duy of the Evangelical Church of Vietnam (South), Vietnam (The C&MA in Vietnam). He has documented significant drift by "reinterpreting" and resultant abandonment of vital teachings of the Simpson's Alliance and the Fourfold Gospel, especially regarding healing, sanctification, the baptism/filling of the Spirit, and the Higher Christian Life.

> The officially distinctive mark of the Evangelical Church of Vietnam (ECVN) is the Fourfold Gospel emblem. It is inherited from A.B. Simpson, the founder of the Christian and Missionary Alliance (C&MA), through the teaching of C&MA missionaries in Vietnam. However, ECVN adapted some of the teachings and reinterpreted the symbols in the Vietnamese context. The reason is that the assimilation of the Fourfold Gospel to the ECVN's theology has been selective through a fundamentalistic perspective and a serious uneasiness about Pentecostalism, and hence, it has become disconnected from its original theological foundation.[6]

1950s—Distancing from Pentecostalism and Baptism in the Spirit

Dr. Harry Turner, President of the Alliance 1954-1960, started in the Alliance, then became a Pentecostal missionary to South America. Coming back to Canada, he pastored in the Pentecostal Assemblies of Canada, but became disillusioned and returned to the Alliance.[7] Eventually, he became an instructor, dean, and Vice President at St. Paul Bible Institute. Trying to distance the Alliance from the Pentecostal excesses, he began to teach that he believed the baptism in the Spirit occurs at conversion with the sanctifying filling occurring subsequent to conversion, although he was not dogmatic about it.[8]

Although a variety of terminology had been used all along, the baptism in the Spirit terminology was curtailed significantly when he became president of the Alliance. Ironically, with the second consecutive tongues-speaking president, this began a shifting of terminology in the C&MA away from Simpson's language of the "baptism of the Holy Spirit" to a more Reformed/Baptistic view. Although the terms "baptism of the Spirit" and "filling of the Spirit" continued to be used synonymously in *The Alliance Weekly* during Tozer's editorship in the 1950s, the term "baptism in the Spirit" often came into disuse.

1960s—Influence of Anglican John Stott and the New Keswick.

The drift was further evident during the time when the official C&MA doctrinal statement was proposed and debated in the early 1960s. A vocal group within the Alliance wanted to do away with the idea of the filling of the Spirit as a crisis or subsequent experience, but eventually the language of crisis and subsequence was maintained. I remember as a teenager in the C&MA in the 1960s the questions of baptism and filling and subsequence being discussed rather hazily.

In the mid-1960s, John Stott, a popular Anglican priest and theologian, spoke at the Keswick conventions, teaching the new Keswick position that the baptism in the Spirit occurs at conversion, especially addressing Pentecostal belief in a subsequent baptism in the Spirit. These addresses were adapted for publication in his book *The Baptism and Filling of the Spirit*. Although Stott was very influential in The Alliance because of his Keswick connections, his teaching contradicted the views of Simpson and early Alliance theology on the baptism in the Spirit. Stott taught a non-Alliance hermeneutic that we should get doctrine from didactic Scripture, not historical Scripture, whereas the Alliance hermeneutic taught from Scripture that *all* Scripture was useful for doctrine (*didaskalia*) (2 Tim 3:16), not just the didactic parts.[9]

Further, he ignored belief in the subsequent baptism in the Spirit taught throughout church history, including by fellow Anglican Jeremy Taylor centuries earlier. A survey of Alliance ministers in the 1970s showed that a third of Alliance ministers had been influenced by Stott's book. So, because of a de-emphasis on theology in The Alliance and historical drift, non-Alliance theology was slowly infiltrating through

Baptistic, Anglican, and Reformed influences, combined with reaction against Pentecostalism.

1970s—"The Alliance Does Not Teach the Baptism in the Spirit Like It Once Did."

So stated one of my first mentors, Rev. Roland Gray, Sr., a retired pastor evangelist who started his ministry in the Alliance in the 1920s and preached on the baptism in the Spirit."[10] In the very first Alliance church where I pastored, Mabel Memmott, an Alliance pastor's widow, told me the exact same thing a decade later: "the Alliance doesn't teach the baptism in the Spirit like it used to." She and another older woman in the church, whose daughter and son-in-law were career missionaries with the C&MA, told me that I was "the most Alliance pastor the church had had in years" because I was teaching the baptism in the Spirit and other old Alliance doctrines.

1979—Reinforcement by a Nyack Professor.

This historical drift became evident through articles in the *Alliance Witness* in 1979 by Nyack professor Dr. Eldon Woodcock. In the first article he presents three views of the baptism in the Spirit: 1) "The baptism of the Holy Spirit occurs when one is baptized with water. . . . This is the Roman Catholic view." 2) "The baptism of the Holy Spirit occurs when a person receives Jesus Christ as his Lord and Savior." 3) "The baptism of the Holy Spirit is a second work of God upon the Christian that occurs after his new birth. It involves an enduement of power for life and service, the bestowing of spiritual gifts and their uses in ministry. It must be earnestly sought. It is accompanied by the initial physical sign of speaking in tongues. This is the standard Pentecostal view."[11]

In his next article he presents his case for #2.[12] However, he either does not know or fails to acknowledge a fourth view—the historic Alliance view—that the third view, minus the belief in tongues as the initial evidence, was the view of A.B. Simpson and the early Alliance, and many other evangelicals who were not Pentecostal (like Dwight Moody, Charles Finney, Oswald Chambers, R.A. Torrey, etc.). Nor does he acknowledge or present the exegetical evidence for this classic Alliance view (which I will share in Appendix 8). Thus, here we have an Alliance professor who actually omits the classic Alliance view and gives no consideration to it at all, either intentionally or out of ignorance of the historic Alliance position. Nor does Woodcock even consider that there are scholarly arguments against his position.

Ironically, the prior summer when I met together with C&MA Vice President Keith Bailey for two hours, he stated that the baptism in the Spirit as the subsequent empowering of the Spirit was Alliance belief. Woodcock's view was actually in conflict with the view of the C&MA Vice President, Simpson, and historic Alliance teaching. Dr. Bailey became one of my mentors through the years.

In an article in the 1999 *Alliance Academic Review* two decades after his *Alliance Witness* articles, Woodcock does finally acknowledge the view of Simpson and early Alliance leaders, as other Alliance leaders likely apprised him of the historic Alliance position. However, he regarded it as "some looseness in the handling of pneumatological terminology in early Alliance literature," averring with some hubris, "my handling of these terms is more precise."[13] While Woodcock may present fuller technical exegesis to support his view, and thus may in some ways appear more precise, on the other hand, other scholarship against his view provides just as precise scholarly handling of the terms agreeing with Simpson's view. I include some of that in Appendix 8 below. The full theological book will engage this more fully and technically.

THE EFFECTS OF ABANDONING BAPTISM IN THE SPIRIT LANGUAGE

Muddying Biblical Support for a Subsequent Sanctifying Crisis Experience of the Spirit.

Many years ago, I was engaged in conversation with a Vice President of the Alliance and a member of the Board of Directors about this problem. They acknowledged that without the use of the "baptism in the Spirit" Scriptures, it is more difficult to provide clear biblical exegesis to support a sanctifying crisis of the Spirit subsequent to conversion. One of the key points connecting the baptism in the Spirit with sanctification was the phrase "and fire" followed by the sweeping away and burning of chaff (Lk 3:16-17). This was a key Scripture viewed by Simpson and early Alliance leaders as the sanctifying or purifying dimension of the baptism in the Spirit. When this language and metaphor was abandoned, Alliance leaders had to resort to and depend upon less clear and less direct Scriptures on the crisis of sanctification.

Historical Amnesia, Resulting in Historical Drift from the Classic Alliance Interpretation.

After a period of ministry outside The Alliance, I desired to return to The Alliance and met with the District Licensing and Ordaining Council where I was living at the time. While they were satisfied with my answers regarding spiritual gifts, some of the Council members questioned my use of the term "baptism in the Spirit." When I gave my scriptural rationale based on what I had learned years earlier in the C&MA, I was surprised when they responded, "We have not heard this interpretation before." Several years later I encountered a district superintendent who also was unaware of the classic Alliance teaching. We have not only experienced historical drift, but also amnesia about who we are and were and what we believe/believed. This generation of leaders does not know our theology and history.

Missing the Meaning and Appropriation of Pentecost Due to Overaction to Pentecostalism.

John R. Rice, not Alliance and known for his fundamentalism, nonetheless did not compromise his belief in the baptism in the Spirit, writing, "Bible teachers retreating before the tongues movement have explained away Pentecost and missed its blessed meaning."[14] Ironically, he wrote this just about the time some Alliance leaders were abandoning the terminology. Rice further writes: "The term 'baptized in the Holy Ghost' is now in reproach.... The term has been seriously abused and misused," alluding to fanaticism and identifying the term solely with tongues.

Decline in Revivals

John R. Rice goes on to assert that the result of the teaching that all Christians have been baptized in the Spirit "has been a decline in revivals. . . . a generation of Christians with little emphasis on the Holy Spirit."[15] Alliance prayer evangelist Armin Gesswein contends even more fervently:

> Wherever dispensationalism gets in, it kills the deep spirit of prayer and revival. . . . But how bracing in this day of need to know that we are still in the dispensation of the Holy Spirit just as in the Acts, and that God can baptize and fill believers with His Spirit, set churches on fire, and through them bring sinner to repentance and to Christ.[16]

Loss of Personally Experiencing the Baptism in the Spirit

Decades earlier, F.F. Bosworth, writing for the Alliance Publishing House, had asserted very similarly:

> I believe that the greatest blow the Devil ever gave the Church was when he got the ministers to teaching that all men are baptized with the Holy Spirit at the time of regeneration—or that receiving Christ is synonymous with receiving His successor, the Holy Spirit. The tragic absence of clear Scriptural teaching on this point has robbed millions of Christian of a joyful attractive, useful, and victorious Christian life. . . . It has been the defeat of thousands of churches. . . . It has robbed thousands of Christians of the supernatural gifts of the Holy Spirit and has kept them from finding their place in the body of Christ.[17]

This is what Dr. Arnold Cook warned of in his book *Historical Drift*: "The failure of one generation to communicate effectively its faith to its children results in loss of personal experience with the living God."[18]

Signs of Recovery and Resurgence 1990s-Present

- *Reemphasis on the baptism in the Spirit.* In more recent years, Dr. Keith Bailey (who had become an informal mentor to me through the years), Dr. Ron Walborn, Dr. Rob Reimer, Dr. David Hearn, Dr. David Chotka, Dr. Kelvin Walker, Dr. David Schroeder, myself, and others have tried to correct this drift by emphasizing the baptism in the Spirit when speaking at Alliance conferences and through our writings.[19]

- *Greater openness to moderate charismatic speakers:* U.S. General Councils in recent decades have featured charismatic leaders like Jack Hayford, John Guest, Jim Cymbala, and Samuel Rodriguez, who are balanced and more like the historic Alliance.

- *A more positive statement on spiritual gifts:* "Expectation Without Agenda." Replacing the old motto, "Seek not, forbid not," which was more negative and often misunderstood and interpreted as stifling the gifts, rather than balancing the gifts.

- *Rekindling the Flame Gatherings.* Brad Bush, Jon Graf, Paul King, Dr. Gary Benedict The Rekindle the Flame Gathering was first held in West Lafayette, Indiana, at Maple Ridge Community Church, May 23-26, 2006, seeking to revive the revival heritage of the early C&MA. Led by Pastor Brad Bush and supported by U.S. C&MA president Dr. Gary Benedict, yearly gatherings were held through 2012, until Brad Bush got sick and passed away in 2015. Dr. Paul King endeavors to continue this vision through conferences and writings.

- *Colleges of Prayer*—led by Dr. Fred Hartley and Dr. Michael Plunkett

- *Redigging the Wells of the Supernatural in the Alliance, 2009-2012*—Dr. Bill Randall, Tim Kayser, and Risen King Community Church, Redding, California

- *Higher Life/Alliance Heritage Renewal Network*—the ministry, books, seminars, and conferences of Dr. Paul King to reemphasize the Alliance Higher Life Heritage, Holy Spirit renewal, healing, discernment, spiritual warfare, and elder-deacon training.

- *Alliance Theological Seminary Holy Spirit conferences* —conducted by Dr. Ron Walborn, Dr. Martin Sanders, Dr. Rob Reimer, Dr. Chuck Davis
- *Soul Care conferences* by Dr. Rob Reimer—focusing on the Holy Spirit and sanctification through inner healing and deliverance.
- *Dr. John Stumbo—Seek Conferences*—on being an Acts 1:8 family
- *Canadian Holy Spirit renewal ministries*—led by Canadian Alliance president Dr. David Hearn, Dr. David Chotka, and others.
- *Others?*—please let me know!

APPENDIX 8: EXEGETICAL BASIS OF THE CLASSIC ALLIANCE VIEW OF SUBSEQUENCE AND THE BAPTISM IN THE SPIRIT

The classic Alliance view of a subsequent baptism in the Spirit has been challenged by some more recent teaching among some Alliance pastors and professors who link Paul's phrase "baptized by one Spirit" to John the Baptist's prophecy of being "baptized with the Holy Spirit and fire." This has been influenced primarily by 1) aversion to Pentecostal linking of tongues to the baptism in the Spirit, 2) Reformed/Baptistic belief on this issue infiltrating the Alliance; 3) the new Keswick influence promoted by John Stott.

In the spirit of being interdenominational and providing a measure of 3rd tier liberty, the Alliance allowed for and respected other terminology for this subsequent experience of the Spirit, However, the classic Alliance position has been that the baptism in/with/of the Spirit is subsequent to conversion. Simpson warned against compromising this position:

- 1909: "Loose views about sanctification, the baptism of the Holy Spirit . . . are out of place on such a platform." [1]

- 1913: "the doctrine of a second work of grace, a spiritual crisis after conversion followed by entire consecration and the baptism of the Holy Spirit, is also becoming obsolete even in evangelical religious circles."[2]

Thus, we must not forget our foundation and our roots. To be honest, The Alliance has not been very good at providing a strong scholarly exegetical defense for its classic position, and in some cases has just given in to opposing views. A comprehensive exegetical study supporting the historic Simpsonian and Alliance terminology of baptism in the Spirit is beyond the scope of this book, but this Appendix addresses some of the typical assertions against this classic Alliance view, providing evidence of valid exegetical support. These will be addressed more fully in the full theological book on Alliance theology. I am also writing a book devoted to the historical-biblical exegetical basis for a post-conversion baptism in the Spirit, tentatively to be titled *Spirit Immersion*. A brief summary appears below.

Exegetical Evidence #1: A Post-Conversion Experience of the Spirit Is Not a Novel, Recent Interpretation.

Contrary to those such as John MacArthur, John Stott, James Dunn who claim this is just a recent charismatic or holiness belief, those who deny a "second blessing" claim it is only a recent doctrine are not aware of the teaching and practice throughout church history, and especially in the earlier church fathers and the Puritans. They also fail to acknowledge or accept the biblical exegetical basis for subsequence presented throughout church history. I presented a paper at an academic conference presenting significant evidence of this interpretation of subsequence from the earliest church fathers and throughout church history, entitled "Historical-Theological Survey of Holy Spirit Empowerment Language, Experience, and Accompanying Phenomena Subsequent to Conversion Prior to the 20th Century."[3] This is a foundation for the book on *Spirit Immersion*.

Exegetical Evidence #2: Holy Spirit Indwelling (Infusion) Precedes Holy Spirit Outpouring (Effusion) (John 20:22; 7:37-39).

Effusion logically follows infusion. There must be an indwelling of the Holy Spirit within before there can be an outpouring of the Holy Spirit from within. John 7:37-39 distinguishes between drinking of the Spirit within (indwelling), known throughout church history as "infusion," and the subsequent rivers of living water flowing out from within (outpouring), known throughout church history as "effusion."

C&MA Greek scholar T.J. McCrossan clarifies that the baptism with the Spirit is an "upon" baptism, not within: "The baptism with the Spirit is always the Spirit 'coming upon' (epi), 'descending upon' (epi), 'poured out upon' (epi), or 'falling upon' (epi), and never, never, never the Spirit coming into (eis) us."[4] The baptism in the Spirit is never expressed as infusion or indwelling, but rather as effusion, pouring out.

The distinction between infusion and effusion has been maintained throughout church history. For instance, Jonathan Edwards, Puritan John Howe, John and Charles Wesley, Isaac Watts, A.W. Tozer, and many others used the term "effusion of the Spirit" to express a subsequent outpouring of the Holy Spirit. An old hymn of Isaac Watts entitled "Effusion of the Spirit" expresses this understanding of the outpouring of the Holy Spirit on Pentecost.

Exegetical Evidence #3: Ontological Reception of the Spirit Within (Indwelling—John 20:22) Is Distinguished from Functional Reception of the Spirit in Power (Empowering —Acts 1:4, 5, 8).

Both John (20:22) and Luke (Acts 1:8ff) use the phrase "receive the Spirit," but mean two different things by the phrase. Luke's pneumatology (doctrine of the Holy Spirit) is functional, receiving the Spirit for the purpose of power (Lk 24:49; Acts 1:8), whereas John's pneumatology in John 20:22 is ontological, the essence of being, that is, receiving the Spirit within—the indwelling of the Spirit. This means that Luke's "receiving the Spirit" does not mean "receiving the Spirit within," but rather "receiving the Spirit in power." Luke and John had different theological agendas, guided by the Holy Spirit.

Biblical languages scholar Howard Ervin demonstrates that John uses the term "receive the Spirit" ontologically of the Spirit's indwelling, whereas Luke uses the phrase functionally of receiving the Spirit in power.[5] Alliance leader Armin Gesswein recognized this half a century earlier, remarking, "they were 'endued with Power from on high,' or 'baptized' with the Holy Spirit. In other words, an experience subsequent to conversion is clearly spoken of. . . . This baptism (Acts 1:5) seems to be a functional rather than a regenerative baptism. Regeneration is not spoken of."[6]

Exegetical Evidence #4: The Book of Acts Is Theological as Well as Historical.

Contrary to John Stott, Wayne Grudem, James Dunn, and others who claim that we cannot derive theology from history, as stated in Chapter Alliance hermeneutics asserts that we can. Other recent scholars have refuted these claims and demonstrated that Luke is a theologian in his own right. Luke presents his theology in his recording of history. Luke gave no such indication in his two-volume Luke-Acts that one was to be excluded from the other or interpreted differently than the other.

As stated in Chapter 2, the Alliance hermeneutic affirms that _all_ scripture is useful for doctrine (*didaskalia*) and practice (2 Tim 3:16), thus believing that we can get doctrine from didactic Scripture (Epistles) and historical Scripture (Acts). Alliance scholar Dr. Bob Willoughby affirms the Alliance position:

> Crucial in arriving at one's understanding of the meaning and significance of Acts 2 for today's believers, is one's hermeneutical methodology. Is Acts 2 only holy-history or does it possess didactic qualities? Does one adopt the position that we look at the book of Acts for history only, relegating doctrine to the epistolary literature of the New Testament. That is basically the position taken, for example, by John Stott. Luke is the historian; Paul is the theologian. Thus, the book of Acts, so descriptive of the "charismatic" power of the Spirit is to be stripped of any permanent doctrinal significance.[7]

Exegetical Evidence #5: The Biblical-Historical Evidence: Most of the Biblical Accounts of Receiving the Spirit Are Post-Conversion Events.

Demonstrating that it is hermeneutically valid to glean Luke's theology within his history of the early church in the books of Acts, we can examine the biblical accounts of "receiving the Spirit" in the book of Acts. James Dunn has tried to demonstrate that all accounts of Spirit reception in Acts were conversions, casting doubt on the genuineness of conversions where reception of the Spirit appears subsequent (especially the Samaritans in Acts 8, Saul in Acts 9, and the Ephesians in Acts 19). Though he is a respected New Testament scholar, other scholars have found his presuppositional hermeneutics and exegesis strained and unconvincing.

One of the principles of hermeneutics is if the plain sense makes sense, there is no other sense. The plain sense of these passages, as affirmed by the church fathers and throughout church history is that the Samaritans, Saul, and the Ephesians were really saved, and their reception of the Spirit was subsequent to conversion. Others will acknowledge this, but then try to explain them as anomalies, not the norm. Again, the plain sense of what Luke writes in Acts is that there are not norms for Holy Spirit reception, only flexible patterns. After through study, early Alliance theologian George Pardington concluded:

> Three facts would seem to be clear: First, conversion, baptism, and the reception of the gift of the Holy Ghost are three separate and distinct things; second, these three things, while separate and distinct, are yet closely related both as doctrines and as experiences; and third, these three things are here stated in their normal order and Scriptural relationship. A careful examination of the book of Acts leads to two conclusions, namely: First, in some instances the Holy Ghost was received at the time of conversion; and second, in other instances the Holy Ghost was received subsequent to conversion.[8]

Here is an overview of the biblical passages regarding a post-conversion reception of the Holy Spirit in power:

- The disciples received the Holy Spirit *within* on Resurrection evening (John 20:22) but the baptism in the Spirit 50 days *after* they were indwelt by the Spirit (Acts 1:4-5, 8; 2:4).

- Those converted on Pentecost are promised to receive the Holy Spirit (Acts 2:38), but Luke does not record that they received the Spirit at that time. However, at a later time *all* were filled with the Spirit in a distinct experience (Acts 4:31).

- The Samaritan believers received the Spirit *after* their conversion through the laying on of hands (Acts 8:15-17).

- Paul was filled with the Spirit through the laying on of hands and healed three days *after* his conversion (Acts 9:17-18).

- The Ephesian believers received the Spirit *after* their conversion through the laying on of hands (Acts 19:1-6).

Only in Acts 10 does it appear that the Holy Spirit was received in power at about the same time as conversion. It would appear that the general biblical pattern is subsequence, but the Holy Spirit cannot be pinned down to a rigid norm.[9]

Exegetical Evidence #6: Use of Aorist Tense to Designate Describe Post-Conversion Events.

Simpson and other Alliance and holiness leaders point to the exegetical basis of such crisis events of the Spirit by documenting the use of the aorist tense, indicating a punctiliar (at a point in time) event in Scripture.[10] Such Scriptures include Romans 12:1-2; Acts 10:44-47; Acts 15:8- 9; 2 Corinthians 6:14-7:1, and several other Scriptures for the decisive experience of the sanctifying baptism in the Spirit, which Simpson considered a transfusion of the life of God within.[11]

Exegetical Evidence #7: Simultaneous Does Not Mean Synonymous.

Ordo salutis, meaning order of salvation, applied here, means the logical and theological order of conversion and the baptism in the Spirit. The two events are not synonymous even if sometimes almost simultaneous, as in Acts 10:44-47. Like Exegetical Evidence #2, there is a logical order that takes place. The two events are not synonymous even if sometimes almost simultaneous. Simpson explains:

> The difference is one in the nature of things rather than in the order of time. The early Christians were expected to pass quickly into the baptism of the Holy Spirit and the fulness of their life in Christ.[12]

> We are willing . . . to concede that the baptism of the Holy Spirit may be received at the very same time a soul is converted. We have known a sinner to be converted, sanctified, and saved all within a single hour, and yet each experience was different in its nature and was received in proper order and by a definite faith for that particular blessing, and this involves the crisis: a full surrender and an explicit preparation of the promise of God by faith.[13]

Simpson makes the point that the baptism in the Spirit involves the distinct crisis of realizing we cannot live the Christian life in our own efforts, but we need to surrender, take hold of His power, not ours, and receive by faith. Though rare, it could happen in the same hour of conversion. Yet it is an act of surrender distinct from the moment of conversion.

Exegetical Evidence #8: The Terms "Baptism" in 1 Corinthians 12:13 and Luke 3:16 Are Not Exegetically Synonymous.

This is highly debated among scholars, but the weight of the evidence by contextual and syntactical exegesis, translators, and commentators is against those who claim they are the same.

The classic Alliance hermeneutic regarding this verse is that the baptism in the Spirit (Lk 3:16) is not the same as baptism by the Spirit into one body (1 Cor 12:13). Baptism by one Spirit into one body is conversion; baptism by Jesus in the Holy Spirit is subsequent to conversion:

> The passage in 1 Cor. 12:13 is best understood as referring, not to the second crisis of the Christian life, the baptism or filling with the Holy Spirit, but rather to the operation of the Holy Spirit by which men and women are baptized into Christ when they first believe on Him, that is, spiritually joined to Christ, being born again by the Spirit. This understanding of the passage leaves no conflict with the other obvious New Testament teaching concerning the necessity of a crisis experience after conversion.—*Dr. J. Hudson Ballard, Ph.D., C&MA Board of Managers*[14]

> We come now to the distinction between the Baptism "by" and "with" the Spirit. . . . 1 Cor. 12:13: 'For by one Spirit we were all baptized into one body.'. . . This is not the Baptism "with" the Spirit; it is clearly the Baptism "by" the Spirit. . . . turn to Matt. 3:11 . . . "He shall baptize you with the Holy Spirit and with fire." Here we have the Baptism not "by" but "with" the Spirit. —*Oswald J. Smith, C&MA pastor*[15]

The Holy Spirit is the instrument or agent by which we are baptized into the body of Christ. It is the Holy Spirit who renews us (Tit 3:5) and bears witness that we are children of God and adopting us into the family of God (Rom 8:16), which is the body of Christ. This is closely related to but distinct from both baptism in water and baptism in the Holy Spirit. Baptism in the Spirit is by Jesus; baptism in the Body of Christ is by the Holy Spirit. A full discussion of this is too extensive for this Appendix but will be included in the full theological book and the book on *Spirit Immersion*. Please contact me if you are interested in seeing this before I can publish the full books.

Exegetical Evidence #9: Scholars Speak of Multi-Dimensional Uses of the Term "Baptism."

- *Dr. Larry Hart, a Southern Baptist professor,* advocates a "multi-dimensional" approach, meaning that "Spirit baptism" can mean different things and describe a variety of experiences, from conversion to Spirit-baptism.[16] Rather than rigidly meaning one thing or the other, it is a kind of both-and approach. This is not dissimilar to the three-in-one baptism that I propose below.
- *Alliance professor/missionary Dr. Randy Harrison* wrote his doctoral dissertation on "baptism in the Spirit" language, concluding that the term can express many experiences of the Spirit. This has been distilled into his book *Overwhelmed by the Spirit.*[17]
- *Welsh Reformed Martyn Lloyd-Jones:* "there are many particular different usages with regard to this word 'baptism,' and the statement in 1 Corinthians 12:13 is but one of them."[18]
- *Princeton theologian Charles Hodge:* "Any communication of the Holy Spirit is called a baptism, ... whether in his regenerating, sanctifying, or inspiring influences, are said to be baptized."[19]
- *Dr. Craig Keener,* Professor of Biblical Studies, Asbury Seminary: "Whichever view we take concerning the chronology of Spirit baptism (some readers, with us, may opt for both), all believers need to know what the Spirit means in practical terms for our relationship with Christ."[20]
- *Reformed Baptist Dr. John Piper* writes of multiple baptisms: "It is right, I think, to ask for a fresh baptism.... I say, "O God, I need a fresh baptism. I need a fresh anointing. I need a fresh filling. I need a fresh outpouring of the Holy Spirit."

I would add to John Piper's words, "That's the language of A.B. Simpson!"

HARMONIZING VARYING VIEWS ON SPIRIT BAPTISM
TRINITY OF BAPTISMS—A PACKAGE DEAL

A solution to the wide divergence of views which has made the best logical, theological, and exegetical sense to me involves integrating insights from Alliance leaders A.B. Simpson, George Pardington, Dr. Randy Harrison, Dr. David Schroeder with early church fathers and other leaders throughout the centuries, especially Ambrose, Basil, Cyprian, Cyril, John of Damascus, Anglican Archbishop Jeremy Taylor, John R. Rice, John Piper, and Dr. Dallas Willard.

Three-fold Conversion-Initiation Package.

Many church fathers viewed the baptism in the Spirit distinct from conversion and water baptism as part of a "3-fold Conversion-Initiation Package." of conversion, water baptism, and baptism in the Spirit.[21] So three different baptisms are mentioned in Scripture. Dr. David Schroeder, former president of Nyack College, shared with me the concept from Dr. Dallas Willard of Matthew 28:19 as being "immersed in Trinitarian Reality." I had previously discovered this concept in the church fathers expressed as a three-fold package deal—a 3-in-1 baptism. This has made the most sense of harmonizing diverse views.

Harmonizing One Baptism with Plural Doctrine of Baptisms.

Ephesians 4:5 speaks of one baptism, yet Hebrews 6:2 speaks of the "doctrine of baptisms" in the plural, creating an apparent contradiction in Scripture. Many explanations are given, but the one that makes the most sense and harmonizes is a trinity of baptisms--a triune (3-in-1) baptism—just as the Trinity of the Godhead. Church fathers Basil and John of Damascus refer to this as "three immersions in one baptism." As God is a Trinity, He loves to give hints of His triune nature throughout Scripture and life. One of these is in a three-fold or triune baptism, closely interconnected but distinct: baptism by the Spirit into the Body of Christ (1 Cor 12:13); baptism by a believer into water (Acts 2:38); and baptism by Jesus in the Holy Spirit and fire (Lk 3:16-17).

TRIUNE 3-IN-1 BAPTISM

3 immersions in 1 baptism (Basil, John of Damascus)
Born again-Born of water-Born of the Spirit[22]

Triune 3-in-1 Baptism			
(3 immersions in 1 baptism—Basil, John of Damascus)			
Baptism *by* (the agent of)	Acts 2:38	John 3:3, 5 3 births	Mt 28:19 Baptism in name of:
the Holy Spirit into the Body of Christ (1 Cor 12:13)	Repent	Born again from above	the Father
a believer in water (Acts 8:36-38)	Be baptized in Jesus' name	Born of water	the Son
Jesus in the Holy Spirit & fire (Mt 3:11; Lk 3:16; Acts 1:5)	Receive gift of Holy Spirit	Born of the Spirit	the Holy Spirit

John R. Rice summarizes it this way:

> In these three types of baptism there were three agents who did the baptizing: (a) John baptized converts *in water*. (b) Jesus baptized the disciples *in the Holy Spirit* at Pentecost. (c) The Holy Spirit baptized the Christians at Corinth *into the body of Christ*. In these three kinds of baptism there were three agents who did the baptizing. In (a), John the Baptist did the baptizing. In (b), Jesus did the baptizing. In (c), it is the Holy Spirit Himself who acts as the agent to take the newborn child of God and put him into the body of Christ.[23]

Note: I am writing a book on this, tentatively to be titled: *Spirit Immersion: A Historical- Exegetical Study of the Biblical Basis for a Post-Conversion "Baptism in the Spirit."*

RESOURCES ON THE C&MA DOCTRINE OF CHRIST OUR SANCTIFIER

Note: This is not a complete listing of relevant sources.

- Gilbertson, Richard. *The Baptism of the Holy Spirit: The Views of A. B. Simpson and His Contemporaries.*
- Gordon, A. J. *The Ministry of the Spirit.*
- Harrison, Randall. *Overwhelmed by the Spirit.*
- McCrossan, T. J. *Speaking with Other Tongues: Sign or Gift —Which?*
- McCrossan, T. J. *Christ's Paralyzed Church X-Rayed.*
- McGraw, Gerald. *Empowered: Dynamics of Holy Living.*
- McGraw, Gerald. *Launch Out: A Theology of Dynamic Sanctification.*
- King, Paul L. *Nuggets of Genuine Gold: Simpson, Tozer, Jaffray, and Other Alliance Leaders on the Spirit-Empowered Life.*
- Nienkirchen, Charles. *A. B. Simpson and the Pentecostal Movement.*
- Pardington, George P. *Crisis of the Deeper Life.*
- Smith, Oswald J. *The Baptism with the Holy Spirit.*
- Stoesz, Samuel. *Sanctification: An Alliance Distinctive.*
- Tozer, A. W. *How to Be Filled with the Spirit.*
- Van de Walle, Bernie. "How High of a Christian Life? A. B. Simpson and the Classic Doctrine of Theosis."

RESOURCES ON ALLIANCE REVIVALS AND BAPTISM IN THE SPIRIT TESTIMONIES

- Bosworth, F. F. *How to Have a Revival.*
- Edman, V. Raymond. *They Found the Secret.*
- Hartley, Fred. *Holy Spirit, Fill Me!*
- Harvey, Richard. *70 Years of Miracles.*
- King, Paul L. *Anointed Women: The Rich Heritage of Women in Ministry in the Christian and Missionary Alliance*

- King, Paul L. *Genuine Gold: The Cautiously Charismatic Story of the Early Christian and Missionary Alliance*
- Reimer, Rob. *River Dwellers.*
- Schroeder, David. *Walking in Your Anointing.*
- Steinkamp, Orrel. *The Holy Spirit in Vietnam.*

BOOKS COMPARING/CONTRASTING VIEWS OF SPIRIT BAPTISM AND SANCTIFICATION

Several books have been written comparing and contrasting various views of Spirit baptism and sanctification. These include the following:

- Alexander, Donald L., ed. *Christian Spirituality: Five Views of Sanctification.*
- Brand, Chad Owen, ed. *Perspectives on Spirit Baptism: Five Views.*
- Lederle, Henry I. *Treasures New and Old: Interpretations of "Spirit-Baptism" in the Charismatic Renewal Movement.*
- Gundry, Stanley N., ed. *Five Views on Sanctification.*

While these are excellence resources for comparing various views, significantly, none of these have discussed or engaged the unique views of Simpson and The Alliance. For The Alliance perspective, you need to go to Alliance sources above.

OTHER GOOD NON-ALLIANCE SOURCES ON SANCTIFICATION AND THE BAPTISM IN THE SPIRIT

- Lawson, James. *Deeper Experiences of Famous Christians.*
- Lloyd-Jones, Martyn. *Joy Unspeakable.*
- Lloyd-Jones, Martyn. *The Baptism and Gifts of the Spirit.*
- Murray, Andrew. *Absolute Surrender.*
- Nee, Watchman. *The Normal Christian Life.*
- Torrey, R.A. *The Holy Spirit: Who He Is and What He Does.*
- Rice, John R. *The Power of Pentecost.*

NOTES

Introduction: Why This Book?

1. Arnold L. Cook, *Historical Drift* (Camp Hill, PA: Christian Publications, 2000), 10.
2. Nguyen Vinh Duy, "A. B. Simpson's Fourfold Gospel in the Evangelical Church of Vietnam: A Study of Selective Theological Assimilation," *Asia Journal of Theology,* October, vol. 35 (2): 171-195; Ernest Wilson, *The Christian and Missionary Alliance: Development and Modifications of Its Original Objectives.* Ph.D. Dissertation, New York University, 1984, 157.
3. Such as some of the word-of-faith like teachings and practices that they eventually modified. See Paul L. King, *Only Believe: Examining the Origin and Development of Classic and Contemporary Faith Theologies* (Tulsa, OK: Word and Spirit Press, 2008). Bernie Van De Walle explores some questionable Christology: See Bernie A. Van De Walle, "Holy Heresy? A. B. Simpson, Sanctification, and Appolinarianism," https://www.academia.edu/27009848/HOLY_HERESY_A._B._SIMPSON_SANCTIFICATION_AND_APPOLINARIANISM. Also, Simpson, Andrew Murray, and others taught that the Holy Spirit did not indwell believers until they are baptized in the Spirit. Few people believe that anymore, although I have heard one district superintendent teach this. On the other hand, some critiques of Simpson are way beyond the pale, such as those of B. B. Warfield, *Counterfeit Miracles*, and David R. Elliott, "A. B. Simpson: A Troubled Mystic." Accessed at https://csph.ca/assets/1998-elliot.pdf.
4. Cook, *Historical Drift*, 5.
5. Scott Russell Borderud, "The Doctrine of Sanctification of The Christian and Missionary Alliance as Represented in Its Statement of Faith of 1964-1965." Doctor of Theology Thesis, University of South Africa, Pretoria, South Africa, November 1992. http://online.ambrose.edu/alliancestudies/ahtreadings/ahtr_s2.html
6. Such as the books by Dr. Samuel Stoetz, Dr. Gerald McGraw, and Dr. Ric Gilbertson on sanctification and the baptism in the Spirit, or on healing by Dr. Keith Bailey, Dr. Drake Travis, Richard Sipley, and myself.
7. Daryn Henry, *A. B. Simpson and the Making of Modern Evangelicalism*: Volume 2 (McGill-Queen's Studies in the History of Religion) (Montreal & Kingston, London, Chicago: McGill-Queen's University Press, 2019), vii. Kindle Edition.
8. Bernie Van de Walle, *The Heart of the Gospel: A. B. Simpson, the Fourfold Gospel, and Late Nineteenth Century Evangelical Theology* (Eugene, OR: Pickwick Publications, 2009).
9. For instance, the foundation of evangelical Lutheran biblical exegesis and exposition is contained in the *Apology of the Augsburg Confession*: "All Scripture ought to be distributed into these two principal topics, the Law, and the promises. For in some places, it presents the Law, and in others the promise concerning Christ,

namely, either when [in the Old Testament] it promises that Christ will come, and offers, for His sake, the remission of sins justification, and life eternal, or when, in the Gospel [in the New Testament], Christ Himself, since He has appeared, promises the remission of sins, justification, and life eternal." *Apology of the Augsburg Confession* (Article 4) (1531).

10. This is what happened in the 1990s with the egalitarian-complementarian (E-C, for short) issue. Both had been co-existing (but not in the popular contemporary secular universalistic sense) in the Alliance for 90 years (see my book *Anointed Women: The Rich Heritage of Women in Ministry in the Christian and Missionary Alliance* (Tulsa, OK: Word & Spirit Press, 2007). I am not sure which side had started the pushing, but the issue rose up in the 1990s, probably in response to the The Council on Biblical Manhood and Womanhood (CBMW), which was formed and issued what is known as the Danvers Statement in 1987.

11. A. B. Simpson, Editorial, *Living Truths (LT)*, July 1902, 1.

12. Simpson, *LT*, July 1902, 1.

13. Simpson, *LT*, July 1902, 1.

14. Simpson, *LT*, July 1902, 2.

15. A. B. Simpson, "Side Issues and Essentials," *CMAW*, Jan 1, 1910, 119-120.

16. Walter C. Kaiser, Jr., and Moises Silva, *An Introduction to Biblical Hermeneutics* (Grand Rapids: Zondervan, 1994), 286.

17. William Sanford LaSor, "The *Sensus Plenior* and Biblical Interpretation," *A Guide to Contemporary Hermeneutics*, Donald K. McKim, ed. (Grand Rapids: Eerdmans, 1986), 58.

18. See Simpson's typology of the tabernacle, divine emblems, typology of the journey of Israel to the Promised Land, Song of Solomon, his typology in interpreting the Parable of the Ten Virgins and the Oil to support a partial rapture theory of the tribulation, etc.

19. A. B. Simpson, *Christ in the Bible (CITB)* (Camp Hill, PA: Christian Publications, 1993), 1:143-148.

20. Simpson, *CITB*, 1:195.

21. Simpson, *CITB*, 4:19, 39.

22. A. B. Simpson, Editorial, *The Christian Alliance & Missionary Weekly (CAMW)*, Oct 31, 1890, 257-258.

1. The Biblical and Historical Basis for the Allliance Hermeneutic

1. The term "ecumenical" in the days of the early Alliance did not have the negative connotations often associated today with watering down the Gospel. The C&MA, in its early days being a non-denominational/inter-denominational para-church organization, was itself considered by Simpson and others to be "ecumenical."

2. In the C&MA, we have used the term "inclusive membership" as a way of including regular adherents or attendees who are not formal members. "Inclusivism" another term that has sometimes been used in Alliance circles to describe

including beliefs from various backgrounds in the Alliance fold, but it has also sometimes been used to refer to a form of universalism, which is not what the Alliance intends or believes.

3. Cited in "The Work at Home," *CAMW*, Dec 30, 1892, 428; David J. Fant, "A Code of Honor," *Alliance Weekly (AW)*, May 20, 1933, 318; Armin R. Gesswein, "The Spirit-Filled Christian, IV," *AW*, Mar 20, 1943, 183.

4. Simpson wrote, "There is nothing that so rends the body of Christ and destroys all unity in Christian life as religious controversy, especially about non-essential matters. . . . There is room for an infinite variety of opinion of minor points, but there is no need to flaunt our opinions in the face of our brethren and provoke them to criticism and controversy. Things which if allowed to rest would never be serious difficulties, when agitated, grow into an exaggerated importance, and Christian love becomes suspended on a lot of side issues, and separated from its true centre. There are, it is true, great essential principles that we cannot compromise, respecting the person and work of Christ, the simplicity of the great salvation, the fullness of redemption, and the future life, but the platform is broad enough to hold the great body of evangelical Christians, and bridge over the hundred little differences that need never have been publicly emphasized. . . . This principle, then, of respecting the conscience of our brethren in things non-essential, is the true secret of toleration and Christian unity." A. B. Simpson, "Consecration, in Relation to Our Duty to the Weak and Errlng," *CAMW*, July 6, 1894, 4, 5. Simpson's entire article was a sermon exposition of Romans 14-15 devoted to liberty and tolerance.

5. "Queries," *CMAW*, June 9, 1900, 385. Simpson's statement here was regarding a doctrinal question as to whether a woman could anoint a sick person for healing.

6. See Stanley J. Rodes, *From Faith to Faith: John Wesley's Covenant Theology and the Way of Salvation* (Eugene, OR: Pickwick Publications, 2013). On the covenanter roots of Anabaptists, see https://gameo.org/index.php?title=Covenant_Theology.

7. "The Work at Home," *CAMW*, Dec 30, 1892, 428.trt.

8. "Is the Christian Alliance an Evangelical Body?" *CAMW*, Apr 29, 1892, 274. Simpson's biographer, A. E. Thompson, gave a date of 1893 for this statement. A. E. Thompson, *A. B. Simpson: His Life and Work* (Camp Hill, PA: Christian Publications, 1960), 129-130. I am not sure if he just missed the year or if there was an additional statement the next year.

9. Richard Gilbertson, *The Baptism of the Holy Spirit* (Camp Hill, PA: Christian Publications, 1993), 54, 285; reaffirmed in the C&MA Board of Managers Minutes, Sept 20-23, 1922.

10. George M. Marsden, *Fundamentalism and American Culture* (New York/Oxford, England: Oxford University Press, 1980), 117, 262. The Presbyterian General Assembly listed the authenticity of the miracles as the fifth point, while millennarians listed the premillennial Second Coming of Christ. The "Fundamentals Essays" followed as a series of 64 expositions from 1910 to 1915, by a variety of leaders expanding upon the intended meaning of these five fundamentals of the faith. R.A. Torrey, ed., *The Fundamentals* (Grand Rapids: Kregel, 1958, 1990).

11. George P. Pardington, *Outline Studies in Christian Doctrine* (Harrisburg: Christian Publications, 1926), 74.

12. C. Allyn Russell, *Voices of American Fundamentalism* (Philadelphia: Westminster Press, 1976), 98.

13. C&MA Board of Managers Minutes, Sept 20-23, 1922.

14. "The Alliance accepts without question the great Fundamentals, specifically as follows: The Verbal Inspiration of the Scriptures. The Trinity of the Godhead. The Deity of our Lord Jesus Christ. The Personality of the Holy Ghost. The Sanctifying Baptism of the Holy Ghost. The Universal Depravity of the Human Race. The Atonement by the Blood of Christ. The Salvation of the Lost by Grace. The Healing of the Body. The Resurrection of the Dead. The Eternity of Punishments and Rewards. The Reality and Personality of Satan. The Pre-millennial Coming of the Lord." W. M. Turnbull and C. H. Chrisman, "The Message of the Christian and Missionary Alliance," on the *Alliance Studies* website at https://online.ambrose.edu/alliancestudies/.

15. Robert Niklaus, cited by Borderud, 8.

16. Prudencio Damboriena, *Tongues As of Fire* (Washington, DC, and Cleveland, OH: Corpus Books), 43.

17. Borderud, "Creeds and the Statement of Faith," excerpted from his Doctor of Theology thesis at the University of South Africa, 1992.

18. Borderud, "Creeds and the Statement of Faith."

2. Alliance Hermeneutical Principles

1. Cook, *Historical Drift*, 61.

2. Bob Willoughby, "Pentecost: An Experience for Today: An Examination of the Baptism of the Holy Spirit in Acts." See John R.W. Stott, *The Baptism and Fullness of the Spirit* (Downers Grove: IVP, 1964), 8-9. Stott claims we should get our doctrine from the teachings of Jesus and the teaching epistles, but not the book of Acts. However, Luke gave no such indication in his two-volume Luke-Acts that one was to be excluded from the other or interpreted differently than the other.

3. A. B. Simpson, Editorial, *CMAW*, Oct 23, 1909, 56.

4. Editorial, *AW*, Oct 31, 1914, 65.

5. John A. MacMillan, "Harmonized Diversity," *AW*, Oct 17, 1942, 658.

6. A. J. Gordon, "The Ministry of Women," *AW*, Dec 15, 1928, 820-821.

3. The Three-Tier Alliance Hermeneutic

1. Similar 3 or 4 tier divisions can be found in other denominations as well. For Baptists, see John S. Hammett, *Biblical Foundations for Baptist Churches: A Contemporary Ecclesiology* (Grand Rapids: Kregel), 177, distinguishing 1st order (essentials for all Christians), 2nd order (defining beliefs for a denomination—like water baptism, Lord's Supper, type of church government) and 3rd order doctrines (beliefs in millennium, rapture, differing views on election and associated issues, etc.). My friend and colleague, David Smith, adds a fourth tier—personal preferences or opinions. While I like David's fourth category, for simplicity's sake, I have

maintained the 3-tier division, which is clear in Alliance documents. I have written a rough, but fuller exposition of Alliance history demonstrating this 3-tier model through quotes from A. B. Simpson and other Alliance leaders.

2. John MacMillan: "Where there is a Christocentric attitude, differences of doctrine and variations in forms of worship are recognized as non-essentials of faith." "Harmonized Diversity," 658.

3. "Great essential principles that we cannot compromise."—A. B. Simpson, "Consecration, in Relation to Our Duty to the Weak and Errlng," *CAMW*, July 6, 1894, 4, 5. "fundamental doctrines"—Pardington, *Outline Studies*, 74. See also C&MA Board of Managers Minutes, Sept 20-23, 1922; Turnbull and Chrisman, "The Message of the C&MA." "Majors . . . positions of key importance vitally necessary to the whole structure."—A. W. Tozer, "A Word in Season," *AW*, May 6, 1944, 231.

4. Simpson wrote an extensive article biblically refuting the carnality of Christ heresy. A. B. Simpson, Editorial, *CAMW*, Jan 13, 1893, 13ff.

5. A. B. Simpson, Editorial, *CMAW*, Mar 31, 1906, 185. This continued to be maintained: "The Alliance has a distinct testimony and message. . . . Primarily our message is Jesus Christ, a living reality and all-sufficient Saviour. In keeping with this it is a message calling to a deeper life, a life of separation, consecration, intercession, and holy service. It is a message of supernatural power, available through our risen Lord for every believing soul. And it is a message of hope in the prospect of His personal return." "Alliance Work in the Home Field," *CMAW*, Feb 3, 1908, 68.

6. A. B. Simpson, *Present Truths or the Supernatural* (Harrisburg: Christian Publications, reprint 1967), 66-67.

7. "Alliance Work in the Home Field," 68.

8. Simpson, *LT*, July 1902, 1.

9. Simpson was firm that the sanctifying filling of the Spirit was not a 3rd tier optional belief for the C&MA: "The great body of Christians united in this movement believe most firmly a definite experience of personal sanctification distinct from the experience of conversion. . . . such a filling with the Holy Ghost consequent upon the full surrender of our will and all our powers as lifts us out of our natural self into the life and power of Christ and makes our whole experience distinctly supernatural and divine. We should deeply deplore any drift from this high and established standard." Editorial, *AW*, Oct 31, 1914, 65. Yet 3rd tier liberty: "It can hardly be expected that all the teachers of sanctification could agree about phases and phrases. But it surely can be an understanding that all antagonisms will be avoided, and that those who hold extreme views . . . will avoid attacking those who differ." Simpson, Editorial, *CMAW*, Mar 31, 1906, 185.

10. Italics mine. Editorial, *The Word, The Work, & The World (WWW)*, Aug/Sept 1887, 111.

11. Simpson, "Consecration," *CAMW*, July 6, 1894, 5. Ulysses Lewis, "Sustentation Fund," *CMAW*, May 21, 1910, 132; *CMAW*, June 9, 1900, 385; "Conference for Prayer and Counsel Regarding Uniformity in the Testimony and Teaching of the Alliance"; Simpson, Editorial, *CMAW*, Mar 31, 1906, 185; A. B. Simpson, "How to Build Up the Alliance," *CAMW*, May 4, 1894, 272.

12. Simpson, "Consecration," *CAMW*, July 6, 1894, 4, 5 (a sermon exposition of Romans 14) devoted to liberty and tolerance. See also A. B. Simpson, Editorial, *AW*, Sept 1,

1906, 129; "The Gospel in Timothy: The Church," *CMAW*, Mar 7, 1908, 385; *CMAW*, June 9, 1900, 385; Simpson, "Side Issues and Essentials," 218; Editorials, *CAMW*, June 26, 1896, 612; "Old Testament Outlines & Outlooks: Genesis, the Book of Beginnings," *AW*, July 29, 1912, 245; "Queries," *CAMW*, Sept 7, 1894, 235; A. B. Simpson, "Some Dangers in Connection with Premillennial Truth," *CMAW*, Jan 14, 1905, 20; A. B. Simpson, "The Soul That Jesus Sought and Found at Jacob's Well," *CMAW*, Nov 26, 1898, 486; Simpson, Editorial, *CMAW*, Mar 31, 1906, 185; Tozer, "A Word in Season," 231.

4. Trinitarian Essentials

1. George P. Pardington, *Outline Studies in Christian Doctrine* (Harrisburg, PA: Christian Publications, 1926), 74.
2. Italics mine. Simpson, "Old Testament Outlines," 245. See also *CITB*, 1:12.
3. Pardington, *Outline Studies*, 100.
4. Jon Tal Murphee, *Divine Paradoxes: A Finite View of an Infinite God* (Camp Hill, PA: Christian Publications, 1998).

5. Christological Essentials

1. Simpson, *CITB*, 5:472.
2. Simpson, *CITB*, 2:223.
3. James Orr, "The Virgin Birth of Christ," *The Fundamentals* (Grand Rapids: Kregel, 1958, 1990), 270.
4. Pardington, *Outline Studies*, 252-285.
5. Pardington, *Outline Studies*, 256.
6. Franklin Johnson, "The Atonement," *The Fundamentals* (Grand Rapids: Kregel, 1958, 1990), 377-385.
7. Simpson wrote an extensive article biblically refuting the carnality of Christ heresy. A. B. Simpson, Editorial, *CAMW*, Jan 13, 1893, 13ff.

6. Holy Spirit Essentials

1. R. A. Torrey, "The Personality and Deity of the Holy Spirit," *The Fundamentals*, 311-315. Compare Pardington, *Outline Studies*, 292.
2. The 1928 C&MA Doctrinal Statement reads as follows: "The Holy Spirit is a Divine Person, the Executive of the Godhead, the Comforter sent by the Lord Jesus Christ to indwell, to guide, and to teach the believer, and to convince the world of sin, of righteousness, and of judgment."
3. Pardington, *Outline Studies*, 293-294.

7. Scripture Essentials (Bibliology)

1. The World Christian Fundamentals Doctrinal Statement reads as follows: "We believe in the Scriptures of the Old and New Testaments as verbally inspired of God, and inerrant in the original writings, and that they are of supreme and final authority in faith and life." *God Hath Spoken: Twenty-five Addresses Delivered at the World Conference on Christian Fundamentals May 25-June 1, 1919* (New York & London: Garland Publishing Co., 1988), 11.

    The 1928 C&MA Doctrinal Statement reads: "The Scriptures of the Old and New Testaments are the inspired Word of God. They contain a complete revelation of His will for the salvation of men and constitute the Divine and only rule of Christian faith and practice."

2. Keith M. Bailey, *Bringing Back the King* (Harrisburg: Christian Publications, 1985), 65.

3. Simpson, *Present Truths*, 24.

4. Although Simpson did not include the word "inerrant" in his statement, it is clear from many other statements from Simpson and other Alliance leaders that inerrancy of the original autographs was intended.

5. H. Wayne House, *Charts of Christian Theology and Doctrine* (Grand Rapids: Zondervan, 1992), 24.

6. Dockery's nine categories include:

    1. **Mechanical Dictation:** *God dictated every word of the Bible.* This view ignores style differences between various authors as well as differing historical and cultural contexts. Proponent: John R. Rice

    2. **Absolute Inerrancy:** *The Bible is true and accurate in all matters.* This view uses the plenary-verbal concept of inspiration, attempting to separate itself from the dictation view while assuring that the Bible is the written word of God. It does not take seriously the human aspect, or the historical contexts, in trying to harmonize the apparent differences and difficulties in Scripture. Proponent: Harold Lindsell

    3. **Critical Inerrancy:** *The Bible is completely true in all that the Scripture affirms, to the degree of precision intended by the original author.* This view does not seek to harmonize every detail. Scientific matters are considered to be treated with phenomenological language rather than technical and scientific thinking. This view allows the cautious use of critical methodologies in interpretation. It takes seriously both the human and divine elements. Proponents: Roger Nicole, J. Ramsey Michaels, D. A. Carson, John Woodbridge

    4. **Limited Inerrancy:** *The Bible is inerrant in all matters of salvation and ethics, faith, and practice, and matters which can be empirically validated.* It is inerrant only in matters for which the Bible was given. This view seeks to be empirical, *i.e.*, guided by observation alone without using science or theory. Some call this view "simple biblicism." Proponent: Howard Marshall

    5. **Qualified Inerrancy:** *The Bible is taken - upon faith - to be inerrant in all matters of salvation and ethics, faith, and practice, and matters which can be empirically validated.* This is the same as the previous statement, except for the faith element. It

attempts to take seriously the human and divine elements. This view is difficult to define. Proponent: Donald G. Bloesch

6. **Nuanced Inerrancy:** *The Bible's inerrancy varies with its types of literature: narrative, poetry, stories, or proverbs.* Some passages require dictation in inspiration, while others, as in poetry, stories, or proverbs, may require only dynamic inspiration. This view takes seriously the human and divine elements. Proponent: Clark Pinnock

7. **Functional Inerrancy:** The Bible is inerrant in its purpose or function. It is inerrant in its power to bring people to salvation and growth in Christian life. Proponents: G. C. Berkouwer, Jack Rogers, Donald McKim

8. **Inerrancy is Irrelevant:** *Inerrancy is neither affirmed nor denied.* The doctrine of inerrancy is pointless, irrelevant, and concerned only with theological minutiæ. Proponent: David A. Hubbard (Fuller Seminary)

9. **Biblical Authority:** *The Bible is authoritative only to point one to an encounter with God.* This view does not take seriously the divine element in the words of the Bible. It freely admits human errors and finds them of no consequence. Proponent: William Countryman.

7. Pardington, *Outline Studies,* 48.

8. A. T. Pierson, *World's Guide to Understanding the Bible* (AMG Publisher, 1994), xii.

9. David H. Moore, "God's Self-Disclosure Inerrantly Recorded," *Alliance Witness,* June 9, 1971, 9-10.

10. T. J. McCrossan, "The Bible: Its Christ and Modernism—What the Bible Claims for Itself," *AW,* Nov 27, 1925, 748.

11. Moore, "God's Self-Disclosure Inerrantly Recorded," 9-10.

12. Arthur P. Johnston, "Making Our Witness Effective," *Alliance Witness,* Feb 17, 1971, 3.

13. Bailey, *Bringing Back the King,* 65-66.

14. As a few examples, see F. B. Meyer, "The Many-sidedness of the Lord Jesus," *AW,* July 20, 1898, 55; A. B. Simpson, "Old Testament Outlines and Outlook," *AW,* Aug 24, 1912, 325.

15. *The Fundamentals—A Testimony to the Truth,* edited by R. A. Torrey, A. C. Dixon and Others, Volumes 2, 9, 10, 27.

"the record for whose inspiration we contend is the original record — the autographs or parchments of Moses, David, Daniel, Matthew, Paul or Peter, as the case may be, and not any particular translation or translations of them whatever."—p. 9

"Some would . . . would argue speciously that to insist on the inerrancy of a parchment no living being has ever seen is an academic question merely, and without value. But do they not fail to see that the character and perfection of the Godhead are involved in that inerrancy?"—p. 9

"does not our concordance, every time we take it up, speak loudly to us of a once inerrant parchment? Why do we not possess concordances for the very words of other books? Nor is that original parchment so remote a thing as some suppose. Do not the number and variety of manuscripts and versions extant render it comparatively easy to arrive at a knowledge of its text. . . . We are not pursuing a phantom in contending for an inspired autograph of the Bible."—p. 10

"those who assert the inerrancy of the scripture autographs do so on the authority of God Himself."—p. 27

16. *The Fundamentals,* 1:179, 201, 217; 2:9, 10, 27; 4:224ff.

17. T. W. Fawthrop, "The Critics Confounded," *AW,* Mar 26, 1938, 197; Simpson, *CITB,* 1:1-3, 295; *CITB,* 3:100; James M. Gray, "Bulwarks of the Faith: What Is the Higher Criticism?," *CMAW,* Mar 1, 1899, 109.

18. As a few examples, see Meyer, "The Many-sidedness of the Lord Jesus," 55; Simpson, "Old Testament Outlines and Outlook," 325. Pardington wrote on the unity of Isaiah against "Deutero-Isaiah" because of Jesus' words. Pardington, *Outline Studies,* 46; See also T. W. Fawthrop, "A Second Isaiah?", 699; "With the New Books," *AW,* Jan 11, 1961, 8; "With the New Books," *Alliance Witness,* May 13, 1970, 14; "With the New Books," *Alliance Witness,* Aug 30, 1972, 14.

19. Moore, "God's Self-Disclosure Inerrantly Recorded," 9-10.

20. H. Robert Cowles, Editorial Voice," *Alliance Witness,* Nov 10, 1982, 30.

21. Andre Bustanoby, "Jots and Tittles: A Case for Inerrancy," *Alliance Witness,* Feb 15, 1967, 6.

22. Moore, "God's Self-Disclosure Inerrantly Recorded," 9-10.

23. Moore, "God's Self-Disclosure," 9-10.

24. Pardington, *Outline Studies,* 45-46.

25. *The Fundamentals,* 2:37. See also Methodist L. W. Munhall, writing for *The Fundamentals,* commented on 2 Timothy 3:16, "The word rendered Scripture in the passage is *graphe.* It means writing, anything written. The writing is composed of words. What else is this but verbal inspiration; and they wrest the 'Scriptures unto their own destruction,' who teach otherwise." L. W. Munhall, *The Fundamentals,* 160. The Fundamentals wrote of verbal inspiration:

    The Scripture cannot be broken —*ou dunatai luthenai.* The verb signifies to loose, unbind, dissolve, and as applied to Scripture means to subvert or deprive of authority. The authority of Scripture is then so complete — so pervasive — as to extend to its individual terms. . . . One may, of course, allege that the Lord's statement of inerrancy implies only that the principal words of Scripture must be taken precisely as they are, but that He does not claim the like authority for all its words. . . . In face of Christ's utterances, it devolves on those who hold that inspiration extends to the thought of Scripture only, but not to the words, or to the leading words but not to the words in general, to adduce very cogent arguments in support of their position. The *onus probandi,* it seems to us, is here made to rest on them." *The Fundamentals,* 1:179.

26. Pardington, *Outline Studies,* 45-46. See also pp. 48, 49. Pardington based his comments on his exegesis of 2 Timothy 3:16 and 2 Peter 1:21, and then quoting other authors discussing proper and improper interpretation of the syntax of the passages. Pardington wrote a fuller exposition of this in the *Alliance Weekly* in 1905. See George P. Pardington, "Outline Studies in Christian Doctrine," *AW,* June 24, 1905, 387. "At Home or Abroad," *AW,* Sept 8, 1928, 578. Andre Bustanoby, "Are the Words Important?" *Alliance Witness,* Mar 15, 1967, 5; Bailey, *Bringing Back the King,* 65-66.

27. William D. Mounce, *Word Biblical Commentary: Pastoral Epistles* (Nashville: Thomas Nelson, 2000), 565.

28. Simpson, *CITB,* 6:57.

29. Pardington, *Outline Studies,* 40, 52.

8. Humankind And Salvation Essentials

1. The World Christian Fundamentals Doctrinal Statement reads as follows:

   IV. We believe that man was created in the image of God, that he sinned and thereby incurred not only physical death but also that spiritual death which is separation from God; and that all human beings are born with a sinful nature, and, in the case of those who reach moral responsibility, become sinners in thought, word and deed. . . .

   IX. We believe in the bodily resurrection of the just and the unjust, the everlasting blessedness of the saved, and the everlasting, conscious punishment of the lost. ," *God Hath Spoken: Twenty-five Addresses*, 11-12.

   The 1928 C&MA Doctrinal Statement reads: "Man was originally created in the likeness and image of God: he fell through disobedience, incurring thereby both physical and spiritual death. All men are born with a sinful nature, are separated from the life of God, and can be saved only through the atoning work of the Lord Jesus Christ. The prospect of the impenitent and unbelieving is existence forever in conscious torment, and that of the believer, is to have everlasting joy and bliss."

2. Pardington, *Outline Studies*, 155.
3. Pardington, Outline Studies, 201.
4. Pardington, *Outline Studies*, 205.
5. *God Hath Spoken: Twenty-five Addresses*, 12.
6. The World Christian Fundamentals Doctrinal Statement reads as follows:

   IV. We believe that man was created in the image of God, that he sinned and thereby incurred not only physical death but also that spiritual death which is separation from God; and that all human beings are born with a sinful nature, and, in the case of those who reach moral responsibility, become sinners in thought, word and deed. . . .

   IX. We believe in the bodily resurrection of the just and the unjust, the everlasting blessedness of the saved, and the everlasting, conscious punishment of the lost." *God Hath Spoken: Twenty-five Addresses*, 11-12.

   The 1928 C&MA Doctrinal Statement reads: "Man was originally created in the likeness and image of God: he fell through disobedience, incurring thereby both physical and spiritual death. All men are born with a sinful nature, are separated from the life of God, and can be saved only through the atoning work of the Lord Jesus Christ. The prospect of the impenitent and unbelieving is existence forever in conscious torment, and that of the believer, is to have everlasting joy and bliss."

7. Pardington, *Outline Studies*, 262.
8. Pardington, *Outline Studies*, 206.
9. "It may be conceded that it (*aionios*) does not etymologically necessitate the idea of eternity, and that sometimes it is used in the sense of age-long to express limited duration. It does, however, express the longest possible duration of which the subject to which it is attributed is capable. So that if the soul is immortal, its punishment must be without end. It is used several time to express the life and duration of God Himself: Rom 16:26; 1 Tim 1:17; Heb 9:14; Rev. 1:8. . . . The most eminent Greek scholars have decided and declare that if these words do not teach

the endlessness of the future punishment, to which they are applied, there are no words in the Greek language to express that meaning Pardington, *Outline Studies*, 210-211.

10. Simpson, *CITB*, 5:420.

9. Church Essentials (Ecclesiology)

1. The 1928 C&MA Doctrinal Statement reads: "The Church consists of all those who have believed on the Lord Jesus Christ, are washed in His blood, and have been born again of the Holy Spirit. It has been commissioned by the Lord to go forth into all the world as a witness, preaching the Gospel to all nations. The local church is a body of believers in Christ who are joined together for the worship of God, edification through the Word of God, prayer, fellowship, the proclamation of the gospel, and observance of the ordinances of baptism and the Lord's Supper."
2. John C. Ryle, "The True Church," *The Fundamentals*, 553.
3. Pardington, *Outline Studies*, 346-347.
4. Riley, "The Great Commission," *God Hath Spoken: Twenty-five Addresses*, 436-437.

10. End-Time Essentials (Eschatology)

1. Pardington, *Outline Studies*, 74.
2. Pardington, *Outline Studies*, 360; Simpson, *CITB*, 6:515.
3. Charles R. Erdman, "The Coming of Christ," *The Great Fundamentals*, 4:265-266, 701.
4. Erdman, "The Coming of Christ," 4:265-266, 701.
5. Simpson, *CITB*, 4:517.
6. Simpson, *Present Truths*, 74-78.

11. The Alliance and the Supernatural

1. A. B. Simpson, "Aggressive Christianity," *CMAW*, Sept 23, 1899, 260.
2. Simpson, *Present Truths*, 66-67.
3. A. B. Simpson, "Our Trust," *CMAW*, May 28, 1910, 145.—
4. Simpson, "Aggressive Christianity," 260.
5. J. Hudson Taylor, "The Source of Power," *CMAW*, June 23, 1900, 416.
6. "Alliance Work in the Home Field," 68.
7. A. B. Simpson, Editorial, *AW*, Oct 12, 1907, 21l
8. W. T. MacArthur, "Watching the Father Work," *AW*, July 15, 1916, 244.
9. "Cleveland Convention," *AW*, May 5, 1923, 172.
10. *The Pioneer*, V, No. 19 (May 1934), 24; cited in Louise Green, "Robert Jaffray: Man of Spirit, Man of Power," *His Dominion*, Vol. 16, No. 1 (March 1990), 5.
11. A. W. Tozer, *I Call It Heresy* (Camp Hill, PA: Christian Publications, 1991), 36.
12. A. B. Simpson, Editorial, *CMAW*, July 6, 1907, 313.

13. Simpson, *The Gospel of Healing* (Harrisburg: Christian Publications, 1915), 57.

14. William C. Stevens, "Jesus Our Healer," *CAMW*, Mar 30, 1891, 183.

15. Armin R. Gesswein, "Dispensationalism," *AW*, Mar 1, 1941, 135, 138.

16. A. W. Tozer, *I Talk Back to the Devil* (Camp Hill, PA: Christian Publications, 1990), 143.

17. Simpson, *The Gospel of Healing*, 19-20.

18. A. B. Simpson, *Missionary Messages* (Harrisburg: Christian Publications, n.d.), 29-30.

19. E. O. Jago, "A Great Crisis!," *Latter Rain Evangel*, Oct 1913, 2.

20. W. C. Stevens, "The Cross and Sickness," *The Pentecostal Evangel*, Aug 23, 1924, 6.

21. *The Pioneer*, V, No. 21 (Nov. 1934), 7; cited in Louise Green, "Robert Jaffray: Man of Spirit, Man of Power," 6.

22. Paris W. Reidhead, Jr., "That I May Know Him (Phil. 3:7-15): A Testimony," July 14, 1953, 5, 16.

23. J. Hudson Ballard, "The Spiritual Clinic," *AW*, Nov. 21, 1914, 126.

24. A. B. Simpson, "Members of One Another," *AW*, Dec 8, 1917, 148; "Christian Altruism," *CMAW*, Aug 7, 1909, 322.

25. Ira E. David, "Spiritual Gifts," *AW*, Sept 29, 1928, 638.

26. John A. MacMillan, "Love's Divine Overflow," *AW*, May 18, 1940, 306.

27. R. S. Roseberry, "The Need of Spiritual Gifts," *AW*, Sept 18, 1948, 695.

28. A. W. Tozer, *Tragedy in the Church: The Missing Gifts* (Harrisburg: Christian Publications, 1978), 33, 42.

29. MacArthur, "Watching the Father Work," 244.

30. MacArthur, "Watching the Father Work," 244.

31. A. B. Simpson, Editorial, *LT*, Apr. 1906, 198.

32. Simpson, Editorial, *LT*, Apr. 1906, 198.

33. Thompson, 195.

34. A. B. Simpson, *The Holy Spirit, or Power from on High* (Harrisburg: Christian Publications, n.d. [1894]), 2:123-124.

35. A. W. Tozer, *God Calls the Man Who Cares* (Camp Hill, PA: Christian Publications, 1992), 56.

36. Stevens, "Jesus Our Healer," 183.

37. A. T. Pierson, *The Acts of the Holy Spirit* (Harrisburg: Christian Publications, 1980), 92.

38. A. B. Simpson, Editorial, *CMAW*, July 9, 1910, 240.

39. A.B. Simpson, Editorial, *CMAW*, July 6, 1907, 313.

40. A.B. Simpson, Editorial, *LT*, Apr 1906, 198; A. B. Simpson, "Gifts and Grace," *CMAW*, June 29, 1907, 303.

41. "Why may we not have all the gifts and all the graces of the Apostolic Church blended in one harmonious whole.... Why may we not have all the supernatural ministries of the early Church? ... even the tongues of Pentecost, without making them subjects of controversy, without judging one another harshly, because each may have all the gifts, and all in such beautiful and blended harmony." Simpson, "Christian Altruism," 322; repeated eight years later, before Simpson's death: "Members of One Another," 148.

12. "The Rallying Point"

1. A. B. Simpson, Editorial, *CAMW*, Sept 5, 1890, 130.
2. A. B. Simpson, "The Four-fold Gospel, or the Fullness of Jesus," *AW*, July 28, 1911, 228.
3. Turnbull and Chrisman, "The Message of the Christian and Missionary Alliance," 1927.
4. Franklin Pyles, *The Whole Gospel for the Whole World*, Kindle, Location 629.
5. "The Work at Home," *CAMW*, Feb 2, 1891, 122. Again in 1910, nearly a quarter of a century after the founding of The Alliance, Simpson reaffirmed the need for the Alliance message to remain strong. A. B. Simpson, Editorial, *AW*, Oct 1, 1910, 8.
6. William T. MacArthur, "Sparks from the Anvil: A Peculiar Flavor," *AW*, May 31, 1930, 341
7. A. B. Simpson, "Fourfold Unity, *CAMW*, Nov 6, 1891, 274.
8. Simpson, "How to Build Up the Alliance," 272.
9. Simpson, "Fourfold Unity," 274.
10. Simpson, Editorial, *CMAW*, Mar 31, 1906, 185; "Alliance Work in the Home Field," 68.
11. "The Work at Home," 122.
12. A. B. Simpson, Editorial, *AW*, May 25, 1912, 113.
13. Editorial, *AW*, Oct 31, 1914, 65.
14. "But it surely can be an understanding that all antagonisms will be avoided, and that those who hold extreme views . . . will avoid attacking those who differ." *CMAW*, Mar 31, 1906, 185.
15. David Yonggi Cho was disgraced through a financial scandal in 2014, taking the fall for his son who was the real culprit. Cho was eventually exonerated and is no longer considered disgraced by most of the Christian community in South Korea, nor by the South Korean government.
16. Pyles, *The Whole Gospel for the Whole World,* Kindle Location 514.

13. Foundations of The Fourfold Gospel

1. A. B. Simpson, "Christ Our Surety," *CAMW*, June 5, 1891, 356. Simpson preached an entire message on the covenants of grace and redemption. See also A. B. Simpson, "The Righteousness of God," Mar 30, 1894, 334; A. B. Simpson, "Chosen in Him," *CMAW*, Mar 9, 1898, 222; A. B. Simpson, "God's Finished Work," *CMAW*, Jan 10, 1903, 19; A. B. Simpson, "The Household of the Lord," *CMAW*, Aug 28, 1909, 365; A. B. Simpson, "Wings, or the Transcendent Life," *AW*, Sept 6, 1913, 55; A. B. Simpson, "Wherefore, Remember," *AW*, Dec 16, 1916, 174: A. B. Simpson, "Justification," July 20, 1918, 242: A. B. Simpson, "The Temptation of Jesus," *AW*, Aug 24, 1918, 322; A. B. Simpson, "Our Standing in Christ," *AW*, July 12, 1913, 226; A. B. Simpson, "In His Name," *CAMW*, June 20, 1890, 387-389.
2. George P. Pardington, "The God of Our Fathers," *AW*, Mar 15, 1913, 380; George P. Pardington, "The Last Supper," *CMAW*, Oct 22, 1910, 55; Frederick W. Farr, "The

Cross and the Throne,' *CAMW*, Mar 6, 1891, 151; Frederick W. Farr, "Spiritual Worship," *AW*, July 25, 1932, 404; Edward Payson, "Sinners Pardoned for Christ's Sake," *AW*, Oct 24, 1956.

3. Charles N. Kinney, "A Letter to the M.T.C.," *CMAW*, Nov 21, 1890, 314. A. B. Simpson, "Christ Our Surety," *CAMW*, June 5, 1891, 356; A. B. Simpson, "Christ as Savior and Sanctifier: Be Definite," *CAMW*, July 1, 1892, 8; A. B. Simpson, "The Pulpit: Business Terms as Types of Spiritual Things," June 23, 1893, 391; Kenneth Mackenzie, 'The Scriptural Basis for Divine Healing," *WWW*, Nov 1, 1885, 295.

4. William E. Boardman, *The Higher Christian Life* (Boston: Henry Hoyt; New York: Sheldon & Co., 1858), accessed online at http://online.ambrose.edu/alliancestudies

5. Simpson, "The Four-fold Gospel, or the Fullness of Jesus," 228.

6. Boardman, 48.

7. A. B. Simpson, Editorial, *CAMW*, Oct 31, 1890, 257-258.

8. Simpson, "The Four-fold Gospel, or the Fullness of Jesus," 228.

14. Jesus Christ Our Savior—The Gospel of Full Salvation

1. A. B. Simpson, "The Gospel Its Own Witness," *WWW*, Feb 1, 1887, 66.

2. A. B. Simpson, "Our Trust," *CMAW*, Sept 10, 1910, 385; J. Hudson Taylor, "The Source of Power," *CMAW*, June 23, 1900, 416.

3. William T. MacArthur, "Sparks from the Anvil: A Peculiar Flavor," *AW*, May 31, 1930, 341.

4. Van de Walle, *The Heart of the Gospel*, 37.

5. Arnold Cook, "My Reflections on My Years in the Christian and Missionary Alliance," accessed at https://www.kneillfoster.com/Cook/main.html

6. Franklin Pyles, *The Whole Gospel for the Whole World: Experiencing the Fourfold Gospel Today* (McMaster Ministry Studies Series Book 3), Pickwick Publications, an Imprint of Wipf and Stock Publishers. Kindle Edition.

7. Thompson, 86.

15. Jesus Christ Our Sanctifier

1. The 1928 C&MA Statement of Faith reads: "It is the will of God that each believer should be filled with the Holy Spirit and thus be sanctified wholly, being separated from sin and the world, and fully consecrated to the will of God, thereby receiving power for holy living and effective service. This is recognized as an experience wrought in the life subsequent to conversion."

2. A. B. Simpson, Editorial, *CMAW*, Oct 23, 1909, 56.

3. A. B. Simpson, Editorial, *AW*, Mar 1, 1913, 337.

4. Editorial, *AW*, Oct 31, 1914, 65.

5. Simpson, *The Holy Spirit*, 2:25.

6. Watchman Nee, *The Normal Christian Life* (Ft. Washington, PA: Christian Literature Crusade, 1957, 1963), 137, 176.

7. Simpson, "The Four-fold Gospel, or the Fullness of Jesus," 228. The crisis nature of
    the sanctifying filling of the Spirit is further demonstrated by the use of the aorist
    tense in key passages, indicating action at a point in time. Regarding the Gentile's
    reception of the Spirit in Acts 10:44-47, Peter comments: "God, who knows the
    heart, showed that he accepted them by giving the Holy Spirit to them, just as He
    did to us. He made no distinction between us and them, for he purified their
    hearts by faith" (Acts 15:8-9). "Showed" or "bore witness" (*emarturesen*) is an aorist
    active indicative, signifying an event which occurred at a point in time. "Giving"
    (*dous*) the Holy Spirit, is an aorist active participle. This is evidence for the "witness
    of the Spirit" as a crisis experience identified with the filling or baptism in the
    Spirit subsequent to conversion. Further, "purified" (*katharisas*) is an aorist active
    participle as well, providing further evidence pointing to a crisis experience of
    sanctification. See also A. J. Gordon, *The Ministry of the Spirit* (Minneapolis:
    Bethany Fellowship, 1964), 116; Pardington, *The Crisis of the Deeper Life*, 109; A. B.
    Simpson, "Baptism and the Baptism of the Holy Spirit," accessed at http://on-
    line.ambrose.edu/alliancestudies/ahtreadings/ahtr_s2.html .

    The language of a second life-changing spiritual experience, regardless of
    terminology, appears throughout church history. Several writers, including
    Jonathan Edwards, William Boardman, George Mueller, and others, have
    described this subsequent experience of the Spirit as a "second conversion." Early
    Alliance leaders usually preferred other terms such as: "A definite second blessing,
    distinct in nature, though not necessarily far removed in time, from the experience
    of conversion"—1906 C&MA Board of Managers document; "a second definite
    work of grace—a crisis as radical and revolutionary as the crisis of conversion"—
    Pardington, *The Crisis of the Deeper Life*, 109.

    Many, especially in the contemporary strongly Reformed camp, have chafed at
    the terminology of "second blessing" as a kind of elitism, but it has been used even
    in Reformed revivalist camps. Older writers like Bernard of Clairvaux, John
    Calvin, Charles Spurgeon, and Scottish Covenanter theologian William Guthrie
    called it the "second operation" of the Spirit. The language of a second life-
    changing spiritual experience, regardless of terminology, appears throughout
    church history. If someone doesn't like the term "second blessing," then they can
    call it something else, but it is a valid term in the Alliance. While elitism can be a
    danger, when it is properly understood as the blessing of dying to self and being
    raised in Christ, it humbles us to realize it is not something we have done, but
    something Christ has done in us and through us. The Alliance has been more
    concerned about experiencing it rather than what you call it. See Simpson, *The
    Holy Spirit,* 2:12.

    Although it is popular today to associate the sealing of the Spirit in Ephesians
    1:13-14 with conversion, this was a frequent term through church history given to
    this distinct post-conversion experience of the Spirit, as amply documented by
    Martyn Lloyd-Jones, many among the early church fathers, as well as the Puritans,
    Spurgeon, and others. See Martyn Lloyd-Jones, *God's Ultimate Purpose; Romans: The
    Sons of God.* In the Nicene and Post-Nicene ages, a variety of terms and metaphors
    continued to be used for a an empowering of the Spirit subsequent to conversion.
    Among the most common were "seal" of the Spirit or "the Lord's signature. These

include Athanasius (296/98-373); Gregory Nazianzen (329-390); General Council of Constantinople (381); Eusebius, church historian; Leo the Great (c. 460). For a variety of terminology used in Scripture, see: "receive (John 7:39); endued/clothed with (Lk 24:49); baptized with (Acts 1:5); come upon (Acts 1:8); filled with (Acts 2:4); poured out (Acts 2:16, 17); shed forth (Acts 2:33; 'poured forth'; fell on, (Acts 11:15); given 'even as he did unto us' (Acts 15:8). These nine [in reality eight] terms refer to the same event, the filling (Acts 2:1-4)." "Three R's of the Holy Spirit," *AW*, Feb 8, 1919, 300

8. Simpson, *The Holy Spirit*, 2:24-26.
9. A. B. Simpson, "The Crisis of the Deeper Life," *LT*, Sept 1906, 523.
10. George P. Pardington, *The Crisis of the Deeper Life* (New York: Christian Alliance Publishing Co., 1925), 131-132; accessed at http://www.cmalliance.org/resources/archives/downloads/miscellaneous/the-crisis-of-the-deeper-life.pdf
11. MacArthur, "Sparks from the Anvil—The Sanctifier," 493. For more on this from other early Alliance leaders, see J. Hudson Ballard, a Secretary of the Board of Managers: J. Hudson Ballard, "The Spiritual Clinic," AW, Nov. 11, 1911, 87; and Alliance theologian George Pardington: Pardington, *The Crisis of the Deeper Life*, 62.
12. A. B. Simpson, "The Crisis of the Deeper Life," *LT,* Sept 1906, 523.
13. A. B. Simpson, "The Baptism of the Holy Spirit: A Crisis or an Evolution?," *LT*, Dec 1905, 710.
14. I often refer strongly Reformed people to Martyn Lloyd-Jones' books on the baptism in the Spirit as an excellent source for a subsequent baptism in the Spirit. His view is very similar to the Alliance in some ways; however, he differs from the Alliance belief in that he does not view it as a sanctifying experience like the Alliance, but he views sanctification as resulting from the baptism in the Spirit. His view is more a reaction against Wesleyan and Keswick views of sanctification rather than against Alliance thinking. Another good strongly Reformed source is John Piper.
15. Simpson, *The Holy Spirit*, 2:24-26.
16. A. B. Simpson, "The Baptism of Fire," *AW*, Apr 19, 1919, 52.
17. See William Franklin, C&MA missionary and district superintendent in William Franklin, "Work at Mukti," *The India Alliance*, Feb 1906, 89; W. M. Turnbull and C. H. Chrisman, C&MA Board of Managers, in Turnbull and Chrisman, "The Message of The Christian and Missionary Alliance."
18. W. T. MacArthur, "Sparks from the Anvil—The Sanctifier," *AW*, Aug 2, 1930, 493.
19. Simpson, *CITB*, 6:13, 14. See also A.B. Simpson, *The Land of Promise* (Harrisburg: Christian Publications, reprint 1969), 37; A. B. Simpson, *Wholly Sanctified* (Harrisburg: Christian Publications, 1925), 27.
20. A. B. Simpson, *The Four-Fold Gospel* (Harrisburg; Christian Publications, n.d.), 39-40.
21. Gilbertson, 285; reaffirmed in the C&MA Board of Managers Minutes, Sept 20-23, 1922.
22. Gerald McGraw, *Launch Out: A Theology of Dynamic Sanctification* (Camp Hill, PA: Christian Publications, 2000).
23. Pardington, *The Crisis of the Deeper Life*, 177-178.

24. A. B. Simpson, *A Larger Christian Life* (Camp Hill, PA: Christian Publications, 1988), 42.

25. William C. Stevens, "Divine Healing in Relation to Revivals," *CMAW*, Feb 28, 1903, 124.

26. Simpson, *A Larger Christian Life,* 64.

27. Simpson, "What Is Meant by the Latter Rain?", 38.

28. Technically speaking, the term "baptism *of* the Holy Spirit" is not accurate. The Greek preposition *en* is used, meaning "in" or "with." So it is more accurate to speak of baptism in the Spirit or baptism with the Spirit. Since the word "baptize" means to immerse or overwhelm, "in" usually seems the best unless one would say "flooded with the Holy Spirit," or as Dr. Randy Harrison, Alliance missionary to CoteVoire, concluded in his doctoral dissertation, "overwhelmed with the Spirit."

29. Pardington, *Outline Studies, 325.*

30. F. N. Senft, 1924 annual report, C&MA Archives.

31. "The Message of The Christian and Missionary Alliance," June 25, 1932, 402-403. Excerpted from Turnbull and Chrisman, "The Message of The Christian and Missionary Alliance."

32. H. M. Shuman, "Annual Report of the President," *AW*, July 9, 1927, 452; H. M. Shuman, "Our Work at Home and Abroad," *AW*, July 20, 1929, 461.

33. Armin R. Gesswein, "The Spirit-Filled Christian, IV," *AW*, Mar 20, 1943, 183.

34. Simpson, *Present Truths*, 65, 86.

35. Simpson, *Missionary Messages*, 27.

36. Simpson, *Wholly Sanctified*, 11, 16.

37. Simpson, *Present Truths*, 65, 86; Simpson, *Missionary Messages*, 27; Simpson, *Wholly Sanctified*, 11, 16; Simpson, "Baptism and the Baptism of the Holy Spirit."

38. Simpson, *CMAW*, Oct 23, 1909, 56.

39. A. B. Simpson, Editorial, *AW*, Mar 1, 1913, 337.

16. Jesus Christ Our Healer

1. "Sawin File on A. B. Simpson: His Work," 346.

2. Replacing the words *"are taught in the Scriptures and are privileges..."* with the following: "as taught in the Scriptures are privileges." The sentence thus reads: "Prayer for the sick and anointing with oil as taught in the Scriptures are privileges for the Church in this present age."

3. The 1928 C&MA Doctrinal Statement reads: "Provision is made in the redemption of the Lord Jesus Christ for the healing of the mortal body in accordance with His Word. The anointing with oil, as set forth in the fifth chapter of James, is to be practiced by the Church in this present age."

4. Gilbertson, 286.

5. Simpson, *CITB*, 3:471; see also Simpson, *CITB*, 4:191, 197.

6. T. J. McCrossan, *Bodily Healing and the Atonement* (Youngstown, OH: Clement Humbard, 1930), 18.

7. Cited in McCrossan, *Bodily Healing*, 18; see F. Delitzsch, *Commentary on the Old Testament: Isaiah* (Grand Rapids: Eerdmans, 1973), 315-320.

8. McCrossan, *Bodily Healing*, 25-26.

9. Simpson, *CITB*, 6:359.

10. Simpson, *CITB*, 1:123.

11. Simpson, *CITB*, 4:197.

12. "The exception should never disprove the rule. One is reminded of this at the present time when the counterfeits, parodies and exaggerations of Divine Healing are being so shamefully exposed and making so many people tempted to grow weary of the very words and phrases which have been so much abused. Nevertheless, we believe in Divine Healing, and more than ever we must stand without fear and despite much ridicule for the sane Scriptural and deeply spiritual truth of the supernatural life of Christ for our bodies. The great adversary has tried to bury these long-neglected truths in a volcanic eruption of fire, smoke, and brimstone. But it is just because of the preciousness and value of the truth that the counterfeit has been so adroitly and wisely advertised." A. B. Simpson, Editorial, *CMAW*, May 19, 1906, 297.

13. McCrossan, *Bodily Healing*, 13, 21, 38, 39.

14. MacArthur, *Charismatic Chaos*, 124-125, 268; Hanegraaff, 249-251.

15. Keith Bailey, *Healing: The Children's Bread* (Harrisburg: Christian Publications, 1977), 43-57.

16. Murray, *Divine Healing*, 54ff.; Oswald Chambers, *If Ye Shall Ask*, (United Kingdom: Marshall Morgan & Scott, 1937), accessed on *The Complete Works of Oswald Chambers*, CD-ROM (Grand Rapids: Discovery House, 2000).

17. Murray, *Divine Healing*, 72; see also p. 17; Douglas, 330.

18. Carter, *Faith Healing Reviewed*, 113.

19. Ibid., 59-60.

20. The 1928 C&MA Doctrinal Statement reads: "Provision is made in the redemption of the Lord Jesus Christ for the healing of the mortal body in accordance with His Word. The anointing with oil, as set forth in the fifth chapter of James, is to be practiced by the Church in this present age."

21. A.B. Simpson, "The Casting Out of Devils," *CAMW*, Nov. 13, 1895, 311.

22. W.C. Stevens, "The Recovery of the Sick," 535.

23. William T. MacArthur, *Ethan O. Allen* (Philadelphia: The Parlor Evangelist, c. 1924), 1-14.

24. MacArthur, *Ethan O. Allen*, 11.

25. MacArthur, "A Reminiscence of Rev. A. B. Simpson," 325-326.

26. MacArthur, "The Phenomenon of Supernatural Utterance," 73.

27. V. Raymond Edman, "Questions You Have Asked," *The Alliance Witness*, Sept. 14, 1966, 18.

28. Stevens, "The Recovery of the Sick," 533, 535.

29. A. W. Tozer, *Born After Midnight* (Camp Hill, PA: Christian Publications, 1989), 43.

17. Jesus Christ Our Coming King

1. Italics mine. Editorial, *WWW*, Aug/Sept 1887, III.
2. A. B. Simpson, "Our Mailbox," *CMAW*, June 16, 1900, 403.
3. H. Grattan Guiness, "The Coming of Christ a Stimulus to Missionary Zeal," *CAMW,* Oct 12, 1896, 307.
4. Gilbertson, 286; C&MA Board of Manager Minutes, Sept 20-23, 1922.
5. Simpson, Editorial, *CMAW*, Mar 31, 1906, 185.
6. A. B. Simpson, "Our Coming Lord: Misapprehensions and Misapplications," *CAMW*, Sept 12, 1890, 153.
7. Gordon Fee explains: "But 'plain meaning' has first of all to do with the author's original intent, it has to do with what would have been plain to those to whom the words were originally addressed. It has not to do with how someone from a suburbanized white American culture of the late 20th century reads his own cultural setting back into the text through the frequently distorted prism of the language of the early 17th century." Gordon Fee, *The Disease of the Health and Wealth Gospel* (Cosa Mesa, CA: Word for Today, 1979), 4.
8. A. B. Simpson, "Our Mailbox," *CMAW*, June 16, 1900, 403.
9. "Queries," *CAMW*, Dec 14, 1894, 571.
10. Pardington, *Outline Studies*, 346.
11. Simpson, *CITB*, 6:326-328.
12. Simpson, *CITB*, 6:4.
13. Guiness, 307.
14. William B. Riley, "The Great Divide, or Christ and the Present Crisis," *God Hath Spoken: Twenty-five Addresses*, 39. For a survey of the evidence of premillennialism among the Early Church Fathers, see Paul L. King, "Premillennialism and the Early Church," *Essays on Premillennialism*, ed. K. Neill Foster and David Fessenden (Camp Hill, PA: Christian Publications, 2002).
15. A. B. Simpson, "Earnests of the Coming Age," *AW*, June 23, 1917, 178, 180.
16. A. B. Simpson, "Divine Healing and the Lord's Coming," *AW*, Sept 22, 1917, 386.
17. Simpson, *The Holy Spirit*, 1:204.
18. A. B. Simpson, *The Love Life of the Lord* (Harrisburg: Christian Publication, n.d.), 195.
19. A. B. Simpson, *CITB*, 3:351.
20. A. B. Simpson, *In Heavenly Places* (Harrisburg: Christian Publications, reprint 1968), 114, 116-118, 125.
21. Simpson, "What Is Meant by the Latter Rain?," *CMAW*, Oct 19, 1907, 38.
22. A. B. Simpson, Editorial, *AW*, May 26, 1917, 114.
23. A. B. Simpson, Editorial, *CMAW*, Feb 11, 1905, 81.
24. Simpson, "What Is Meant by the Latter Rain?," 38.
25. Simpson, "What Is Meant by the Latter Rain?," 38, 50.
26. Simpson, "Divine Healing and the Lord's Coming," 386-387.
27. Simpson, "Divine Healing and the Lord's Coming," 387.
28. A. B. Simpson, "Living Under the Powers of the World to Come," *AW*, Feb 21, 1914, 324.

29. Erdman, *The Great Fundamentals*, Vol 4, 268.

18. Third Tier Principles for Open Questions

1. Simpson, "Consecration," July 6, 1894, 5. See also: "The Alliance branches every-where have been tried and sifted and have settled now to bed rock with a loyal people and are building right on the Fourfold Gospel in Christ, who is all and in all, -a platform broad and deep enough for any child of God. There is nothing better." Ulysses Lewis, "Sustentation Fund," *CMAW*, May 21, 1910, 132.
2. "Our Mail Box," *CMAW*, June 9, 1900, 385.
3. Simpson, Editorial, *CMAW*, Mar 31, 1906, 185. "It was distinctly understood when the Alliance was organized that there was to be no controversy on the questions of church government, baptism, feet washing, Calvinism, Arminianism, etc., on which the various evangelical bodies are divided, but we were simply to agree to differ."
4. A. B. Simpson, "The Phases and Phrases of the Higher Christian Life," *CMAW*, Oct 28, 1899, 348.
5. Simpson, Editorial, *CMAW*, Mar 31, 1906, 185.
6. Tozer, "A Word in Season," 231.
7. Simpson, Editorial, *AW*, Sept 1, 1906, 129; Gilbertson, 286; C&MA Board of Manager Minutes, Sept 20-23, 1922.
8. MacMillan, "Harmonized Diversity," 658.
9. "Conference for Prayer and Counsel Regarding Uniformity in the Testimony and Teaching of the Alliance."
10. ". . . open questions about which the Alliance is not giving a special testimony These open questions include various doctrines about which Presbyterians and Methodists differ, such as God's purpose in election, falling from grace, methods of church government, etc. It is not within our province in the Alliance literature and conventions to argue these questions of difference between the various evangelical denominations, nor is it judicious for our correspondents or teachers to agitate them, as unfortunately they do occasionally. We have plenty of room in the special testimony of the Alliance. Christ our Saviour, Sanctifier, Healer, and Coming Lord, to give out all the messages the Holy Spirit has for us." Simpson, Editorial, *AW*, Sept 1, 1906, 129.
11. Gilbertson, 286; C&MA Board of Manager Minutes, Sept 20-23, 1922.
12. Simpson, "Christian Altruism," 322; "Members of One Another," 148.
13. These principles have been cited from the following sources: Simpson, Editorial, *CMAW*, Mar 31, 1906, 185; Simpson, "The Phases and Phrases of the Higher Christian Life," 348; Simpson, Editorial, *CMAW*, May 25, 1912, 113; A. B. Simpson, "The Sword of the Spirit, " *CMAW*, Oct 5, 1894, 319; quoted in May Mabette Anderson, "Who Shall Abide?", *CMAW*, Jan 11, 1908, 244; A. B. Simpson, Editorial, *AW*, May 30, 1914, 130; Mary B. Mullen, "Some Danger Lines," Nov 2, 1907, 75.
14. A. W. Tozer, *The Warfare of the Spirit* (Camp Hill, PA: Christian Publications, 1993), 105.

15. In another article Simpson writes: "There is often needless controversy about phases of truth and phrases in which it is expressed. We hear the 'Second Blessing,' 'Entire Sanctification,' 'a clean heart,' 'eradication,' 'separation,' 'a deeper life,' 'the rest of faith,' 'the consecrated life,' 'the baptism of the Holy Spirit,' 'the fulness of Jesus,' 'Christian perfection,' 'perfect love,' and simple hearts become perplexed while dogmatic people become warlike over these various lines of battle. Perhaps after all we shall find when we reach the land of perfect light that these various parties were nearer together than they dreamed, and that amid an infinite diversity of expression there was s substantial oneness of spirit. After all the great thing is not so much what we say but what we are and what Christ is to us. The finest theories and the most Scriptural phrases do not constitute the divine life. Let us learn to recognize the Christ life behind every variety of temperament and theological expression. At the same time, we shall find it very safe to keep close to Bible terms. If we meet God on His own very Word we shall find that He will meet us in blessing." Simpson, "The Phases and Phrases of the Higher Christian Life," 348.

16. Gilbertson, 286, C&MA Board of Manager Minutes, Sept 20-23, 1922.

17. Simpson was asked, "Do you believe the Anglo-Israel theory, or is it accepted by the Christian Alliance?

    ANSWER.-We do not believe the theory, but some excellent members of the Christian Alliance, we believe, do hold to it. It is not a matter essential to fellowship in the Four-fold Gospel, and while we do not deem it profitable to discuss these side issues in the Alliance, we do not deem it of sufficient importance to interrupt our perfect communion with those who hold these views. We would not advise our Alliance people to become occupied with any of these questions, or to allow the work lo he distracted from its great central purpose and side-tracked by anybody. "Queries," *CAMW*, Sept 7, 1894, 235.

19. The Open Question Hermeneutic Applied to Theological Issues

1. *CITB*, 1:13.
2. *CITB*, 1:13.
3. *CITB*, 1:13, 14.
4. *CITB*, 1:18.
5. Simpson, "Old Testament Outlines," 245. See also *CITB*, 1:12. I am not sure how views that say God directed, ordained, and devised the changes, path, and *telos* of creation but used evolutionary processes as the mechanism would be treated. That would take further investigation.
6. Pardington, *Outline Studies*, 100.
7. L. A. Harriman, "Backsliding," *CMAW*, Aug 4, 1906, 66-68; C. B. Woodruff, "Backsliding—A Reply," *CMAW*, Oct 6, 1906, 210-211.
8. Simpson, Editorial, *CMAW*, Oct 6, 1906, 211. See also Simpson, Editorial, *CMAW*, Sept 1, 1906, 129,

9. "The point at issue is a hyper scholasticism carrying doctrinal points to divisive fruitage." Specifically mentioned were "extreme Calvinistic views." Official letter from the Secretary of the Alliance dated October 23, 1922, that was attached to the end of the Board of Managers Minutes of October 21, 1922, page 168.

10. There is some question as to whether the Alliance position is compatible with a strong "limited atonement" view. Certainly, Simpson did not accept limited atonement, moving away from his strong Calvinistic background on that point.

11. Simpson, *CITB*, 4:128-132. Others who held a partial rapture theory included Dr. Ira David from the C&MA; friends of Simpson—J. Hudson Taylor and Otto Stockmayer; the Stone Church, a Pentecostal church in Chicago with whom the Alliance maintained friendship and fellowship; and others: G. H. Pember, J. A. Seiss, Robert Govett, G. H. Lang, D. M. Panton, Watchman Nee, G. Campbell Morgan.

12. Kenneth MacKenzie, "Helps to Truth Seekers," *AW*, Aug 7, 1926, 519.

13. Simpson, *CITB*, 5:99-106.

14. A. B. Simpson, "Our Coming Lord: Misapprehensions and Misapplications," *CAMW*, Sept 12, 1890, 153.

15. J. A. MacMillan, "British Israelism—A Latter-Time Heresy," Part I, *AW*, Sept 1, 1934, 548ff.; Part II, Sept 8, 1934, 564ff.; Part III, Sept 15, 1934, 580ff; Part IV, Sept 22, 1934, 596ff.; Part V, Sept 29, 1934, 612ff.

16. Simpson, *In Heavenly Places*, 114, 116-118, 125.

20. The Open Question Hermeneutic Applied to Church Government Issues

1. "The Gospel in Timothy: The Church," 385.

2. Dialogue on C&MA Workers page, Facebook, May 19, 2021.

3. King, *Anointed Women*, 26.

4. MacKenzie, "Helps for Truth Seekers," *AW*, Apr 13, 1929, 238.

5. King, *Anointed Women*, 26, 31, 33, 36, 45, 59, 79, 80, 82, 128, 186, 189, 190=192, 195.

6. King, *Anointed Women*, 116.

7. "Nathan Bailey, Correspondence to G. J. Schumaker of the IRS dated, Sept. 4, 1964, cited in Wendell W. Price, "The Role of Women in the History of the C&MA, San Francisco Theological Seminary, 1977, 66.

8. Correspondence with Dr. Franklin Pyles and Rev. David Freedman.

9. Gordon, "The Ministry of Women," *AW*, Dec 15, 1928, 820-821.

10. Ironically, in 1999 the US General Council, forgetting its heritage, voted to switch to a strict complementarian view, no longer permitting women to serve as pastors.

11. Gordon, "The Ministry of Women," *AW*, Dec 15, 1928, 820-821.

12. Kenneth MacKenzie, "Helps for Truth Seekers," *AW*, Apr 13, 1929, 238.

13. "Women Who Helped in the Gospel," *CMAW*, June 18, 1897, 592.

14. *CMAW*, June 9, 1900, 385, cited in Andrews, "Restricted Freedom," 229; J. Hudson Ballard, "The Spiritual Clinic," *CMAW*, Aug 19, 1911, 333.

15. MacKenzie, "Helps for Truth Seekers," *AW*, Apr 13, 1929, 238.

16. T. J. McCrossan, *Speaking with Other Tongues: Sign or Gift—Which?* (Christian Publications, 1927), 5.

17. Henry Wilson, "Our Children's Bible School," *CMAW*, Feb 21, 1903, 105; "Dr. Wilson and the Children," *CMAW*, May 10, 1905, 363; Gordon, "The Ministry of Women," 820-821.

18. This section was excerpted from *Anointed Women*, 60-61.

19. Kenneth MacKenzie, "Helps for Truth Seekers," *AW*, Apr 13, 1929, 238.

20. Gordon, "The Ministry of Women," *AW*, Dec 15, 1928, 820-821.

21. **Resources for Further Study**

    King, Paul L. *Anointed Women: The Rich Heritage of Women in Ministry in the Christian and Missionary Alliance.* Tulsa, OK: Word & Spirit Press, 2009.

    King, Paul L. "Faultlines and Quantum Leaps: An Alliance Historian and Theologian's Critique of Andrew Ballitch's Critique of Dr. John Stumbo and National C&MA Leadership on Women in Ministry—A Critique of 'A Radical Question for a Conservative Church: Should The Christian and Missionary Alliance Call Women 'Pastors'? by Andrew S. Ballitch." Available at www. paulkingministries.com

    King, Paul L. "Response by Dr. Paul L. King to the C&MA Ministry of Women Proposals:

    Addressing Historical and Biblical/Theological Inaccuracies in Elder Authority and Women in Ministry Issues," 2021. Available by request from Paul King.

    King, Paul L. "An Academic Response to the "Two Views on the Use of the Title Pastor Within The Christian & Missionary Alliance" (referencing the Two Views Paper distributed prior to General Council 2021). Available by request from Paul King.

    King, Paul L. "The Issue of 'Elder Authority'—A Response to the C&MA Ministry of Women Proposals at Council 2021." Available by request from Paul King.

21. The Alliance Open Question Hermeneutic Applied to Worship Practices

1. Simpson, Editorial, *CMAW*, Mar 31, 1906, 185; Simpson, "Side Issues and Essentials," 218.

2. Simpson, "Side Issues and Essentials," 218.

3. Editorial, *CAMW*, June 26, 1896, 612.

4. Simpson, "Side Issues and Essentials," 218.

5. A. B. Simpson, "The Soul That Jesus Sought and Found at Jacob's Well," *CMAW*, Nov 26, 1898, 486.

Appendix 1: The Niagara Creed of 1878

1. https://www.efcc.org/am-site/media/sof-niagara-creed-14-points.pdf. Listed along with Alliance distinctives, The Apostles Creed, and The Great Fundamentals. C&MA Board of Managers Minutes, Sept 20-23, 1922.

Appendix 4: Christ's Humanity, Kenotic Theories And The Alliance

1. Donald G. Bloesch, *Jesus Christ: Savior and Lord* (Downers Grove, IL: IVP, 1997), 61.
2. Adapted from H. Wayne House, *Charts of Christian Theology and Doctrine* (Grand Rapids: Zondervan, 1992), Chart 30, 58-59. House is an evangelical theologian and biblical scholar who has taught in conservative evangelical institutions such as LeTourneau College and Dallas Theological Seminary and has served as the president of the Evangelical Theological Society.
3. Millard J. Erickson, *Christian Theology,* Second Edition (Grand Rapids: Baker Books, 1983, 1984, 1985, 1998), 751.
4. J. Rodman Williams, *Renewal Theology* (Grand Rapids: Zondervan, 1996), 1:323.
5. Simpson, *CITB*, 6:163.
6. A.W. Tozer, *Tozer on the Son of God—A 365 Day Devotional* (Chicago: Moody Press, 2020), February 1.

Appendix 5: Understanding Double Baptism

1. Simpson, "Baptism and the Baptism of the Holy Spirit."
2. Cited in Kilian McDonnell and George T. Montague, *Christian Initiation and Baptism in the Holy Spirit: Evidence from the First Eight Centuries* (Collegeville, MN: The Liturgical Press, 1991, 1994), 305, 308, 312, 314.
3. Jeremy Taylor, *The Whole Works of the Right Rev. Jeremy Taylor*; Volume 3 (London: Henry Bohn, York Street, Covent Gardens, 1851), 240.

Appendix 6: The Alliance and Historic Views on Spirit Baptism

1. Paul L. King, "Historical-Theological Survey of Holy Spirit Empowerment Language, Experience, & Accompanying Phenomena Subsequent to Conversion Prior to the 20th Century," presented at the 45th Annual Meeting of the Society for Pentecostal Studies, Washington, DC, March 2019.

Appendix 7: Decline and Recovery of C&MA Spirit Baptism Emphasis

1. A. B. Simpson, Editorial, *CMAW*, Oct 23, 1909, 56.
2. Cook, *Historical Drift*, 10.
3. Ernest Wilson, 157.
4. Ernest Wilson, 157, 168.
5. Ernest Wilson, 225.
6. Duy, "A.B. Simpson's Fourfold Gospel in the Evangelical Church of Vietnam," 171-195.
7. See Paul L. King, *Genuine Gold* (Tulsa, OK: Word & Spirit Press, 2006), 222, 245-246.
8. Harry L. Turner, *Voice of the Spirit* (St. Paul: St. Paul Bible College, 1949, 1951), 37, 38, 66. Dr. Harry Turner, a former Pentecostal missionary and pastor, rejoined the Alliance, eventually becoming president of the C&MA 1954-1960. His negative experience with Pentecostals seemed to sway him to distance the Alliance from Pentecostalism by teaching that the baptism in the Spirit was a once-for-all event for the Jews, repeated for the Gentiles in Acts 10, as opposed the position of Simpson and the earlier Alliance. He was not adamant about his position, and still acknowledged a post-conversion crisis or filling, allowing, "Others wish to term this experience the baptism of the Spirit. We have no objection if you arrive at the true filling of the Spirit. We believe that in God's purpose baptism of the Spirit and the filling of the Spirit are two distinct doctrines, but God is not so much concerned with the tag as He is with the goods" (p. 73). He does not discuss or engage the views of Simpson, Pardington, and other Alliance leaders on their views, even though he cites them in regard to a post-conversion experience. For the most part, his argument is based on the silence of the use of the term "baptized in the Spirit." Curiously, he does not relate 1 Corinthians 12:13 to the baptism in the Spirit as most of those who argue against a subsequent Spirit baptism. Nor does he discern the difference in "receiving the word" vs. "receiving the Spirit." Though his paper is thoughtful, it is not convincing, although since he became president of the C&MA, his view was apparently not challenged.
9. See John R.W. Stott, *The Baptism and Fullness of the Spirit* (Downers Grove: IVP, 1964), 8-9. Stott claims we should get our doctrine from the teachings of Jesus and the teaching epistles, but not the book of Acts. However, Luke gave no such indication in his two-volume Luke-Acts that one was to be excluded from the other or interpreted differently than the other.
10. Rev. Gray was my first mentor and like a grandfather to me. In the 1920s he ministered with former Assemblies of God evangelist Alonzo Horn, who joined the Alliance. In some of those meetings, holy laughter, miraculous healings occurred, including healing the blind and deaf and goiters instantly disappearing. He also cautioned about "spurious tongues" and other manifestations.
11. Eldon Woodcock, "Baptism into the Body," *Alliance Witness,* Jan 10, 1979, 22.
12. Woodcock claims, "Many recent theologians have discerned the Holy Spirit's role as a fresh empowering of believers to overcome their sinful tendencies and to serve the Lord effectively. Some label this a baptism of the Holy Spirit. However, this

involves a confusion of two distinct ministries of the Holy Spirit. None of the seven explicit New Testament references to the baptism of the Holy Spirit asserts or suggests that Spirit baptism is directly associated with the promise and reception of power. What is the relationship between the baptism of the Holy Spirit and the Holy Spirit's empowering believers? Spirit baptism is distinct from Spirit-empowering. Spirit baptism occurs only at the new birth, hut His empowering may occur then and or many times afterward." Eldon Woodcock, "Spirit Baptism," *Alliance Witness*, Jan 24, 1979, 22. Note: The seven references include four parallel references to baptism in the Spirit (Mt 3:ll; Mk 1.8; Lk 3:16: John 1:33); Acts 1:5, in which Jesus refers back to the prior four references; Acts 11:15-17, which refers back to the prior reference; and I Cor 12:13, which does not use the exact same language, but is similar. However, this statement is not entirely accurate for several reasons:

First of all, he makes his claim on the logical fallacy of an argument from silence: "None of the seven explicit New Testament references to the baptism of the Holy Spirit asserts or suggests that Spirit baptism is directly associated with the promise and reception of power." Such a statement is

weak unless supported by other evidence. We will show in the next point evidence to the contrary.

Secondly, he fails to acknowledge the following context of Acts 1:5, in which three verses later Jesus specifically relates the baptism in the Spirit with the promise of power (which Jesus also mentions: "wait in Jerusalem until you are clothed with power from on high" (Lk k 24:49). So the baptism in the Spirit is indeed directly associated with receiving power. Acts 11:15-17 refers to the same promise of power through the baptism in the Spirit.

Third, Woodcock claims: "Spirit baptism occurs only at the new birth." The evidence does not prove this. Five out of the seven references give no such hint. In Acts 11, Spirit baptism does occur at new birth, but it does not prove that it occurs *only* at new birth. It does not prove that the two are synonymous, only that they can occur simultaneously. First Corinthians 12:13 does occur at new birth, but whether that is the same as new birth is debated vigorously among scholars.

Finally, although the language of I Cor 12:13 is similar, it is not the same, so it cannot automatically be considered the same without further investigation. Woodcock does not even consider the scholarly arguments against his position. Thus, Woodcock is making an artificial distinction between Spirit baptism and Spirit-empowering, not based on a consensus of exegesis.

13. Eldon Woodcock, "Being Filled with the Spirit," *Alliance Academic Review* (Camp Hill, PA: Christian Publications, 1999). 94.

14. John R. Rice, *The Power of Pentecost of the Fullness of the Spirit* (Murpheesboro, TN: Sword of the Lord Publishers, 1949), 88.

15. Rice, *The Power of Pentecost*, 149, 151.

16. Armin R. Gesswein, "Dispensationalism," AW, Mar. 1, 1941, 135, 138.

17. F. F. Bosworth, in the "Introduction" of Oswald J. Smith, *The Baptism with the Holy Spirit* (New York: Christian Alliance Publishing Co., 1925), 7.

18. Cook, *Historical*, 10.

19. Dr. Bailey distinguished between baptism by the Spirit into the body of Christ at conversion (I Cor 12:13) and the subsequent baptism with the Spirit. Keith Bailey,

"The Promise of the Father," message preached at Southwestern District Leadership Retreat, Mar 26, 1996.

Appendix 8: Exegetical Basis of the Classic Alliance View of Subsequence and the Baptism in the Spirit

1. Simpson, *CMAW*, Oct 23, 1909, 56.
2. A. B. Simpson, Editorial, *AW*, Mar 1, 1913, 337.
3. Paul L. King, "Historical-Theological Survey of Holy Spirit Empowerment Language, Experience, & Accompanying Phenomena Subsequent to Conversion Prior to the 20th Century," presented at the 45th Annual Meeting of the Society for Pentecostal Studies, Washington, DC, March 2019.
4. T. J. McCrossan, *Christ's Paralyzed Church X-Rayed* (Youngstown, OH: C. E. Humbard, 1937), 118. Luke 24:49 and Acts 1:8 use *epi* and *eperchomai*. Acts 8:16—fall upon (*epipipto epi*); Acts 10:44, 45—came upon (*epipipto epi*), poured out upon (*epi . . . ekchuno*); Acts 11:15—fell upon (*epipipto*); 19:6—came upon (*erchomai*).
5. Howard M. Ervin, *Conversion-Initiation and the Baptism in the Holy Spirit* (Peabody, MA: Hendrickson Publishers, 1984), 26, 136, 139; Howard M. Ervin, *These Are Not Drunken As Ye Suppose* (Plainfield, NJ: Logos, 1968), 25-33.
6. Armin R. Gesswein, "The Spirit-Filled Christian, IV," *AW*, Mar 20, 1943, 183.
7. Bob Willoughby, "Pentecost: An Experience for Today: An Examination of the Baptism of the Holy Spirit in Acts."
8. Pardington, *Outline Studies*, 324-325.
9. Dunn tries to make us believe that the Samaritans, Paul, and the Ephesians weren't really converted until their reception of the Spirit. Nowhere does Scripture indicate that laying on of hands is needed to be saved. Stott, Dunn, and others would have us believe that we cannot derive doctrine from history, i.e. a doctrine of subsequent Spirit baptism. How then, can they derive a doctrine of reception of the Spirit at conversion from Acts? Further, if we cannot derive doctrine from Acts, how can we derive it from the Gospel of Luke? That is a case of wrongly dividing the word of truth. Paul makes asks an implicit doctrinal question when he asked the Ephesians if they had received the Spirit when they believed. There are too many subsequent "anomalies" for them to be anomalies. Reception of the Spirit at conversion is the anomaly. The church fathers also viewed these events in Acts as a pattern for a distinct act of receiving the outpouring of the Spirit.
10. Simpson, for instance, makes frequent reference to the use of the aorist tense in verbs describing the crisis event of the Holy Spirit distinct from conversion. A. B. Simpson, "Forward," *CAMW*, Oct 17, 1890, 226; A.B. Simpson, "Risen with Christ," *CAMW*, Apr 3, 1891, 211; A. B. Simpson, "Sanctification and Growth," *CAMW*, July 17, 1891, 38; A. B. Simpson, "The Fullness of Jesus," *CAMW*, Jan 17, 1896, 54.
11. A. B. Simpson, *The Four-Fold Gospel* (Harrisburg: Christian Publications, n.d.), 39-40. The crisis nature of the sanctifying filling of the Spirit is further demonstrated by the *principle of grammar and syntax* by the use of the aorist tense in key passages, indicating action at a point in time. Regarding the Gentile's reception of the Spirit

in Acts 10:44-47, Peter comments: "God, who knows the heart, showed that he accepted them by giving the Holy Spirit to them, just as He did to us. He made no distinction between us and them, for he purified their hearts by faith" (Acts 15:8-9). "Showed" or "bore witness" (*emarturesen*) is an aorist active indicative, signifying an event which occurred at a point in time. "Giving" (*dous*) the Holy Spirit, is an aorist active participle. This is evidence for the "witness of the Spirit" as a crisis experience identified with the filling or baptism in the Spirit subsequent to conversion. Further, "purified" (*katharisas*) is an aorist active participle as well, providing further evidence pointing to a crisis experience of sanctification.

12. Simpson, "The Crisis of the Deeper Life," *LT,* Sept 1906, 523.

13. Simpson, "The Baptism of the Holy Spirit: A Crisis or an Evolution?," *LT*, Dec 1905, 710.

14. J. Hudson Ballard, "The Spiritual Clinic," *AW*, Jan. 16, 1915, 254.

15. Smith, *The Baptism With the Holy Spirit*, 19.

16. Larry Hart, "Spirit Baptism: A Dimensional Charismatic Perspective," *Perspectives on Spirit Baptism: Five Views*, Chad Owen Brand, ed. (Nashville: Broadman, 2004), 105ff.

17. Randall A. Harrison, *Overwhelmed by the Spirit: A Biblical Study on Discovering the Spirit* (Entrust Publications, 2013).

18. Martyn Lloyd-Jones, *God's Ultimate Purpose* (Grand Rapids: Baker, 1978), 267-268.

19. Charles Hodge, "Commentary on 1 Corinthians 12:13," *Hodge's Commentary on Romans, Ephesians, and First Corinthians*. https:https://www.studylight.org/commentaries/hdg/1-corinthians-12.html. See also T. J. McCrossan, *Christ's Paralyzed Church X-Rayed, 118.*

20. Cited in George M. Flattery, *A Biblical Theology of the Holy Spirit in the New Testament: John-Paul* (Springfield, MO: Global University, 2009), 34.

21. The *Treatise on Rebaptism* as calls it "the mystery of the faith being divided," explaining "sometimes found in some sort divided, and separated, and arranged, and ordered just as if they were by themselves" and at other times "entire and complete." If they have not been baptized in the Spirit, they are no less converted or saved, but have not been "consummated" and are not "perfectly Christians" or "might have had a faith somewhat imperfect *Treatise on Rebaptism*, Chapters 3, 5. For Pseudo-Dionysius, "the consecrating gift and grace of the Divine Birth in God is completed in the most Divine perfectings of the chrism. Pseudo-Dionysius the Areopagite, Section X. "Muron" is Dionysius' term for anointing oil or chrism.

22. See Appendix 5. Many contemporary interpretations of John 3:3-8 conflate born again and born of water and Spirit together as the one and the same, but several church fathers make distinctions between them. Anglican archbishop Jeremy Taylor also strongly supported this ancient interpretation of John 3:5: born of water = water baptism/born of the Spirit = baptism in the Holy Spirit. See Taylor, 239, 240, 249.

23. Rice, *The Power of Pentecost*, 102.

OTHER TITLES BY PAUL L. KING

Made in the USA
Columbia, SC
21 July 2023

20602082R00146